More praise for *Beyond Forgiveness*

"Stay with it, and let this book open your heart, that best of all changings. Hard work, no question, but so worth it. The good and brave stories being told here—like the monk's tears on the head of the sullen teenager (that open this book), like James O'Dea's tears in the metro reading Thomas Merton (that close it)—will give you courage, heat for the leap, the phone call, the meltdown."

—Coleman Barks, author of *Rumi: The Big Red Book* and *The Essential Rumi*

"You cannot read this book without taking up a spiritual challenge; the challenge is to see even the most painful of the wrongs that are done to us in a larger, more transparent, and perennial context. This book is full of stories of spiritual courage and a transcendence that passes all cultural and religious boundaries, to show us the universality of what is truly spiritual about humanity. Phil Cousineau has a remarkable instinct for topics that pulse with the painful yet vital spiritual heartbeat of our time."

—Stephen Larsen, Ph.D., author of *The Fundamentalist Mind: How Polarized Thinking Imperils Us All* and coauthor of *A Fire in the Mind: The Life of Joseph Campbell*

"If we harbor thoughts of violence or hatred, or seek revenge or retribution, we are contributing to the wounding of the world; if we transform those thoughts into forgiveness and compassion, and then move beyond them to actually make amends or restitution, we are contributing to the healing of the world. This timely, powerful and compassionate book by Phil Cousineau helps show us the way."

—Deepak Chopra, author of *The Book of Secrets* and *The Path to Love*

"Nothing will help us survive the present age more than the realization that we must break the cycles of violence, when our souls long for healing, forgiveness often proves to be an inadequate solution to the soul's desire for longer lasting reconciliation. I've long believed another step is required for our transformation, one that Phil Cousineau reveals here as being on the other side of forgiveness, in the ancient ritual of atonement. I believe this book is the vital next step in the making of a strong modern myth of deep reconciliation. It is a profoundly important book and I give it my blessing."

—Robert A. Johnson, author of *He, She,*
Transformation, and *A Slender Thread*

"*Beyond Forgiveness: Reflections on Atonement* is an inspiring, practical, and compelling book, relevant for our times. Cousineau provides a profound and provocative book that has us ponder where we might need to forgive ourselves and others; and to look at atonement and what it ignites in the human spirit."

—Angeles Arrien, Ph.D., author of *The Second Half of Life*

BOOKS BY PHIL COUSINEAU

The Hero's Journey: Joseph Campbell on His Life and Work, 1990

Deadlines: A Rhapsody on a Theme of Famous and Infamous Last Words, 1991

Riders on the Storm: My Life with Jim Morrison and the Doors (by John Densmore with Phil Cousineau), 1992

The Soul of the World: A Modern Book of Hours (with Eric Lawton), 1993

Soul: An Archaeology: Readings from Socrates to Ray Charles, 1993

Prayers at 3 A.M.: Poems, Songs, Chants for the Middle of the Night, 1995

Design Outlaws: On the Frontier of the 21ˢᵗ Century (with Christopher Zelov), 1996

Soul Moments: Marvelous Stories of Synchronicity, 1997

The Art of Pilgrimage: The Seeker's Guide to Making Travel Sacred, 1998

Riddle Me This: A World Treasury of Word Puzzles, Folk Wisdom, and Literary Conundrums, 1999

The Soul Aflame: A Modern Book of Hours (with Eric Lawton), 2000

The Book of Roads: Travel Stories, 2000

Once and Future Myths: The Power of Ancient Stories in Modern Times, 2001

The Way Things Are: Conversations with Huston Smith on the Spiritual Life, 2003

The Olympic Odyssey: Rekindling the True Spirit of the Great Games, 2004

The Blue Museum: Poems, 2004

A Seat at the Table: The Struggle for American Indian Religious Freedom, 2005

Angkor Wat: The Marvelous Enigma (photographs) 2006

Night Train: New Poems, 2007

The Jaguar People: An Amazonian Chronicle (photographs), 2007

Stoking the Creative Fires: 9 Ways to Rekindle Your Passion and Imagination, 2008

Fungoes and Fastballs: Great Moments in Baseball Haiku, 2008

The Meaning of Tea (with Scott Chamberlin Hoyt), 2009

City 21: The Search for the Second Enlightenment (with Christopher Zelov), 2009

The Oldest Story in the World: A Mosaic of Meditations on Storytelling, 2010

Wordcatcher: An Odyssey into the World of Weird and Wonderful Words, 2010

The Song of the Open Road (photographs), 2010

Beyond Forgiveness: Reflections on Atonement, 2011

beyond forgiveness

beyond forgiveness

Reflections on Atonement

Edited by Phil Cousineau

FOREWORD BY HUSTON SMITH

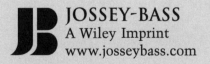

JOSSEY-BASS
A Wiley Imprint
www.josseybass.com

Published by Jossey-Bass
A Wiley Imprint
989 Market Street, San Francisco, CA 94103-1741—www.josseybass.com

Readers should be aware that Internet Web sites offered as citations and/or sources for further information may have changed or disappeared between the time this was written and when it is read.

Limit of Liability/Disclaimer of Warranty: While the publisher and author have used their best efforts in preparing this book, they make no representations or warranties with respect to the accuracy or completeness of the contents of this book and specifically disclaim any implied warranties of merchantability or fitness for a particular purpose. No warranty may be created or extended by sales representatives or written sales materials. The advice and strategies contained herein may not be suitable for your situation. You should consult with a professional where appropriate. Neither the publisher nor author shall be liable for any loss of profit or any other commercial damages, including but not limited to special, incidental, consequential, or other damages.

Jossey-Bass books and products are available through most bookstores. To contact Jossey-Bass directly call our Customer Care Department within the U.S. at 800-956-7739, outside the U.S. at 317-572-3986, or fax 317-572-4002.

Jossey-Bass also publishes its books in a variety of electronic formats. Some content that appears in print may not be available in electronic books.

From "Yom Kippur 1984" in *Adrienne Rich's Poetry and Prose: Poems, Prose, Reviews and Criticism*, selected and edited by Barbara Charlesworth Gelpi and Albert Gelpi. Copyright © 1993, 1975 by W.W. Norton & Company, Inc. Reprinted with permission.

From "Voices from Lemnos, IV, Chorus" in *Opened Ground: Selected Poems 1966-1996* by Seamus Heaney. Copyright © 1998 by Seamus Heaney. Reprinted by permission of Farrar, Straus and Giroux LLC.

Library of Congress Cataloging-in-Publication Data
    Beyond forgiveness : reflections on atonement / edited by Phil Cousineau ; foreword by Huston Smith.
       p. cm.
     ISBN 978-0-470-90773-3 (pbk.); 978-0-470-94003-7 (ebk); 978-0-470-94004-4 (ebk); 978-1-118-02670-0 (ebk).
      1. Forgiveness. 2. Atonement. I. Cousineau, Phil.
    BJ1476.B49 2011
    179'.9—dc22

                                        2010040033

Printed in the United States of America
FIRST EDITION
PB Printing 10 9 8 7 6 5 4 3 2 1

CONTENTS

Forgiveness is better than revenge.

—*Heraclitus (535–475 BCE)*

Find someone like yourself. Find others.
Agree you will never desert each other.
Understand that any rift among you
means power to those who want to do you in. . . .
This is the day of atonement; but do my people forgive me?
If a cloud knew loneliness and fear, I would be that cloud.

—*Adrienne Rich, "Yom Kippur 1984"*

How can a novelist achieve atonement when, with her absolute power of deciding outcomes, she is also God? There is no one, no entity or higher form that she can appeal to, or be reconciled with, or that can forgive her. There is nothing outside her. . . . It was always an impossible task, and that was precisely the point. The attempt was all.

—*Ian McEwan,* Atonement

To Bob Schnekenburger,
my foreman at Industrial & Automotive Fasteners, in Detroit,
whose stories about serving as a Green Beret in Vietnam
were my first painful lessons in the need
for finding truth and reconciliation
in all our wars

atonement as a spiritual path

HUSTON SMITH

Being persuaded to repent doesn't mean simply to feel sorry. It requires backing up—full speed astern—to reverse the human tendency to go one's own way, as the following story of a twentieth-century Zen monk shows.

This monk lived as a recluse in a hut on the side of a mountain. His only possessions were his robe, his straw sandals, and the bowl with which he begged for his food in the nearby village. The evening after a thief stole his sandals and bowl, he wrote:

> The moon still shines
> in my window. Unstolen
> by the thief.

His freedom from attachments, as demonstrated in this haiku, was one of the reasons the villagers revered him.

One day, as the monk was on his daily walk seeking food, a mother invited him into her home to share the noonday meal with her and her son, whom (she explained before they entered the house) she hoped the monk could straighten out, for the lad was a delinquent and was clearly headed for trouble.

When the son was called, he barely acknowledged the monk's presence, and he stared sullenly at the table throughout the meal. The monk too remained silent as they all ate. But as the monk was preparing to leave, the son did deign to do his duty. As he stooped to tie the monk's straw sandals, he felt a drop of warm water fall on his head. Looking up, he saw tears streaming down the monk's face. The monk's compassion for what was in store for the young man prompted him to mend his ways.

This true story offers a beautiful example of the "power made perfect in weakness" that St. Paul extolled in the New Testament, and it sets the right tone for the interpretation of atonement I am attempting to give. Apart from God, who *is* love, love is a response to incoming love. And the most powerful demonstration of the sender's love is to let the receiver know that the sender suffers the pain the recipient suffers—in God's case infinitely, for there is nothing halfway about God.

In the Zen story, when the tear fell, the son realized—and actually experienced—the sorrow, the pain, in the monk. The weeping of the monk was a salvific act because it opened the heart of the son and kept him from being totally self-centered. The monk's tear brought into the son's heart the pain of another.

This story illustrates how compassion allows us to feel what someone else feels, which in turn allows us to forgive them, and to forgive ourselves, as we travel on the spiritual path.

What the wisdom traditions tell us is that we are in good hands. Out of gratitude, we are called to relieve each other's burdens, and to forgive each other, which is why there is an emphasis on forgiveness and atonement in all the world's religions.

I recall a former student of mine, Douglas George-Kanentiio, a member of the Iroquois tribe, telling me at the 1999 Parliament of World's Religions, in Cape Town, South Africa, that the great gift he had received from our time there was his encounter with the Truth and Reconciliation Commission organized by Archbishop Desmond Tutu and Nelson Mandela. He said he was so inspired by what the South Africans had accomplished through their acts of forgiveness and restitution and commitment to nonviolence that he wanted to try to apply their recommendations to his own people's situation. The

Iroquois had experienced violence, discrimination, and racism similar to what the black South Africans had endured, and now it was important for his people to reach new ways of forgiveness and restitution, as well as reviving traditional forms of restorative justice. To bring together people who need reconciliation requires a recognition and acceptance of our own shortcomings, our flaws, our imperfections. At the heart of atonement, which has at its root the idea of *reconciliation*, is the recovery of our wholeness.

The power of the acts of forgiveness and atonement is the recognition of the flaw in all of us, without exception, as well as the realization of our ultimate unity. When we are "at one," we are united, side by side, and together. Our sense of ourselves as separate is illusion, what our senses report. As the ancients told us, the senses are false witnesses. In poetic idiom, "Life is real, life is earnest / And things are not as they seem."

It is as if we were gazing on a cloudless sky through a transom in which nine panes of glass are held together by two horizontal and two vertical bars. Looking through that transom, we see the sky as consisting of nine pieces. But of course the sky itself is not so divided. And neither are we.

Welcome to Phil Cousineau's important book.

the next step in forgiveness and healing

PHIL COUSINEAU

Throughout history people have had to make difficult, even heartrending decisions about how to respond to the suffering they have endured at the hands of other human beings—or to the pain they themselves have inflicted upon other people.

Over and over, we are confronted with the dilemma of how to respond to the cruelty and suffering that can pervade our lives. Do we forgive, or do we retaliate? Should we make peace or exact revenge? Can we live alongside our enemies, or do we seek retribution? And what about the harm *we* have caused? Is it possible for us to ever undo or make up for the damage we may have wreaked on the world?

From the earliest times different cultures have resolved their conflicts and meted out justice in their own way. Traditionally there have been two widely diverging paths—punishment or reform—which are rooted in retribution and forgiveness, respectively. The first is antagonistic and adversarial; the second, compassionate and cooperative. The difference between the two is dramatic. As the Chinese proverb has it, "If you are hell-bent on revenge, dig two graves"—one for your enemy and one for you. Revenge buries us in bitterness; hate immerses us in anger.

While retaliation has earned the lion's share of attention over the centuries, more measured responses to both personal and collective conflicts have also been practiced. The instinct to be vindictive may be as old as stone, but the impulse toward reconciliation runs like an ancient underground river. And like water dissolving stone, if it flows long enough, so too can acts of compassion dissolve anger, the showing of remorse prompt forgiveness, and the making of amends alleviate guilt.

None of these paths is easy.

Nor do we find much encouragement, in a world riven by seemingly endless cycles of violence, to ask for forgiveness, still less to offer our own to someone who may have hurt us. But if we miss the moment for real reconciliation, we miss the chance to heal and move beyond the bitterness or guilt that can suffocate our lives.

Despite all the injunctions to exact revenge, from the hijacking of religious beliefs to testosterone-driven media violence, an impressive range of alternatives remains. Many distinguished scientists and philosophers now call into doubt the long-held belief that human beings are hardwired for violence, doomed by what anthropologist Robert Ardrey infamously called "the territorial imperative," victimized by what has been named "the demon seed phenomenon," or paralyzed by the "selfish genes" that reputedly determine our fate.

Instead there is ample and encouraging evidence that "Trend is not destiny," as the eminent microbiologist René Dubos boldly concluded in *A God Within*.

Antonio Damasio, professor of neuroscience at the University of Southern California and director of its Brain and Creativity Institute, believes that our early ancestors were far more likely to survive if they were able to respond to a friend who needed help, or felt compassion for an enemy who was writhing in pain. Similarly, cultural historian Susan Griffin believes that strong research reveals that human beings can and do change even their most deeply engrained violent and selfish behavior. In her Pulitzer Prize–winning book *A Chorus of Stones: The Private Life of War*, she writes, "It is perhaps a choice each of us makes over and over, even many times throughout one day, whether to use knowledge as power or intimacy."

Indeed evidence is mounting that the urge to act selflessly and live cooperatively was among the transcendent forces that helped our ancestors wrench themselves away from the grip of brute instinct, and bound us together into tribes and communities. In our own time, many political and spiritual leaders have exhorted us to practice forgiveness because it helps to cultivate the powers of empathy that helps solidify our relationships with others. While anger and violence may have spilled the most ink, from Homer's epics to Cormac McCarthy's novels, sophisticated forgiveness practices based on compassion, reprieve, amnesty, clemency, mercy, absolution, restitution, and restorative justice have also commanded great attention and exacted enormous influence. In ancient Greece the word *metanoia* referred to a sudden change of mind but also to *repentance*. *Change* is the operative word, the heart of the drama that reveals how we might creatively and compassionately respond to violence.

Twenty-five hundred years ago, the Buddha said, "Anger will never disappear so long as thoughts of resentment are cherished in the mind. Anger will disappear just as soon as thoughts of resentment are forgotten." "Forgive them, for they know not what they do," Christ said as he died on the cross. The Koran states, "Hold to forgiveness, command what is right; but turn away from the ignorant." To Mother Teresa we owe, "People are illogical and self-centered. Forgive them anyway." Dag Hammarskjöld, the Nobel Peace Prize laureate, said, "Forgiveness is the answer to the child's dream of a miracle by which what is broken is made whole again, what is soiled is again made clean." In the spring of 2009, Zainab Salbi, an Iraqi-American who works with women victims of war, said, "I think we need to forgive for our own health and healing. Without forgiveness, it's hard to move on." Recently, Huston Smith, the beloved historian of religion, wrote, "So the power of the act of forgiveness is the recognition of the flaw in all of us."

And yet there lingers a disturbing feeling. To forgive is noble; to be forgiven can be a reprieve. But surely there must be more to reconciliation between aggrieved peoples; otherwise, individuals, families, and entire cultures wouldn't have been whiplashed by cycles of violence throughout history. As indispensable as forgiveness has been to the healing process, another equally profound action is needed for real reconciliation, which Arun Gandhi, grandson of Mohandas Gandhi, calls "the other side of the coin." Turning over the coin of forgiveness, we discover *atonement*, the semi-hidden, much overlooked half of the reconciliation process. Atonement is the act that *proves* the depth of our desire to be forgiven, or to forgive; it is the process of making things right, the restoration of some semblance of balance in our lives.

"If someone steals my pen and uses it for a year," Archbishop Desmond Tutu said in 1987, "but being contrite, comes to me and returns my pen and begs for forgiveness, my response is to ask for compensation for the use of my pen, for the ink used and for some indication of contrition/repentance by the offender."

To paraphrase Tutu's famous injunction in the fight against apartheid, "Forgiveness makes the future possible," while atonement makes the *present* possible. A gesture as simple as replacing a stolen pen or as complex as war reparations makes the present moment not just better but *tolerable*. Without offering those who wrong us, however seriously, the chance to make amends, or granting ourselves the opportunity to atone for any hurt we have caused, we remain stuck in the past; we suffer from a kind of "soul rust" and are unable to live fully in the present moment. The real work in conflict resolution is bringing these two practices of forgiveness and atonement together, whenever they have been split apart like cordwood, until we can say, in the spirit of the Irish bard Van Morrison, that "the healing has begun."

Or as the soul singer Sam Cooke sang, plaintively, sorrowfully, and yet hopefully, after witnessing the first civil rights marches, "A change is gonna come."

Reconciliation

In *Atonement*, Ian McEwan's "symphonic novel of love and war, childhood and class, guilt and forgiveness," an elderly novelist attempts, through the alchemy of her storytelling, to atone for a tragic mistake she made as a thirteen-year-old girl:

> How can a novelist achieve atonement when, with her absolute power of deciding outcomes, she is also God? There is no one, no entity or higher form that she can appeal to, or be reconciled with, or that can forgive her. There is nothing outside her. . . . It was always an impossible task, and that was precisely the point. The attempt was all.

When I first read those lines, shortly after the book was published, I was immediately catapulted back in time to 1975, to the six months I spent working as a volunteer at Ashdot Ya'akov, a kibbutz in Israel's Jordan Valley. Every two weeks a large contingent of German students arrived at the kibbutz to work with us in the date groves, banana fields, and chicken coops. I was told by the *kibbutzniks* that the students had been sent there by the German government to ensure that the next generation would better appreciate Jewish culture, and never again demonize it. When I asked an old kibbutznik named Udi, who worked with me in the very date groves he had planted in 1909, how he felt about working alongside young German volunteers, he gritted his teeth and revealed to me that seventy out of seventy-two members of his family had perished in the grisly concentration camp at Auschwitz. "It is very, very hard for me to forgive, but this is a beginning, a hard beginning, but a beginning. . . ."

Since then Germany has continued its efforts to atone for the horrors of the Holocaust. It has paid out billions of dollars in reparations, returned thousands of items of stolen property, and made other amends, such as passing laws against political extremism and making it illegal to display symbols of Nazism.

Fifteen years after my stint on the kibbutz, in the winter of 1990, I received a phone call from a filmmaker from Mill Valley, California. Gary Rhine told me he was making a documentary film about the Wounded Knee massacre and its aftermath among the Dakota Sioux. Would I help? (How could I say no?) I gladly looked at the rough cut and was deeply stirred by the footage, but I had to know something before I signed on. *Why* was he making the film? Without hesitation, Gary told me that he was Jewish and that his family in Europe had been decimated by the Nazis during World War II. There was nothing he could do about that now, he confided, but he *could* do something about what he called the "American Holocaust," the wanton destruction of American Indians and their culture. He could help them tell their stories, and over the course of a few documentary films, he wanted to try to train some young Native Americans to tell their own stories with cameras. Together, over the next thirteen years, we made six films about the American Indian struggle for religious and political freedom. In his own remarkably selfless way my friend "Rhino" was offering to atone for the entire culture—a powerful act of reconciliation offered to the Five Hundred Nations for the transgressions of the past five hundred years. As he was fond of saying, "People don't change when they see the light; they change when they feel the heat." And the most effective heat, he believed, came when people shared their stories because it was the most effective way to realize that we have more in common than we ever dreamed of.

The Root Meaning of "At-One-Ment"

Early in the fourteenth century the word *atone* appeared in print for the first time. At that time it simply meant "to be in accord with, to make or become united or reconciled." Or as the mystics said, "To become one again with our Oneness." Two centuries later, the word was adapted and expanded by William Tyndale (1494–1536), a leader of the English Reformation and an early lexicographer. Tyndale had been frustrated by the lack of a direct translation of the biblical concept of reconciliation with God, and to better convey this core belief of his faith he combed ancient Hebrew and Greek manuscripts before finally combining two words, *at* and *onement*. For Tyndale, the new compound word reflected what he believed to be the numinous power of the sacrifice on the Cross symbolized the reconnection of humanity with the divine. Today, to atone generally means "to make amends for" but also carries connotations of being "at one with, in harmony."

Remarkably, the idea even shows up in the world of modern art. The influential art critic Arthur Danto regarded Barnett Newman's epic 1948 painting *Onement I* as conveying exactly this notion of unity and ultimate harmony. What Newman painted was, as Danto wrote, "the condition of being one, as in the incantation 'God is one.' It refers, one might say, to the oneness of God."

The myriad shades of meaning of the word are reflected in the solemn Jewish holiday Yom Kippur, the Day of Atonement, a time of ritual rest, fasting, and prayer in which observants seek forgiveness for any transgressions committed over the previous year, amend behavior, and make repentance for the purpose of reorganizing their personal and community life to augment the process of change. Rabbi Michael Lerner says, "The great message of these High Holy Days is that change is possible—we are not stuck." For centuries these holidays have been a cause, Lerner explained to me, of "great joy for the force of healing and transformation that God makes possible," and they allow us to acknowledge that "this world is co-created by all of us, and we atone for all of it."

Beyond the Judeo-Christian traditions, many indigenous cultures, from American Indians to New Guinea tribesmen, enforce strict rituals and ceremonies aimed at restoring the balance of life undone after battles, indiscretions, or violations of taboos. In the powerful documentary film from Australia, *Breaking Bows and Arrows*, a New Guinea Bougainvillean tribesman named Frances Boisibere painfully confesses to a vengeance killing in a nearby village, then fulfills the requirement for the traditional reconciliation ceremony. "So we could have peace and they have peace, too," Boisibere says, "and so we do not pass [revenge] on." What kind of peace? Boisibere says it is the kind that comes from their old peacemaking rituals that "clear the conscience, lift the heaviness, eliminate heartache, and have done with our sorrow."

Over time the understanding and practice of atonement has evolved from its theological underpinnings to more generally refer to *an act that rights a wrong, makes amends, repairs harm, offers restitution, attempts compensation, clears the conscience of the offender, relieves the anger of the victim, and serves justice with a sacrifice commensurate with the harm that has been done.*

If performed willingly and honestly, atoning acknowledges the harm and the grief of the victim that, if not dealt with, often leads to a wider cycle of revenge in communities. Anger and shame are open wounds that can fester for decades—as I can attest to after one unforgettable exchange with the wife of a Vietnam War veteran. She confided to me that her husband's one trip of atonement back to Vietnam, in which he helped build an orphanage, had healed him more than twenty years of psychotherapy.

The profound truth lurking inside this active, almost alchemical aspect of atonement is beautifully borne out by Goethe, in the Atonement section of his poem "Trilogy." There, he elegantly describes how the "lightened heart" offers itself willingly and with joy in "grateful payment" for a sweet gift of "music and love." Five concise lines are all it takes for the great German poet to reveal repentance as the secret heart of atonement. The word itself derives from the Old French *repentir*, to feel deep regret, through the Latin *paentiere*, to make sorry, from the earlier Greek *paena*, pain and payment, as in the offering of blood money. So atonement *costs* us something—pride, humility, time, money. If it doesn't involve a sacrifice of some kind, it isn't real atonement.

Twenty-five hundred years ago, the Greek playwright Aeschylus asked, "What atonement is there for blood spilt upon the earth?" All over the earth people are still wondering the same thing. For many, the example of Mohandas Gandhi's practice of *satyagraha*, or nonviolence, has proved to be the modern answer to Aeschylus' plaintive cry because it has helped transform our attitudes toward peacemaking. Stories about Gandhi's personal responses to violence read like modern parables. One such contemporary story is Khaled Hosseini's powerful novel *The Kite Runner*. Amir is an exiled Afghani writer, living in San Francisco, who has been racked with lifelong guilt over his betrayal of his best friend, Hassan, the son of the family servant, when they were boys growing up in Kabul. When his friend's father calls Amir and pleads for him to return to Afghanistan, he recoils with fear. But when Amir is told, "And now there's a way to be good again," he recognizes the chance for redemption. At great peril, Amir returns to the harrowing violence of his homeland, and despite great risk to his life, he finds a way to atone for his youthful betrayal. As Richard Corliss wrote in his review of the movie in *Time* magazine, it is a story that "makes you believe there may be justice in the world," which is a clear and concise way to describe the effect of going beyond forgiveness to an act of atonement. It has the uncanny power to restore balance and justice.

When the virulent apartheid government in South Africa was overthrown in 1994 by the potent combination of strong international condemnation and domestic resistance, President Nelson Mandela, Archbishop Desmond Tutu, and the Truth and Reconciliation Commission startled the world with their approach to reconciliation and peacemaking. As Tutu's biographer, John Allen, wrote in *Tutu: Rabble-Rouser for Peace*, the new democratically elected leaders offered their former persecutors "amnesty in exchange for truth [and] healing in place of retribution." One of the first moves Mandela made as president has become emblematic of the black South African efforts to transcend the impulse to exact revenge. Turning to his own former prison guards on Robben Island, where he was incarcerated for over twenty years, Mandela offered them jobs as ferry pilots and prison guides when the island became a tourist site.

"This kind of justice," Tutu said later that year, "seeks to rehabilitate both the victim and the perpetrator, who should be given the opportunity to be integrated into the community he or she has injured by his or her offense."

Today many courts are echoing the commission's vision of restorative justice. That vision was an outgrowth of traditional African peacemaking practices, which in turn were rooted in an ancient tribal belief in the ultimate interconnection of all people. Nowhere is this better expressed than in the African proverb, "I am because you are; you are because we are."

In 2000 a judge in Atlanta sentenced four white-racist arsonists to rebuild the black church they had deliberately burned down. In 2007 a judge in New Hampshire ordered nine college students who had drunkenly trashed poet Robert Frost's home to apologize, clean up the mess, and then take classes with Frost's biographer, Jay Parini, to learn why their crime was so disrespectful and had caused so much grief.

In 2007 the government of Brazil created the Amnesty Commission in an effort to seek forgiveness from hundreds of victims of torture during military rule in the mid-1970s. But the government too has gone a step further, offering what the Rev. Fred Morris, himself a torture victim, calls a "lump sum of money and a lifetime pension as a gesture of compensation." What this atonement process is accomplishing, he concludes, is to help the entire country "regain its dignity after the horrors of the military regime."

The Indian rights lawyer James Botsford reports that in Wisconsin, the Tribal Judges Association has been working with the Indian Law Office of Wisconsin Judicare over the past few years to encourage the reemergence and revitalization of peace-making in their tribal courts and tribal communities.

"Forty tribal people," he writes, "from eight of Wisconsin's eleven tribes have gone through a week-long certification course in mediation and taken supplemental training on Indian specific cultural components in peacemaking. Several tribal courts here have begun using peacemaking/mediation as a way for parties to resolve their conflicts without litigation." The difference, he explains, is that the Western way of justice is firmly based on adversarial law, whose goal is an outcome only one side needs to feel is just. Unfortunately, he adds, the approach emphasizes winning to such a degree that it demands a loser. "Punishment," he adds, "penalty, and judgments force us to miss opportunities to educate, grow, learn and heal."

Over the years, Botsford has described to me several inspiring examples of the revival of tribal peacemaking, or what the Indian elders playfully refer to as "original dispute resolution." One story from a reservation community stands out. It seems that there was a particularly incorrigible Native kid who deliberately broke an old woman's window and spray-painted her house. Recently, Botsford wrote to me:

> A Peacemaking session was convened with all the stakeholders in this kid's life. They gathered in a traditional Talking Circle. A feather was passed around and around until all was said that had to be said. By then it was learned that the kid was acting out, angry that his home life was lousy, even dangerous. His father was a drunken jerk, and beat the kids and their mother. The kid's grandparents were summoned to meet along with tribal clan elders. Together, they decided that the reprobate of a father needed to make some serious adjustments in his behavior, and he was required to apologize to his wife and his kids. Instead of exiling the boy to the juvenile detention center, which was many miles away, he was told to apologize to the old woman, repair her house, and to fetch her groceries for six months. But

that's not all. When the elders learned that the kid liked working with wood he was assigned to a tribal elder, what we would
call a mentor, who was a woodworker. Since then all of his healing and atonement has been monitored by a periodic review with
the tribal elders.

Uncannily, not long after I read Botsford's story I came
across an article in the *Irish Times* that seemed to be a poignant
echo of these nascent attempts at restorative justice. Addressing
the need to allow a second chance to youths guilty of petty
crimes in Ireland, Eammonn Mac Aodha wrote to the editors,
"While society must be protected from those who might pose it
a threat, it is vital we let people get on with their lives once
they have atoned."

The Next Step

For me, *Beyond Forgiveness: Reflections on Atonement* resembles one of those Age of Exploration ships that explored vast,
uncharted, dangerous seas in search of spices, treasure, and knowledge. The era's mapmakers often sketched dragons in the blank
spaces of the Seven Seas, where no Europeans had ever sailed.
On some maps, underneath those creatures you can still read
playful captions, such as "Here Be Dragons" or "Sleeping Beauties
Lie Here," poetic suggestions that unmapped worlds might reveal
marvels to be embraced rather than perils to be avoided.

Such is the spirit in which the following fifteen essays and
interviews in this book are offered. While a great deal has been
written and published about forgiveness in our time, the idea of
moving beyond it to atonement is mostly uncharted territory for
modern people. For many, the most recognizable equivalent of
atonement in our time is what Archbishop Tutu called *restitution* during the Truth and Reconciliation Commission hearings
in South Africa. The contributors to this volume offer a series of
exhilarating discoveries within our court systems, international
negotiations, business transactions, and personal relationships

that provide powerful alternatives to lives spent plotting revenge or lashing out with reprisals. These authors help us realize that in dispute resolution we always have a choice when confronting the seemingly intractable conflicts that trouble the world. We can view our disputes either as monstrous beasts or as slumbering beauties, as if peaceful reconciliation is waiting to be awakened.

While still a member of the Truth and Reconciliation Commission, which he helped found, Archbishop Tutu wrote:

> Unless you deal with the past in a creative and positive manner, then you run the terrible risk of having no future worth speaking of. The past can have a baleful or beneficial impact on the future. South Africa will be seriously undermined if those who benefited from the obnoxious apartheid system, perceived as the oppressors, will not ask for forgiveness for the awful things done under apartheid and if the victims, the oppressed, do not offer forgiveness.

As *National Geographic* magazine reports in its June 2010 issue, the "day of reckoning" in South Africa came in the early 1990s, but its repercussions are still unfolding. Deon Snyman, a Dutch Reformed Church minister, says, "Those who supported the system of apartheid need to apologize in a way that will feel sincere. Then they need to make amends in a way that restores some of the dignity and some of the material opportunities that had eroded under that system." His solution is a powerful illustration of the need to move beyond forgiveness, as noble and vital as that is, to the next and clinching stage of reconciliation, which is needed to end the cycles of violence seen in his country. What is still needed, he says, is "community-led restitution—the creation of such emblems of remorse, a school, a clinic, or a skills-training center."

Since November 2009, human rights groups have been demanding that in cases where political prisoners have been considered for presidential pardons, their victims must be given a chance to tell their story. Many of these victims appearing in court wore a T-shirt that read, "No reconciliation without truth, reparation, redress."

On February 23, 2010, the South African Constitutional Court ruled in favor of the victims, many of whom have since been able to regain some of their dignity by telling the world what happened. As one woman, who had been tortured under apartheid, said after her day in court, she feels she is no longer a victim and can move on with her life.

Creative and positive, ceaseless and courageous, atonement is, as Senator Ted Kennedy wrote in his memoirs just before his passing in the summer of 2009, "a never-ending process." Never-ending, but never less than worthy, because atonement speaks to the secret part of us that needs to *prove* we are sorry for committing a terrible wrong, to show some proof that our words—"I'm sorry"—are not empty, but will be backed up by an *action* that stops the soul rust threatening to corrode our lives.

For Senator Kennedy's fellow senator Robert Byrd, remorse took decades to unfold. In the early 1940s, Byrd had been an "Exalted Cyclops" in the Ku Klux Klan, an association he later regarded as "an immutable stain," and which he feared would irreparably harm his legacy. Nonetheless, as Frank Rich, in an op-ed piece in the *New York Times* in the summer of 2010, wrote, "His résumé in racism was dwarfed not just by his efforts to atone for it but by his legislative achievements on many fronts during his epic Senate career."

Our sense of sustainable justice demands action if the gap between forgiveness and atonement, apologies and restitution is not closed, if our contrition is not expressed by a *meaningful* act that reconciles the offender with his or her victim.

Consider the report from the *Melbourne Herald-Sun*, in July 2010, that when Archbishop Denis Hart apologized to victims of sexual abuse by Catholic clergy, the Forgotten Australian Action Group's spokesperson Louise Goode remarked, "It's farcical if it isn't followed by the action of atonement, which needs to be expressed in a financial way. The apology must come with redress and compensation." The Melbourne Victim's Collective said the apology, though sincere, was just words, and that "concrete and practical reform" were needed, such as abuse education for clergy and parishioners alike.

Similarly, Financial Times.com called for "acts of atonement" from the British government for the deaths of fourteen Irish Catholics on "Bloody Sunday," in Londonderry in 1972. Atonement is also called for in the "one man crusade" by Efraim Zuroff, the Israeli director of the Simon Wiesenthal Center, for war crimes against Jews by Lithuanian partisans during World War II. "The Lithuanians," Zuroff told CNN in 2010, "squandered the best chance they had to get that burden of guilt off them. And now it's going to take them 100 years to get rid of it. The only way to succeed is through education, documentation, research—and a lot of pain."

As Zuroff points out so succinctly, part of the power of atonement is that it has the potential to lift our guilt, accept responsibility for wrongs committed, and assuage our pain, no matter how much time has passed.

According to the *Providence Journal*, in Rhode Island, Brown University has begun "fulfilling its vow of atonement." After intrepid researchers uncovered the university's unsettling ties to the early slave trade, it has moved steadily forward in a series of amends. Brown is expanding its African studies department, establishing a fellowship for the study of the slave trade, hiring seventy-nine-year-old Nigerian novelist Chinua Achebe as a teacher, and bringing in historian Jane Lancaster to "revise the university's history." A slave memorial is planned for the campus.

But atonement and amends are not limited to academia and religious organizations. Redemption in one form or another has long been a recurrent theme in the movie industry, from Luc Besson's *Joan of Arc* to Robert Bresson's *Pickpocket*, Roland Joffé's *Mission*, Sidney Lumet's *Verdict*, Jane Anderson's *Prize Winner of*

Defiance, Ohio, Marc Forster's *Kite Runner*, and Clint Eastwood's remarkable *Gran Torino*. In this last film, Eastwood's character, a grizzled Korean war vet, retired Ford factory worker, and recent widower named Walt Kowalski is confronted by his Hmong next-door neighbor. She has brought her brother Thao over to his house because "he wants to make amends" for trying to steal Walt's beloved car, his 1972 Gran Torino. At first Walt balks, as many do when offered restitution, but eventually he relents, allowing the boy to wash his car and make repairs to the dilapidated Hmong house across the street. Against all odds, the resentment and suspicion, the guilt and shame dissolve, and one of the most unusual and touching friendships in recent movie history is born, which precipitates a startling, cathartic atonement in the final scene.

What all the above stories, anecdotes, and research have in common can be compressed into a single observation that my old friend, the late mythologist Joseph Campbell, told me was the core of all the great wisdom traditions throughout history: "The ultimate metaphysical realization is that . . . *you and the other are one.*"

the revival of an ancient awareness

RICHARD J. MEYER

When I first encountered the famous speech by Chief Keokuk (Kiyo'kaga), I felt many deep and conflicting emotions, including shock, inspiration, awe, and confusion. I asked, and I continue to ask, how this tribal Sauk chief could say these words while he and his nation were being sentenced to the Trail of Tears. His words brought tears to my eyes:

> The many moons and sunny days we have lived here will long be remembered by us. The Great Spirit has smiled upon us and made us glad. But we have agreed to go. We go to a country we know little of. Our home will be beyond a great river on the way to the setting sun. We will build our wigwams there in another land. . . . In peace we bid you good-bye. . . . If you come to see us, we will gladly welcome you.

How could he even think of a future where "we will gladly welcome you"? What spiritual source had this leader tapped?

Over the years, I have admired many individuals who have dealt with "unforgivable" tragedies and dire circumstances. How did they perform the seemingly impossible act of forgiveness? How did the Kennedy family forgive the assassins of Jack and Bobby? How could Jacqueline write a letter to Lee Harvey

Oswald's widow while she was planning the funeral of her husband, the fallen president? Skeptics might believe that the letter was contrived by aides; and yet, even if that were true, had I been her I would not have had the will to sign it.

How did Abraham Lincoln invite his opponents to be members of his cabinet and later pen the immortal words of his Second Inaugural Address, on August 4, 1865:

> With malice toward none, with charity for all . . . let us strive on to finish the work we are in . . . to do all which may achieve and cherish a just and lasting peace among ourselves and with all nations.

How did Lincoln write these words—and *mean* what he wrote—and even more, how was he able to act upon them? How was Azim Khamisa, an immigrant investment banker, able to view the thirteen-year-old murderer of his son, Tariq, as a second victim of the senseless crime? Why does a rape victim seek out her attacker and initiate an atonement process?

In my life, I have experienced a world where someone not only holds a resentment but acts on it, and where some still hold on to a slight from childhood. Perhaps it is easier to forgive the big things—the unforgivable things—while the smaller hurts remain as a low-grade infection. Yet I know that not dealing with a petty infection is analogous to the way that stealing a dime makes it easier for me to steal a dollar, and stealing a dollar makes it easier for me to steal a hundred.

I am convinced that reducing anger in my life is very important. A very steep path suggested by a mystic states, "We are encouraged to *eliminate* our anger." That same mystic went on to make the point that at first our anger can be likened to words we carve in the rocks of a cliff. In time, the wind and rains eliminate these words. As we progress, we learn to write our words in the sand of the seashore; in a day or two the tides wash them away. Then, finally, we learn to write our anger in the water.

If we can learn to write our anger in the waters of life and allow it to flow away—if we are truly able to forgive—I believe we become "bulletproof," immune to the desire for violence or revenge. Nothing else is able to hurt us. (As modern science has discovered, we learn that resentments also create a destructive physical change in our bodies.)

The Origins of This Book

The inspiration for this book began when I read Marianne Williamson's book *Healing the Soul of America*. Her prayers of atonement seemed like the exact medicine we all need.

Later, as a board member for a social profit organization, the Metta Center for Nonviolence Education, I asked that the idea of a book devoted to the subject of atonement be placed on the agenda. It was—but at the very bottom. But a board member who had to leave early paused and said, "Before I leave, I want to hear about this atonement project." Surprised, I described my vision, and it was very well received.

A month later, attending a space launch at Cape Canaveral, Florida, I was politely asked at dinner what our social profit organization, Metta, was doing. I said that we were exploring the concept of a book on atonement. As the word "atonement" came from my mouth, the eight people at the table all stopped speaking, and several of them seemed to have dropped their forks. Had I struck a raw nerve?

I ended the conversation by saying, "We need to invite everyone, 'All the King's horses and all the King's men,' as well as all the Queen's horses and all the Queen's women, so to speak, to participate in our atonement project."

With time and patience, the project has flowered with beautiful blossoms in the form of the contributions from many wonderful authors who have added to this anthology. This seems only right since the word *anthology*, editor Phil Cousineau points out, originally meant "a gathering of flowers."

A Personal Note

In the arena of personal atonement, the authors in this anthology describe many moving stories of wrongs that have occurred in their lives, along with solutions that have arrived as part of the healing process. As we expand our awareness to a less personal and more national level, we believe it will be easier to identify wrongs that have occurred collectively and have a more authentic way to achieve genuine atonement.

But a difficult question remains. On the collective level of forgiveness and atonement, are we responsible for wrongs that were perpetrated hundreds of years ago by our ancestors?

Marianne Williamson points out, as related in Michael Nagler's essay, that when you purchase a business, you purchase both its assets and its liabilities. I agree. These liabilities continue to compound and create a blockage that in turn hampers our ability to move forward. Our mistakes, like most, were most likely based on fear. It does not matter. We want to move forward. We understand that our government would have a difficult time announcing its mistakes. This is because our government is only a reflection of the people, and many of us have been slow to embrace atonement. Likewise, we also understand that other countries have committed grave errors that have hurt our nation—and other nations. But we, as individuals, choose to move forward. Each of us can use the techniques of the great religions of the world and some of the ideas presented in this book. If all the individuals of our nation were to join in this cause of Atonement, our nation would follow, as would the world.

This volume reviews some of the poor choices of our ancestors, and some of our contemporaries. The essays have inspired me to review my participation in any discord, past and present. Ideally, this book will inspire you to become more engaged, more reflective. It is designed to raise questions more than answers: *Why am I afraid to do more? What could I have done better? When was the last time I asked God or my fellow human beings for forgiveness? What can I do to rectify my own shortcomings in my own individual sphere? How can I make things right?*

Those of us involved in what I think of as the Atonement Movement realize that this process may be painful, and that by necessity it may have political and religious implications. But we believe too that in every situation that calls for reconciliation, all of us, regardless of political or religious orientation, can move forward through bold acts of self-forgiveness, forgiveness of others, and atonement. If we can do that, together we will heal the world.

PART ONE

forgiveness and beyond

Hope for a great sea-change
On the far side of revenge.
Believe that a further shore
Is reachable from here.
Believe in miracles
And cures and
healing wells.

—*Seamus Heaney*

CHAPTER 1

forgiveness as spiritual liberation

MICHAEL BERNARD BECKWITH

> Whatever liberates our spirit without
> giving us self-control is disastrous.
>
> —Johann Wolfgang von Goethe

Michael Bernard Beckwith is the founder of the Agape International Spiritual Center and cofounder of the Association for Global New Thought, and of the Season for Nonviolence. As revealed in this interview, he is deeply committed to helping others break free from the patterns of violence and revenge that we have all inherited and to sparking the belief that people can change, as well as "grow, develop, and unfold." Real forgiveness, he has said, is "giving up the hope that the past could have been any different."

At Barack Obama's inauguration in 2009, he said, and I'm paraphrasing, that in order to move forward, the Israelis are going to have to see things from the Palestinian point of view, and the Palestinians are going to have see things from the Israeli point of view.

This is a page out of Gandhi, and one out of Martin Luther King Jr., on real forgiveness and compassion, which means seeing things from the other person's perspective. Oftentimes when we forgive, we hold on to our perception, and we forget that someone else has a different perception.

To me real forgiveness takes place not only when amends are made—when that sense of atonement has happened—but when I can *see* from the other person's perspective.

When I was a young boy, I became a Boy Scout. One day I was walking home with a friend of mine. Suddenly, we noticed a house on fire. We looked inside and saw a man who was unconscious, lying on his couch. We saw smoke everywhere, but we couldn't wake him up. We ran down the street trying to knock on people's doors to say, "We need to use your phone." But people saw only these little black kids, and they didn't want us to come into their homes. Finally, somebody said, "Wait here. I'll call the police, and I'll call the fire department." And they did. Soon after, we saw the fire truck coming down the street, so we ran down to meet it. We were standing on the island, pointing to the house. A fireman came out of the truck and said to us, "Get out of the way, you little niggers!"

Just like that.

I was ten or eleven years old at the time. It hit me like a ton of bricks on my chest. We were Boy Scouts. We were wearing our uniforms. We had visions of saving this man and being recognized in some way.

When we heard those words, we were floored. We stuck around long enough to see them break down the door and bring out the man on a stretcher with an oxygen mask on his face. The fire department even saved his dogs.

At the end of the day, no one had died; the firefighters had saved the man. But I especially remember that day, because that day I quit the Boy Scouts. I never went back. I felt a little anger in me and thought that maybe there was something wrong with me. But I began a quest. It was that incident that actually helped set me on my path of deep introspection, and of being somewhat of a revolutionary and taking a stand to change society.

As the years went on, I was called to forgive this fireman. But I didn't release the angst and the resentment that were in my belly. Then one time when I was doing some forgiveness work, the memory of that fireman "came up" again for some reason. I thought that I had already forgiven him and moved on, but evidently I hadn't.

Suddenly, I left my body. I rose up, and I entered into the body of the fireman. I saw him, and then I heard him say those words, "Get out of the way, you little niggers!" Of course, there was ignorance and prejudice in him, but I realized then that what had really been on his mind was, *These kids are in the way.* He was just trying to get to the fire. From his point of view, there were two little niggers, but his more pressing thought was, *I've got to get to the fire, and they're in the way.*

What happened that day when I was doing the forgiveness work was that I suddenly saw something from the fireman's perspective—and it increased my ability to be forgiving.

Forgiveness as Practice

Forgiveness is very powerful, and it's necessary for our well-being. But other steps must be made, when possible, to make amends. Of course, if persons are dead or you can't get in touch with them, you still have work to do within your own being.

It's very powerful when something happens and you are willing to see things from the other person's point of view, and your perception expands. That's the birth of compassion: to walk a mile in the other person's moccasins. But there must be a willingness to do that. Instead, people are often unwilling to do it, saying, "No, *I'm* right. *This* is what happened; this is my point of view. I'm going to forgive you for what you did." In fact, you might not share my point of view, my perception, while I assume you do. I think that getting over that misunderstanding is very big in the practice of forgiveness.

Regarding forgiveness becoming a practice, I think that a person needs a practice, period. The ego is so dominant that we are always prone to be *right*, to understand *our* side of the equation. We need a spiritual practice that is constantly expanding our paradigm, our point of view, so that we're not seeing things through the ego but through the heart of compassion, our spiritual perception.

We need a prayer practice, and we need a meditation practice. We need to practice philanthropy, generosity. We need to *practice*. These things have to become a practice until they become a way of life.

At-One-Ment

The act of atonement, the experience of *at-one-ment*, allows you to be conscious that you've never really been cut off, that you've always been one with the only power there is. Unfortunately, though, there is a perception and an experience of being cut off from the whole, based on slights that have been done, and on the lack of making amends. This is "unforgiveness." But when we begin doing the inner work of making amends, of self-forgiveness, and of forgiveness of others, we have the realization that *we are at one* with something that we can never really be cut off from, except in our perception.

We can think of it this way: there's a perception that the sun sets. But actually the earth just turns on its axis; it's only a perception that the sun is gone. In reality, it is shining on another part of the earth. *It's all perception.*

The pain and the suffering is the story we tell ourselves. I ask people, "What is the story you are telling yourselves?" With unforgiveness the story we are telling ourselves is that we are lacking something because of something someone did or did not do. We *are* missing something—a story that explains the truth of who we really are and goes beyond mere perception to the truth. In reality we are always connected, even when my perception is telling me that because you did something to me, I am missing something if I am disconnected. That's my perception; that's my experience.

In fact, you cannot determine my destiny; only my perception can determine my destiny. When I forgive you, I take my power back. When I give you back affirmative energy for something you may have done, I own my power—and now I own my destiny. My destiny is not in the hands of what you did or did not do to me. If we accept responsibility for our actions, we emerge out of being a victim. I'm not denying that somebody did something bad. I'm not sweeping it under the rug. I'm not letting them off the hook in any way, shape, or form. But I am allowing a bigger destiny in me to unfold. I am not a victim of what somebody did to me, or what they've said about me, or called me. I'm not victimized by any of that. I forgive it. I own my own power. *And I move forward on my journey.*

The Giving Within For-Give-Ness

To use a Christian analogy, people say that Jesus taught, "You should turn the cheek if someone smites you; you should turn the other cheek if they wrong you." Many people interpret this as saying that if someone hits you, you should turn the other cheek and let them hit you again. I don't think he meant that. I think he meant that you are supposed to give back a different form of energy. If you are given hate or indifference, you are to give back love, patience, and compassion. Turning the other cheek means you're giving back another energy. If someone gives you negative energy, you give back positive, affirmative energy—such as forgiveness. If someone has done something wrong or destructive to you, you give another energy back. Instead of "giving as good as you get," you give back a higher form of energy.

This is the giving within for-give-ness.

You should disengage then from the ego's point of view, which is always saying that you're right, and that as you've been given negative energy, so you should *double* it back on the other person.

This is oftentimes where nations live: in revenge.

But the *practice* of forgiveness is a higher state of consciousness because you're acknowledging that someone may have done something wrong, destructive, or not life-enhancing, but you are still going to give back an *affirmative* energy in their direction. That is really a state of consciousness that the reptilian brain is not going to relate to!

Collective Forgiveness, Collective Atonement

I look at collective atonement from two perspectives. One is from the individual who has been victimized. For instance, when I speak to African Americans about the evils that have been heaped upon us as a race, I speak about not using that history as an excuse to not move forward. I speak about forgiveness. I speak about not severing ourselves from the energy of what has been done *for* us. And I speak about not looking for someone outside of ourselves to just give us something.

When I speak to the larger population, I talk about compassion, about what happened, about what can be done in the service of forgiveness—making atonement, moving forward—whether that's affirmative action or reparations.

I have two perceptions then for two different groups of people. It's not a blanket situation. I'll say to myself, *Don't look for anything from anybody. This is the hand you've been dealt. This is what's happened. There are glass ceilings. There is racism, bigotry, prejudice. Move forward as best you can. Take what you have and go forward, forgiving.* And then to people in so-called power I say, "You have to understand what has happened, and then you have to find a way to move from the consciousness of compassion to make amends." In other words, I don't lump it all together.

I invite my congregation to practice forgiveness before they go to bed at night. That is, I invite them not to wait until the day they die to judge their entire life. I invite them to look at themselves on a daily basis and ask: "What mistakes did I make? Are there amends that need to be made? Did someone do me wrong? Is there some forgiveness that needs to happen?" Then, forgive themselves. That way, they're going to bed free, clean, and clear. Unforgiveness is not piling up and creating static that prevents one from hearing the voice of God. Forgiveness becomes a way of living.

If we allow hurt and pain to pile up, we know metaphysically, from the mind-body connection, that we will be dealing with a lack of creativity, a lack of energy, and disease, and all because we're allowing this filter we look through to become more and more clouded.

There are many times during the year, in the Jewish, Christian, and Buddhist traditions, when you do your forgiveness through special rituals, but I think it's very powerful to practice forgiveness and self-forgiveness every night.

On the Journey

When we're stuck on our journey, lost in the forest, or trapped in the labyrinth, it's because, generally speaking, we have done something wrong and we're covering it up. It's like what happens when something toxic is in our body. The body has a protective mechanism; it creates a cyst. Within the cyst is mercury or some other toxic substance that the body does not want in the bloodstream. The average person says, "I have a cyst. That's a bad thing." Actually a cyst is nature's way of keeping us safe. Psychologically, we develop defensive and compulsive behaviors, coping mechanisms that keep a deep hurt from being totally felt. That way we can function, somewhat.

When we begin to develop a spiritual practice, we become stronger and stronger in the awareness that we live in a friendly universe, that God is *for* us and not against us. When that becomes more real to us, we start to dissolve the cyst; in other words, we start to dispel the coping and defense mechanisms, the compulsive behaviors that are sapping the energy from our natural creativity, our loving and giving selves.

The way we function in the world when we have a spiritual practice of affirmative prayer, meditation, contemplation, introspection, study, fellowship, or sacred service, is that we start to unravel our stories about being a victim, being powerless, being separated. The cysts or coping mechanisms are then no longer necessary. We become a more fully enfranchised expression of the infinite. We have more power. We are no longer separated: we achieve at-one-ment.

The Real Work

The most important work we do is not the formal prayers, the meditation time. These are important, but the real work happens during the rest of the day. This is when you contemplate the content of your awareness, when you actually look at the thoughts that are emerging. You notice that very often the thoughts you have are a reflection of the everyday. But that world is an illusion; it has all kinds of decadent values, and is oftentimes a reflection of the mass ego, which is full of fear, doubt, worry, and separation.

If you are able to look at those "worldly" thoughts as they're emerging, and you're not resisting them, not trying to make them go away, and not getting attached to them, then you can slowly disempower them. As they lose their power, you begin to be aware of another world—a spiritual world.

If I could wax spiritual for a moment, this is the world that God sees, a world of beauty, a world of harmony.

The Long View

If you then step back for a moment, you find that God is still God; apple trees are still doing apples; peach trees are still doing peaches. Nothing has really changed in the world. The only thing that has changed is your perception, which has been limited. The economic system is immature, and at best it does not reflect the plenitude of the universe. You can try to bail out that system as much as you want, but it's always going to have a hole in it, at least until it comes into harmony with the spiritual system, which we are far from at the moment.

If we look at our thoughts on a regular basis, we will see which thoughts are reflecting the worldly—and which thoughts are reflecting our soul. When we begin to participate in the more soulful thoughts, our life begins to change. We give birth to creativity, to compassion, to patience, to love. And we give birth to forgiveness. Now these are not emotions; these are nondual qualities that are of the presence of God that is within us. So I teach people to have a definite formal time for practice, because what we do during the rest of the day is where the rubber meets the road.

The Death of the Ego

The ego doesn't know the difference between spiritual growth and annihilation. When we have a moment of atonement, it's like a little death. We're actually dying to a perception that we've been holding on to. If we then say, "I forgive," it really means, "I'm changing." *I'm* changing—not the other person. The other person may have done a dastardly thing, but if I am willing to go deep within my soul to forgive that individual, then *I am changing*, not him. But we are afraid of change, afraid of transformation, because of that little death, which is really the death of our ego, our perception, and our perspective.

There's a forgiveness story that I heard originally from the great Howard Thurman. The way I tell it and share it means it is now my story.

A man wants to forgive someone who has done him wrong. But he is having difficulty doing so—at least, he is aware of this—so before he goes to bed, he says a sincere prayer and asks for assistance with forgiveness. As the man falls asleep, he is visited by an angel. While he's in the lucid dream state, the angel teaches him that all forgiveness is really *self*-forgiveness. He learns that forgiveness releases toxins, poison; it releases the resentment within you. When you forgive someone else, he learns, you're really doing yourself a service.

When the man wakes up the next day, he's more prone to forgive the man who had done him wrong. But that night when he's about to go to sleep, he realizes there is still rancor in his heart. He hasn't quite gotten there. So he prays again, "Please, Lord, I really want to know how to forgive."

As he falls asleep, he's visited again by the angel. This time the angel takes him out of his body and brings him to the very moment of conception of the man who had done him wrong. The angel takes him through the time line of the man's life and shows him the conditions the man was raised under, the teachers he had, the things that happened to him, all the way up to the moment when the infraction occurred. Then the angel shows him that what this man did—the wrong he committed— was the highest and best thing he could have done. Moreover, the angel shows him that if the man could have known better, he would have done better. *This was the best that he could do in that moment. Forgive him.*

When the man wakes up, he realizes, "Wow—that was the best he could do. Even though it was bad. Even though he hurt people. Even though he caused me suffering. Based on his limited perception, his limited point of view, that was the best he had to offer."

But the next night the man still has an inkling of unforgiveness lurking in him. So he gets down on his knees, and he really goes at it: "God, I really want to be released from this unforgiveness. Help me."

Praying, he falls asleep. The angel comes for the third time and again takes him out of his body. This time the angel parts the veil of eternity, separates the veil of time and space, so that the man can see the moment when God is actually creating a soul. Then he *gasps*, because he sees that that man who is being created, the man who wronged him, is *himself*.

Behind the veil, the man can finally see that we're all one. And so he is able to come back to the waking world with the awareness that the man who wronged him *is* him. All forgiveness is self-forgiveness. Finally, he is able to release the rancor, the animosity, the anger, and the resentment that were in his own heart.

The Moment of Moments

At moments, you know you are more than your biological imperatives, more than your DNA, more than what you inherited from your culture. Something about you is eternal. You begin to have that spiritual epiphany, that *Aha!* When that realization takes over, it can be said that you are coming into your spiritual maturity. And it is in that spiritual maturity that forgiveness has its beginnings.

Look at Rwanda. You now have people whose families were slaughtered living next door to the people who did the slaughtering. They have entered into a forgiveness pact, and they are working side by side.

We can go through the whole civil rights movement, and through the many experiences of the Dalai Lama. If one individual can rise above the limited perception of unforgiveness, it means that deep within us we all have the capacity to touch the essence of forgiveness.

The Roots of Atonement

In South Africa, Nelson Mandela invited to sit with him at a banquet a man who had urinated on him when he was in prison on Robben Island, off the coast of Cape Town. Mandela also hired his ex-jailers to act as tour guides and serve as ferry operators to and from Robben Island. With these acts he was granting forgiveness and inviting atonement. He was turning the other cheek, giving one form of energy for another.

No one would have thought it out of sorts if Mandela and others had slapped those ex-guards around the prison, or embarrassed them, or staged a war tribunal. But by forgiving them and by actually committing a *positive* act, he was displaying a very high state of consciousness. Likewise, Dr. Martin Luther King Jr., in the 1960s, kept individuals from shooting and sniping, saying, "We're going to give love for hate. Know that our cause is just. We're going to forgive and we're going to continue to withstand the blows, and continue to love our enemy until we convert the enemy to a friend."

In contrast, look at what happened after 9/11, at a time when everyone was showering the United States with such compassion. The president said, "We're going to hunt them down and kill them." Then he said, "Now go shopping." He proffered consumerism and unforgiveness in the same breath. It was a throwback to the old cowboy movies: "We'll circle the wagons and kill everybody."

The high states of consciousness shown by Dr. King and Nelson Mandela raise the question of whether it helps inspire the general population when a public figure behaves in such exemplary ways. I think it's actually a double-edged sword. On the one hand, it gives us a tremendous example; on the other, people sometimes confer a kind of specialness on these figures. They forget that they were ordinary people, too. Gandhi was an attorney; King was a twenty-six-year-old Baptist minister; Mandela, in jail for twenty-seven years, had very little education but for the books he read there. These weren't specially anointed people. These were people who dug deep within themselves and discovered that ineffable, timeless dimension of reality, and gave it permission to come forward.

I always say then that "if they can do it, we can do it. Don't put them way up there. Definitely acknowledge them, praise them, have a holiday." But we lose the significance of their actions if we make them too special. What they are examples of is the *possibility* of forgiveness—and of atonement, because they allowed those who had mistreated them to make things right, to make some form of restitution.

Soul Force

In Gandhi's writings, *ahimsa*, literally, "the avoidance of violence," refers to a life of causing no harm, and it is the best path for learning forgiveness. It is a kind of soul force. If you go back to New Testament scriptures, Jesus says, "Pray for those who curse you. Do good to those who spitefully use you." He's saying that if somebody does you wrong, do something good for that person. That is what activates your soul force. It also requires a high state of consciousness, because when somebody does you wrong you want to get them back! But that only increases the cycle of violence and the disenfranchisement from the divine source. If you can rise up then and actually forgive, you're stepping into real spiritual power.

When enough individuals do this, the collective begins to shift. After 9/11, the president had the opportunity to lift the consciousness of the planet—and he blew his moment on stage, and as a politician, by asking for revenge. He reflected the lowest common denominator of society, which is hate, the desire to go out and get them. These may be very normal ways of being in the world, and our spiritual leaders ask us to go to a level that may *not* be the norm—but this higher state of forgiveness is supremely natural from a spiritual point of view.

One time when I was with James Lawson, the civil rights activist, he told me a story. He had been with Dr. King at a function, and as they were about to sit down, a man walked up and asked, "Are you Dr. King Jr.?" King answered, "Yes, I am." And the man spat on him. Dr. King stopped, pulled out a handkerchief and wiped off the spittle, folded the handkerchief neatly, and handed it to the man saying, "I think this belongs to you." His expanded awareness of love allowed him to choose. If he had had a limited perception, he might have struck the man—and everyone would have said, "Well, what did the guy expect? He spit on him!" But King's expanded awareness of love, of peace, of forgiveness gave him more options. And by contrast, he showed that if you have limited awareness, you have fewer options.

The president, after 9/11, had limited perception and limited options, and so did the people he was representing. Other questions could have been asked: "Who did this? Why was this done?"

Of course, we still have to defend ourselves. No one is denying that. But we went into the wrong country! The people who attacked us came from Afghanistan, but we said, "Let's go into Iraq!"

Forgiveness in Our Communities

Community is very important. It offers us a way to be reminded, a way to practice these spiritual principles. You take what you learn in the community and then go out into the larger world. Often the community teaches you that it's easier to forgive somebody you don't know than somebody you run into all the time. You'll hold a grudge against your best friend, but a stranger you'll forgive, for you equate what your best friend did as betrayal. In community, we're given a wonderful opportunity to practice forgiveness. Pretty soon we're able to say, "The world is my community." I love what Dr. Thurman said: "It's impossible to love humanity in general; you can only love humanity in particular." It's abstract to say you love humanity when you can't love the person right next to you, or forgive the person who cut you off on the freeway. You love, in particular, the people you see every day. That's how you love humanity: by forgiving and loving the people that you bump up against every day. It's the friction that causes you to grow.

The Spiritual Challenge

Challenges are our spiritual liberators. They make you strong; they activate qualities in you that were lying dormant, like certain seeds in the forest that will never germinate unless there's a fire. The shell is so hard that only the intensity of fire will break it open. There are qualities that lie dormant in us until there's a challenge big enough to break them open. Beyond the reasons for the challenge, then, there is a redeeming value to certain challenges that make us go within.

I remember years ago speaking at a spiritual community where the congregation actually wanted me to be their minister. There was a small group, however, that didn't want to have an African American in that position, and they demonized me, and said all manner of things that had no reality at all. They talked about race and how property values were going to go down; they said, "those people park their cars on the sidewalk." They threw the book at me. The experience was a challenge that forced me to go down to a level of myself that I never would have plumbed if everything had been hunky-dory. What they said about me forced me to go to a level of forgiveness that made me really fall in love with these people who were calling me bad names.

Over the years, many of these people have come to me in the spirit of atonement, wanting to make amends. I had to allow them to atone for what they had said and done. In turn, I have spoken in public about the depth of love I wouldn't have gotten to if they had first said, "Oh, we love you, Michael. Come on in." Because of the things they said about me, the hard shell covering up the seed of forgiveness cracked in the fire, and I found depths of love in me that I never knew existed.

Phil Cousineau conducted this interview with Michael Bernard Beckwith in Culver City, California, on January 23, 2009.

the wisdom of atonement

JACOB NEEDLEMAN

> Use the present to repair the past,
> and prepare the future.
>
> —*George Ivanovich Gurdjieff*

For the philosopher, professor, and prolific author Jacob Needleman, the path to the well-lived life goes through the asking of profound questions, including the perennial ones about justice. In this interview, Needleman explores atonement as a way of deeply examining the past and making the necessary sacrifices to fix it, if it needs repair. His thoughts on the search for the profound depths of the reconciliation process help illuminate the limitations of forgiveness and the need to move beyond it to concrete acts of making amends. Never one to settle for a quick fix or any easy answer to any deep problem, he is quick to point out that sacrifices are required for what he calls the "deep action" of real atonement. For Needleman atonement is far from an abstract idea, Instead, it is a "metaphysical obligation," even a gift, passed between the victim and perpetrator that helps make possible a more harmonious, more just, even wiser life.

How do I understand my task as a philosopher? What is my approach to the kinds of problems that come with the question of forgiveness and remorse and atonement? These are deep questions of the human spirit, the human soul, the human life. I find that many of the great questions of our lives, if not all of them, have implications for our views of the whole universe, of reality itself, of what it means to be a human being in the universal scheme.

What is the meaning of our life? What is the point? Why are we here? Why do we suffer? Why do we live, why do we die? What can we know? These are the great questions of the human heart, the questions that really have no answers, or it seems that are unanswerable by what we in our culture generally have come to consider answers. In fact the only really interesting questions are the unanswerable ones.

And yet answers exist—just not in the way we tend to search for them. Over the years I have found that when there is a real question, like the one about the relationship between forgiveness, atonement, and reconciliation, I need to open up the question as deeply as possible. I believe it is more gratifying to deepen the real question, in order to show its connection to other things in life, than to simply settle for an acceptable answer.

When two or more people share a question of the heart, it creates a uniquely human bond between them. To deeply question life together results in a certain finer quality of human energy passing between people. We tend to think that what does pass between people should only be things like subjective love, touch, helping each other, being physical in different ways, saying nice things, being pleasant with each other. But when we look back on cultures in different places, we see many things they communicate in their rituals and customs that we don't understand, things that seem difficult and complicated. We, by contrast, seem to have settled for comfort, for convenience, and for communication at a surface level, which is exaggerated now with electronic communication that supposedly brings people together. But it only brings small parts of them together, while the bigger parts are left lonely and untouched, causing terrible discomfort, yearning, and dissatisfaction.

Something needs to pass between people that is not passing. What is it that is *not* passing between us? It's my belief that many of the customs and rituals of the past were meant to help people navigate the metaphysical depths of their inner life and outer, everyday life, simultaneously. And we have lost that.

Repairing the Past

This is my way of *placing* a question, of sharing it with another person, and jumping into it from another angle, in this case the deep question about atonement, or what Gurdjieff calls "to repair the past."

The Jewish tradition says that only the victim has the right to forgive. For people to say, "Let's all forgive the Nazis," is from the point of view of the Jewish tradition meaningless. In fact, it's even an insult. Who are we to forgive people who murdered and butchered millions of men, women, and children? That's something that's so realistic in Judaism—asking, what are the inner conditions necessary for *the real feeling of forgiveness?* Comfortably sitting here in my home in Oakland, California, I can perhaps forgive the Chinese for killing Tibetans, but can the Dalai Lama? If *he* can, then that's big.

This means that real forgiveness has to cost you something, and so does atonement. Maybe atonement *is* the cost of forgiveness. But what is it that makes it cost? What do you pay when you atone? I'm paying something when I atone, but what is it? I can't just say, "I'm sorry." Nonsense! "I'm sorry I killed your son. Please forgive me." Nonsense!

Why? Maybe it has to do with how people express themselves, whether the forgiveness comes from their guts, the cosmic part of the human being. It was like that for Azim Khamisa (Chapter Ten), who found forgiveness for his son's murderer while holding his son in his arms in the grave. At that moment the energies of the universe entered into this man. He's a saint at that point. If your child enters into your hands, and you're standing in his grave, then for that moment you become a saint—you can't help it—either that, or you go crazy.

This painful depth is where real forgiveness and atonement live.

My Russian grandmother was a fierce woman; she was like a tank. Tough, strict with her children. She made her life out of nothing when she came over here. She had six sons and one daughter, and the daughter, who was very beautiful, was just nineteen years old when she was killed crossing the street in front of our house. That beautiful young woman helped me learn how to walk. I had loved her as a small boy. I remember being taken to the cemetery when they buried her and hearing this terrible commotion. I had to close my eyes. My grandmother, who was wrapped in black rags, was so distraught over this girl's death that she jumped into the grave while they were lowering the coffin and shoveling dirt inside. She was screaming and shrieking like a mad woman, trying to pull her daughter out of the grave. Her big strapping sons could barely pull her off. I opened my eyes and saw this old woman digging her nails into the coffin, trying to shake her daughter out of death.

This, too, is where forgiveness and atonement live. Not necessarily in the realm of death but in the realm of the real forces of human life. Atonement is action; atonement is one of those forces that *act*. There might be an inner aspect, which can be huge, but there must be an action as vivid as the physical merging of a mother with her dead daughter when she jumps into the grave.

If Atonement Is Rejected

The Jewish tradition teaches that when you have offended another human being, the one who has committed the offense has got to go to the person who has been injured and seek forgiveness. Then he has to atone. The person who has been hurt may or may not forgive him, and then the other person can try a second time, and again he may or may not be forgiven. But if he is denied a third time, then this kind of solution may no longer be possible. Much is said about this in the traditional texts—more than we can go into here.

Of course, it is cruel not to forgive the person seeking forgiveness; this needs to be emphasized. It's cruel not to forgive someone who is genuinely seeking forgiveness and is willing to pay for it in some sense of the word. It is cruel not to allow the offender to make a payment, to atone. And there's no atonement without forgiveness from both sides.

Sometimes it's hard to go down into personal experience. Very hard. It's easy to say that anger is bad for your health, but it's hard to let it go. We need not underestimate how difficult it is when real harm is done, when a real sonuvabitch screws you over. When somebody hurts someone you love. Marriage is full of this kind of thing; so is divorce. It's not something that can be controlled by the mind, by the emotions. It's easy to say, "Yes, I forgive her, the bitch. I forgive her. It's all right."

No, the hurt runs deeper than that, hence the feelings of vengeance and resentment. The anger is there, in what Gurdjieff calls "the essence." Not so much in the personality. In a way, deep anger, which is a powerful old Teutonic word, is not personal. I don't know what else to call it other than "impersonal anger," which is not an idea, but a force. Christ got deeply angry. He chased the moneychangers out of the temple. He said there would be wailing and gnashing of teeth; he said, "I came to bring not peace but a sword." He was not a pussycat. People have this Caspar Milquetoast version of Christ forgiving everybody. But his forgiveness was strong; it did not come cheap.

He said, "If any man come to me, and hate not his father, and mother, and wife, and children, and brethren, and sisters, yea, and his own life, he cannot be my disciple." What did he mean by that? It sounds perverse. But I feel that it's connected to something profound, deep down in the soul, something about the influences that imprison the life of the soul. Christ the tiger.

With atonement, the big forces of the universe have to be involved; otherwise, to talk of reconciliation is cheap, superficial, hypocritical. But today we don't live much of our lives in conscious relation to big forces in the universe. We have to confront them when we meet death, and birth; then the forces overwhelm us, and sometimes they wake us up. But on the whole our life is pretty comfortable. We do have forces of money that bother us, but they're all mixed up with other things that may take away from the primal, instinctual, and sensual forces within us, among which are the power to love and the power to hate. Now hating what is hateful is in my opinion a worthy thing—that is, if you hate not from your ego but from an impersonal place, as when hating the brutal injustices of the world.

The Question of Remorse

There are hundreds of stories from the Nazi concentration camps, but there is one I must tell now. I know a woman whose mother had been put onto one of the German death trains and sent off to one of the camps. When they arrived, the warden said that everyone had to take a shower. All of the prisoners went into the room with the shower and took their clothes off, but this woman said to herself that something was wrong. As it turns out, she was right. When the showers were turned on, out came hot, scalding water. The Nazis boiled them alive. A thousand people, men, women, and children were boiled to death. This woman pretended to be dead underneath them, and somehow managed to survive.

How can you *not* hate that? It would be stupid to say, "Oh, well, I forgive them." It would be inhuman not to hate that. You could say, "I don't hate them, but I do hate their act." Well, I don't know about that, although I respect impersonal hatred. Sometimes our hatred comes from a deep place that is hard to understand. How we should respond to that remains an open question. Even when it's personal, though, it's not so simple.

But how can anyone atone for the kinds of inhuman acts that took place in the camps? There is an important point here about atonement and reconciliation that has to do with remorse. If you look at the world, can you really feel that there's any hope, that hope is taking hold anywhere? Maybe you can say yes in a few places around the world. But when you're finished thinking about Iraq, you have to think about Rwanda. And when you're done thinking about that, you have to think about what's happening in our own neighborhoods: the violence, brutality, ignorance, coarseness, and stupidity. The more I learn about the Nazis, the more I feel ashamed of being human. I feel like I need to apologize to somebody, to God, to something else; and that I need to atone for those rotten people. What is so different between us? Real forgiveness and atonement touch on the subject of the origin of human evil. Where does it come from? And what is remorse, because atonement without remorse is cheap.

Can those who turned on the boiling water ever achieve atonement? I do not think so. Here one might say, "Only God can atone for such deep crime." Here Judaism and Christianity meet and fuse.

When I was writing about slavery in my book *The American Soul*, I realized that although the civil rights movement was very important in giving black people the rights that others have, it nevertheless would not bring what was really needed until real remorse was felt.

After the book was published, I was interviewed one day on a national call-in show. I began by talking about my idea of the meaning of America, that it creates a protected space for people to come together in a search for conscience. A man called up, who was clearly a black man and who sounded like he may have been driving a truck in who-knows-where. He asked, "What about slavery, Professor?" I felt on the spot. I was scared because he was an African American, and here was I, a Jewish-white professor. On call-in shows you have to speak quickly. I said to myself, *What the hell, just say what you said in the book.* So I did: "Unless Americans actually feel remorse about what's been done," I said, "the other changes are not going to go deep enough, and they aren't going to make the difference that has to be made." I waited for him to say, "That's a cop-out." But instead the man said, with his voice crackling, "That's the best answer I ever heard."

It's one thing to say that we have to make reparations for slavery, though of course that would solve some social problems.

But you know real remorse when you see it. An admission of remorse would be a great gesture, a meaningful gesture, and it would be important. It would be like a missing piece in the forgiveness and atonement process, because remorse is what allows us to go into atonement and take action with respect to a wrong that has been committed.

The Privilege of Repairing the Past

For atonement to occur you need to have taken action, deep action. But what's the phenomenology of real atonement? What does it mean? I read so much about forgiveness. Why does it leave me feeling empty? I've been around long enough to know that forgiveness alone is not going to bring change on any significant scale for the human race. We may need to repair the past, but what kind of repairing? In the sense that Gurdjieff spoke about. I think Gurdjieff was speaking about a man or a woman needing to change something in the family line because something had gone wrong, maybe with the mother, the father, the grandparents. Maybe the grandfather had committed a crime; maybe an injustice had been done to his children. If so, the bloodline has to repay somewhere; it has to repair that offense.

Gurdjieff once said to one of the young men in his group, "You are in that bloodline. You've been given the privilege of having to repair the past." I think this means something more than doing some good deed. But what did he mean? What kind of inner and outer action is needed in order to "repair the past"?

We might ask the same question about the need for collective atonement and amends with Native Americans because we nearly destroyed their cultures, though thank God they are restoring them. How can we make up for this incredible crime? We can't bring these people or their cultures back to life. How can we possibly atone for what we did to them? Not by just giving lip service to it, but by doing something—again, by *acting*.

What I suggest in *The American Soul* is that we have to give back to the earth what Native Americans gave to the earth; we have to be to the earth what they were to the earth. That's one thing we can do to atone for what we did. We can give back to the earth what we took away from the earth by nearly destroying them.

When we look at communal cultures, we see that the entire community has to participate in the atonement, or participate in the punishment; everyone has to make amends in some way. By yourself, you may not feel that you can atone, but maybe you can with the community. How do we get to that communal responsibility from this culture where we feel personally, individually, responsible? What is lacking in us that we're unable to live this truth, this communal atonement?

Atonement as Awakening

The story about Azim Khamisa, the man in the grave holding his twenty-year-old son's shrouded body, really stands out for me because he was in an awakened state at that moment. He was *awake*, in Gurdjieff's sense. How can the rest of us come to that awakened consciousness without having our son die? Isn't that the whole meaning of real spiritual development?

I don't mean to cheapen anything about what happened to Khamisa, because there are people who go mad over tragedies like that. But almost anyone can wake up if they are standing before the death of a loved one—or are encountering their own impending death. This shows that we do have this immense capacity in us to awaken, but will we wake up only because of something that happens *to* us? Can we not awaken on our own, so that we live closer to that state of being so alive? One awakened person is so powerful; maybe we don't need the whole world to awaken. Maybe we just need a small number of awakened human beings to have a powerful influence in the world.

As Gurdjieff said, we are asleep. One symptom of our sleep is that we can't keep promises. Nietzsche says man is the creature that can make promises. But how many serious promises can any of us really make and keep? It is a sign of a good man that he always lives up to his promises. Why is that?

To understand this, you have to become acquainted with these good, tough philosophers like Nietzsche. He teaches that morality of a certain kind is a system of self-deceptions. You tell yourself you're going to do better next time. Nonsense. You *aren't* going to do better next time. Maybe you don't even know what you want, but you're making promises to yourself and to others. I explored this in a class I taught. One of my texts, which at first only amused everyone, was Dr. Seuss's *Horton Hatches the Egg:* "I meant what I said and I said what I meant / An elephant's faithful one hundred per cent!" What does that really mean? What does it mean that so many of us so easily fail to keep our promises?

My context here is, What kind of a human being are we talking about who needs to atone? Can atonement be understood as something that only an awakened human being can do? Or is atonement also an instrument toward awakening, something we pay that helps us to wake up in our life, at least for a short while?

If the football player Michael Vick, who was imprisoned for operating an illegal dog-fighting business in his own home, had shown real remorse and paid, say, two million dollars to an animal rights group, he would probably have changed his being, at least for a little while. He would have earned a self-respect he never knew was possible, because real self-respect comes from making a hard gesture, a tough payment. That's why Vick's example is apt, because the relationship between atonement and money is interesting—very real, as it is in the Talmud and the Mishnah. How much money does it take? In his case it would have to be more than, say, twenty thousand dollars; it would take a million, or two million dollars, enough for it to hurt. Making amends has to be a sacrifice; it has to hurt.

And what is real self-respect, anyhow? I ask my students sometimes, "Did you ever do something for another person that really cost you something, and you never let it be known that you did it?"

Almost none of them ever raise their hand. What does that say about human nature?

We have this fashionable theory about human nature being purely self-centered. But that is not really true. Man is built to give, built to serve. That's the essential part of our nature. Human nature can't be reduced to the selfish gene. We now have interesting research in anthropology about altruism that shows how natural generosity is to the human spirit. What that tells us is that unless we're able to give, we're never going to be happy.

The Gift

A few years ago, I was teaching a class at a business school in Mexico. During one class, we were talking about what it means to be a good man, and a student, thirty-five, who had a little boy of five, told the class this story. "You know," he began, "I was decorating the Christmas tree with my son in the living room when there was a knock at the front door. We went to answer it, and there was a beggar boy. In Mexico beggars are perfectly acceptable, not like in America. The boy was about the same age as my son, and so my son and I went back to the living room and I said to him, 'Give him one of your toys.' My son picked up one of his old, beat-up toys. 'No,' I said. 'Give him your favorite toy.' My little boy balked. 'No,' I said, and I was gentle but firm. 'Give him your favorite toy.' Finally, my son picked up a toy he had just gotten for Christmas, and while I waited in the living room he went down to the front door. A few seconds later, he came running back, radiant, shouting, 'Daddy, can I do that again?'"

What did that boy discover about what we are and who we are? I think it was the joy of selflessness. It's there inside us, waiting, but the culture puts a crust around it for selfish reasons, telling us to *get, get, get*. Then the culture puts a crust around the crust, saying, "You have to be nice." We're brought up in a culture of human relationships—Cosmo magazine, and so on—that asks, "Are you getting enough out of the relationship?" instead of, "Are you giving enough?" But it never tells you that what you have to get to is underneath the crust, which is your heart, longing not to get but to give. The little boy was no guru, but he knew something. He discovered a part of himself, and he'll never forget it.

And where does that discovery come from?

There's a word in Greek, *metanoia*, that means "to change the mind"; it also can be translated as "repentance." What that means is payment. We all have to pay a price to be a part of the human family.

There's a memorable sarcastic saying by Nietzsche: "Man does not desire pleasure; the Englishman does." For Nietzsche, the essence of man was the will to self-mastery. The will to power was the will to transform one's emotions, one's self. But we moderns have lost that sensibility. We're here to get pleasure; we're here to get ahead. Charity is superficial most of the time. People get tax write-offs for giving to charity. This is a big subject: the need to struggle, to overcome, to become, to develop one's inner world.

How do we atone for the harm we've done if we haven't mastered ourselves?

Remorse in an Implacable World

What do we do with what is implacable in the world? Let's say I've come to you to atone for the harm I've done to you. From an objective point of view I'm offering you a gift. But let's say you don't want the gift; you're not going to accept it. Can we still speak of that as a gift? I don't think of it as a gift. I don't know what to think of it. I think of it as an objective obligation. It's metaphysical, not only psychological. If I recognize I have done something wrong and I tell you I was wrong and I feel it— and you see that I feel it—then if you're sensitive that's almost enough for us to be reconciled. But maybe I can *also do* something, if there's anything that can be done. Even if my offense is irreparable with action, at least I have come to you with my head bowed. I've given up my egoistic position of superiority; I've put myself below you. And I am asking for your forgiveness, for I was wrong. It takes a lot of courage to do that. It's not hard if you're sitting back in your chair just thinking about it, but it's very hard to go to that guy you've been working with for twenty years, with all the hierarchies and constant competition, go into his office or home, sit down, and say, "I was wrong. I'm really sorry."

If you are the victim, the aggrieved party, you have a choice. What is the obligation? It's not an easy question to answer. *But sometimes just living with a real question makes you more human than getting an answer.* When you really live with a great question, it opens your heart; it opens your mind. *We're most human when we're in question.* Man does not suffer from his questions but from his answers.

Now let's mix it up. What do two people do when they both feel they've been wronged by the other? This happens often. You don't forgive the person, and the person doesn't forgive you. But if you have done your best, then you're clean. It's the same thing with remorse. Remorse comes after you've done your best to come clean and still you've failed. Only it's not the guilt trip that arises when you've made a half-hearted attempt and, having failed, you feel you could have done better. Remorse is a state in which you recognize that your very being is at stake. It's a consciousness of your objective *lack*. Yes, action could come out of that, but first know that remorse is a powerful inner force. There's nothing to *do*, in one sense, except to be remorseful.

The Gift of Atonement

There's something mysterious about the phenomenology of a gift, about what is passed between the giver and the receiver. All of us know people who won't accept a gift, or if they do, they immediately want to pay us back. They say, "Oh, thank you; now I have to give you something."

No, I don't want anything back necessarily. I want to give you something; I want you to receive it. But if you keep saying you need to pay me back, then that's a false kind of balance. Isn't that interesting?

Atonement may also be like this. I've given you the gift of simply putting myself in front of you, so now the question is whether you are going to accept that gift. It's very hard when people quarrel in business, in marriage, or in the family and each feels the other to be at fault, until finally one refuses the gift of forgiveness or the offer to atone for the harm.

If someone has deeply hurt my daughter, sexually or emotionally, and I am devoted to protecting her because she is the apple of my eye, I may not be able to forgive that person. I was supposed to be her protector. I could forgive him if he had hurt me, but he hurt my own daughter. How does one look at that? This analogy helps us understand that a problem with atonement and forgiveness often comes down to the fact that what has been hurt, which I value, is not me.

The problem often comes because everyone in the community, more or less, has to accept the reality of something called atonement—or the possibility of it. When they don't, you can still try to atone, but they're not going to accept it necessarily or recognize it as the gift it really is. It's very easy to think you can repair the world through an act of atonement, but in fact it's difficult if the guy next to you doesn't agree with you.

Some years ago, I was with Anthony Bloom, the Russian Orthodox archbishop in London. I told him about an experience I had had in a Greek Orthodox church in Athens. A huge head of the Cosmic Christ was on the ceiling, and I had the feeling that the whole of life is constantly pouring down a gift to me. I wondered how could I respond to this gift? It was overwhelming. I asked Anthony about this state of not knowing how to respond, and he said something beautiful and immediate.

He asked, "What is the proper response to a gift?" I waited a few moments in silence. Then he said, "The proper response to a gift is to accept it!" Then he went on to say that all real spiritual work is to make ourselves able to accept the gift that is being offered us. As it is, we are stiff-necked people who find it hard to accept these divine gifts. What is it, he asked, that prevents us from accepting the gift, the grace, the energy of God that are being given to us?

Again, all of these thoughts are just a way of opening the question of atonement, thinking of it as a gift between those who have committed some harm, and those who have been hurt.

Phil Cousineau conducted this interview with Jacob Needleman in Oakland, California, on August 24, 2009.

we can work it out

heart, mind, and action in the struggle for atonement

MICHAEL N. NAGLER

> Yes, I have been a wretched person, but I have
> redeemed myself. And I say to you and all those
> who can listen and will listen that redemption is
> tailor-made for the wretched, and that's what I used
> to be. . . . That's how I would like my legacy to be
> remembered as: a redemptive transition, something
> that I believe is not exclusive just for the so-called
> sanctimonious, the elitists. . . . It's accessible for
> everybody. That's the beauty about it.
> —"Tookie" Williams, radio interview, 2009

As former chairperson of the University of California's Peace and Conflict Studies program and one of the world's most respected scholars of peace and nonviolence, Michael Nagler is uniquely qualified to explore what it means for individuals and nations alike to move "beyond forgiveness." In this far-reaching essay he describes the dynamics of the "spreading movement of reconciliation and atonement," which he defines as a combination of apologizing and making concrete reparations. But Nagler goes beyond abstract collective concerns to the concrete and personal. "We can atone," he writes, "by rooting out the attitude of disregard, not to say dehumanization, in our hearts and minds that permitted such crimes to happen."

The Reverend Charles Freer Andrews, familiar to those who have seen Attenborough's *Gandhi* and known to Indians of Gandhi's era as "Deenabandhu," the "kin of the poor," once heard that an Indian policeman had been seriously beaten by his superiors and was practically paralyzed, although not from the beating itself. Completely loyal to the British regime, he had been unjustly accused of cutting a telegraph wire as an act of sabotage. Andrews went to call on him, but the policeman at first refused to see him, saying he never wanted to talk to another Englishman. Nonetheless, Andrews did get in, and in an act of great power in India, prostrated himself before the stricken man and begged for forgiveness. The policeman got up from his bed, a cured man.

That's atonement. It shows that one can atone for an act one did not directly commit; but more than this, it reveals something of the dynamics of atonement. The emotional struggle Andrews must have gone through to prostrate himself before an Indian at that time—even today most Westerners would not be able to do it without some inner struggle—and the paralyzed man's dramatic reaction tell us something about the combination of inner state and outward action, of actual and symbolic gesture, that makes real atonement happen.[1] The point is often missed.

It only came home to me when I was traveling in Atlanta some years ago and heard that a black church had been burned to the ground by four racists. When I picked up the story, they were being duly sentenced—to rebuild the church. It struck me then, and I have often observed since, that in the spreading movement of reconciliation and atonement this is not always the case.[2]

In post-apartheid South Africa, whose Truth and Reconciliation Commission (TRC) became the paradigm for more than twenty such efforts around the conflict-tormented world today, precisely this element of concrete action, of physical *restitution*, was missing. Offenders were simply asked to make a public admission of their "political" crimes during the apartheid era and, when they did so, were promptly pardoned. They were never asked to *do* anything to make amends, which in my opinion is the only way to satisfy both the victims *and* their offenders.

To be sure, the TRC process was preferable any day to exacting vengeance, which often only makes a conflict spiral out of control and always leaves behind more problems than it "resolves." The process made it possible to rebuild a nation from that traumatic past. Nonetheless, the TRC experience was not uniformly successful, and at least part of the reason was that it sought reconciliation solely on the level of emotion—if that.

Those who have seen the documentary about the TRC called *Long Night's Journey into Day* will remember, alongside many truly heartwarming episodes of genuine repentance, offenders, both white and black, who exploited the opportunity cynically, without any real change of heart. This is a difficulty accompanying any attempt to impose atonement by law: if such an emotional struggle is not easy to undertake, it is even harder to prove that it has been done in a genuine spirit. It is easy enough to fool even oneself, not to mention others. One can make every effort to repent and still not be able to overcome a *reservatio mentalis* (mental reservation) deep within oneself. While the TRC must be given credit for a great deal, there is reason to think it could have done much more, for even when an emotional transformation is genuine, it is somehow only complete when it's expressed in action—ideally, as in Atlanta, in rebuilding what one has destroyed.

Collective Atonement

When it came to light in 1988 that the cruiser *Vincennes* had shot down Iran Air Flight 655 over the Persian Gulf, killing all 290 civilian passengers onboard, including thirty-eight non-Iranians and sixty-six children, then–vice president Bush stated, "I don't care what the facts are. I will never apologize for the American people."

Elise Boulding, the Quaker sociologist and pioneer of peace and conflict studies, has written, "Failure to grieve over its shortcomings is a serious problem for the United States and contribute[s] to anti-American attitudes in the rest of the world."[3] This is a soul-damaging failure; an explicit intention of this volume—or at least my main purpose for contributing to it—is to address just this problem. One does not have to read far into Howard Zinn's *People's History of the United States*, not to mention almost anything by Noam Chomsky, to understand that this nation has a large backload of negative karma (or in more native terms, the residue of the law that "As ye sow, so shall ye reap"). Even if one does not accept the operation of such a principle, it is a simple though often conveniently forgotten fact that victims don't like being victimized and tend to fight back when they get the chance.[4] Especially if those who hurt them do not apologize.

There are millions of Americans today who though they may never read the likes of Zinn or Chomsky, are dimly aware that as a nation we have inherited a backlog of debt—toward Native Americans whom we found here, and the Native Africans we dragged here, just to mention two glaring examples. I among others strongly believe that America cannot go forward until we find some way to face and overcome this legacy; in a word, to atone for it.

Yet—and this is the key point—it is emotionally very difficult for nearly anyone to confront his or her guilt. Most modern reformers, in their understandable outrage, do not understand this. Gandhi understood it to the core. As the great British historian Arnold Toynbee said, "He made it impossible for us to go on ruling India, but he made it possible for us to leave *without rancor and without humiliation*" (emphasis added).

A large part of Gandhi's power lay in his ability to see the wrongdoings of his opponents outside a moral framework, to take them out of the domain of morality and "judgmentalism."[5] It followed from his principle, fundamental to nonviolence, to separate the doer from the deed or, as we would say, the sinner from the sin. It enabled him to resist wrongdoing all the more effectively, for it made it possible, as Toynbee points out, for the wrongdoers themselves to own responsibility for their actions without stigmatizing themselves as wrongdoers—exactly what Vice President Bush and the Americans who followed him were not courageous enough to do.

Pride stands in the way of atonement; but, I will argue, shame is not the antidote to that pride. What is needed is restitution. The offender must be made aware that what he did or is doing is wrong, but simultaneously he must be helped to see that he can atone for it. A most dramatic case (to my knowledge not historical though certainly characteristic) is in one of the final scenes of *Gandhi*, where the Mahatma tells a guilt-stricken Hindu who has killed a Muslim child in revenge for the murder of his own son, "I know a way out of hell," namely, to adopt an orphaned child about the same age as his own son, "but be sure that he is a Muslim and that you raise him as such."

To make something like this work, we must be able to see a torturer as a person who has carried out torture, not as a "torturer"—that is, torture must be something he *did*, not something he *is*. We who would nurse America or anyone else free from its hurtful past must always be aware of this.

As Ted Nordhaus and Michael Schellenberger have recently argued,[6] Americans today are on the whole so saturated with gloom and doom—the rising threat of terrorism, global climate change, collapsing economies—that more evidence of their guilt will only drive them deeper into the kind of denial that made George H. W. Bush popular—a denial that leads to counteraccusations and other conflict-exacerbating behaviors. All the more reason that bringing up the burden of moral guilt without simultaneously showing a path to concrete restitution for that guilt will be counterproductive.

As we have begun to see, behind the dynamic of atonement lies the fundamental question of who we think we are. Here it is relevant that recent work in psychology and in the neurosciences has given striking support to the declaration, made by the wisest humans for eons, that when we hurt others we hurt ourselves. Swami Vivekananda has said, "Western civilization has in vain endeavored to find a reason for altruism. Here it is. I am my brother, and his pain is mine. I cannot injure him without injuring myself, or do ill to other beings without bringing that ill upon my own soul."[7] This is a law of nature, it would now seem, not a lofty, unrealistic sentiment.

Marco Iacoboni, the neuroscientist who has worked extensively on "mirror neurons," writes, "We have evolved to connect deeply with other human beings." This means, of course, that "although we commonly think of pain as a fundamentally private experience our brain actually treats it as an experience shared with others," a fact that has led psychologist Rachel Macnair to contribute a new concept which she has named perpetration-induced traumatic stress (PITS), the stress induced by injuring another in any context. The subjective complement of posttraumatic stress disorder, PITS has been documented extensively in soldiers, executioners, perpetrators of domestic violence, and yes, abortion practitioners.[8] We would not have it any other way. If it were possible for human beings to harm others without feeling hurt themselves, our regeneration would be impossible.

We can therefore take it that anyone who has knowingly caused another harm—be it in a domestic blowup or in the systematic damage done by an "economic hit man"; that is, whether physical or structural—is herself suffering, and should be approached with an intention to relieve that suffering rather than condemn. She may or may not be aware of her own hurt, and it is not always our job to make her so. For as I have been saying, to pull the protection away from another's conscience without providing an emotional and pragmatic escape route is not only a kind of cruelty itself; it is usually counterproductive.

That being said, however, we must remember that it takes two to restore a relationship. While it is counterproductive to rouse an offender's guilt feelings without giving him a concrete way to atone (that is to own the offense without being identified with it), the victim of an offense wants to be heard; he wants his suffering to be acknowledged.

Many years ago I attended one of the early meetings that would lead to the peace-building institution we know today as Unarmed Civilian Peacekeeping.[9] Mubarak Awad, an important player in the mostly nonviolent First Intifada of Palestine, was on hand for that meeting. I shall never forget his response when we asked him if they wanted us internationals around: "Yes. Do not tell us what to do, but be with us. We are not afraid to die; but we do not want to die alone, with no one watching."

As a society, we are holding ourselves back by failing to understand this need. What we call "closure" in the criminal justice system, where the victims or relatives of victims are encouraged to believe that they will feel satisfied by the suffering of those who offended them, betrays a serious misunderstanding of human nature. What victims really want is acknowledgment of their pain and *restoration of the relationship with the one who hurt them*.

Jane Goodall, Frans de Waal, and others have reported that when, say, a female chimpanzee has been attacked by a male she will follow her attacker, importuning him for some gesture of affection. She does not want revenge; she wants to restore the relationship.

Similarly, when Helena Norbert-Hodge was in Ladakh, she reports, there would sometimes be a theft, say, of a sack of rice— no small matter in that spare environment. The entire village would know who took it; yet, to Norbert-Hodge's surprise no one would try to confront the thief. What she came to understand was that in a small human circle like a Ladakhi village you cannot afford to alienate others with whom you live and on whose cooperation you depend. The *relationship* is paramount, not justice—whatever that is. The word *atonement* derives from "at-one-ment," after all.

As Gandhi discovered when he was still practicing law in South Africa, the real point of the law is to "unite parties who have been riven asunder." This is part of the reason that victims want recognition of their suffering rather than revenge for it: they want the reality of their feelings acknowledged so that the other can be in genuine rapport with them.

It can be extremely frustrating when a society is so ignorant of this principle, including its application to offenders. When twelve-year-old Polly Klaas was abducted from her home in my town, Petaluma, California, the entire nation was shocked and searched for her everywhere until her molester and, alas, killer finally stepped forward. I am not here concerned with the judicial punishment that was meted out to Richard Allen Davis, but with a smaller incident that occurred during the frantic search for Polly. The owner of a copy service in Petaluma had volunteered to furnish thousands of posters for the searchers, and was doing so—until someone dug up the fact that he had once been a sex offender himself. Yet he was the best person to have been allowed to perform that service. What was the good of denying him atonement?

Why, too, when the German government asked if they could build a museum of modern Germany near the Holocaust Museum in Washington, D.C., were they not allowed to show that they do repudiate their past mistakes? Who is helped by keeping them locked in guilt? Do we not realize that such barriers to atonement, while bringing scant comfort to their victims, only lock the offenders into their offender identity, making it more likely that they will commit such acts again?

In their studies of trauma (this will apply to both offender and victim), John Wilson and Terence Keane argue that "sustained empathy, as part of any treatment modality, is essential to facilitate posttraumatic recovery."[10] In Ann Wolbert Burgess and Lynda Lytle Holmstrom's follow-up study of rape survivors, "the women who had made the best recoveries were those who had become active in the anti-rape movement."[11] Logically—though

I have not run across studies of this—at least the same would be true of perpetrators; namely, that to help victims of crimes similar to what one has committed oneself could be a powerful form of restitution. There are anecdotal reports that what the copy service owner in Petaluma was trying to do was instinctively correct.

An interesting example of this is provided by the case of a German girl who at age fourteen had become obsessed by guilt and self-hatred over her country's Nazi past. Her parents sent her finally to visit Auschwitz, where the following occurred:

> After seeing the devastation I started crying and I couldn't stop. The kind guide . . . held me in her arms and gently stroked my hair and said that it was not my fault because the Jews who died didn't know who I was or even my grandfather [who had been a Nazi]. It took awhile, but I finally understood. The gift that finally took away my shame and guilt was the love that Marta showed me. She, who was of Jewish ancestry . . . was able to love me well. I felt that if she could overcome her hatred of Germans I could stop hating myself. I am now working in the tourist business as a guide here in Germany so that I may be an instrument of change.[12]

By contrast, Governor Arnold Schwarzenegger refused to pardon Stanley "Tookie" Williams, who had been a founder of a violent gang; while in prison, Williams wrote children's books and became a strong voice to prevent other African American youth from following his erring footsteps. The governor may have done something politically strategic for himself (though in the long run I don't believe even this will be true), but he earned outrage from the civilized world for refusing to acknowledge that a man who offended had *already* atoned. All that the governor accomplished was to cheat society of Williams's extremely helpful services—and, of course, to send a message that atonement is not possible, which is a devastating lie. "Our

God is a god of vengeance": that is as serious a heresy as one can entertain.

Four Principles of Atonement

What have we said so far? We have turned up several principles in the dynamic of atonement:

1. Think amorally. Abandon revenge and retribution. When the Hebrew Bible has God say, "Vengeance is mine," it is implied that only God has the wisdom and the detachment to use it, when it must be used, as an educational tool.

2. The goal in atonement is to relieve offenders of their guilt *and* victims of their resentment.

3. Atonement is about the restoration of relationships. This holds true at whatever level we approach the healing process—interpersonal, international, or intrasocial, the latter being where the struggling restorative justice movement is based, and precisely on relationship work in opposition to the retributive work of the present system.

4. Action as well as emotion must be part of the healing process. As Shakespeare's Claudius reveals:

> "Forgive me my foul murder"?
> That cannot be; since I am still possess'd
> Of those effects for which I did the murder,
> My crown, mine own ambition and my queen.
> May one be pardon'd and retain th' offence?

A remarkable example took place in South India very recently, where a couple who had been active with Gandhi and his follower Vinoba Bhave worked for many years to get restitution for a horrible act: the burning to death of forty-four peasant men, women, and children in 1968 by angry landholders from whom the peasants had demanded higher wages. This is the story:[13]

> In June, three cars pulled up to LAFTI's [Land for Tillers Freedom's] headquarters in Kuthur. . . . They came bearing garlands, and fruit, and papers. Lots of papers. They were here to gift their land—*all of it*—to Krishnammal and the people she serves, an act of restorative justice so surreal as to be almost unfathomable to people who have not followed the course of the struggle for these four decades. The beatings, the imprisonments, the hardships and deprivations, the days, month, years, and decades of "No conflict, no compromise"—Krishnammal's motto—have now resulted in an act of contrition and atonement that is virtually beyond the imagination. To be sure, the landlords and their descendents are not now about to endure poverty. Most of them have gone off to India's burgeoning cities, where the majority [is] sure to prosper. Others have gone to America and elsewhere to seek their fortune. "I don't wish to deprive them," says Krishnammal, "they too have marriages and births and occasions of their own to celebrate, and they must be allowed that privilege." But the land, and the scene of horrific struggles, and the commitment of a very, very small band of Gandhian organizers identifying themselves completely with the condition of the people, now belongs to the people, and, specifically, the women who till it.

Note that the landowners came bearing garlands—a symbol of veneration—but also something very tangible: the deeds to large tracts of their land, given to the poor landless farmers of the region. The event emphasizes a final point that is quite relevant to our own situation: ideally, atonement takes place between offender and victim, but of course that is not always possible, especially if the crime in question is murder. Atonement is still necessary, and it is possible by means of restitution to the family of the victims, as in President Ronald Reagan's official apology and reparation to Japanese Americans interned during World War II, or in cases of families of any victims who have suffered damages. Just as in Charles Freer Andrews's case with which we began, the person atoning need not be directly guilty of the offense but may in some way represent it or be willing to take it on. Doing good relieves the burden of having done harm. Andrews was not the one who had injured that Indian civil servant, but it was he who healed him.

What Is to Be Done?

My friend Marianne Williamson had been preaching every Sunday to her Unitarian congregation that reparation to the descendants of African slaves was a good thing. One of her parishioners came up to her and said, "You know, I love you, and I love most of what you say, but this reparation business doesn't make any sense to me." Marianne said, "Look, when you take over a business, it has certain assets and liabilities, and you take on both. It's like that: America has many assets, but this tragic legacy of slavery is one of its liabilities." He got it.

Apologizing and making concrete reparations to the descendants of Native Americans and African Americans may well be one way of setting our needed redemption in motion, but I want to suggest another, which can work more broadly for these and many other mistakes. We can atone by rooting out the attitude of disregard, not to say dehumanization, in our hearts and minds that permitted such crimes to happen.

I am writing these lines in Nicaragua, where I am visiting family. When we watch the weather reports on television—or even more, the news reports—I am always startled to see that Nicaraguans thinks of themselves as part of the world. They're as interested in the weather on Lake Ontario as they are in that of Lago de Managua; in disturbances in Cairo as well as León.

Conclusion

I am prepared to accept that (North) America has a special role to play in the world, which is why I have written this essay. But we can only play that role if "special" does not mean "separate." Whatever "exception" we may enjoy, it is not an exemption from the assets and liabilities of being human. Barack Obama came to office—thankfully—on a platform of "change." But with regard to this important matter of *attitude*, of self-definition, change has so far not been very deep. For example, while he offers more funding for education than his benighted predecessor, his avowed reasons for doing so are part of the tired old paradigm that says, "If we are going to out-compete others, we have to out-educate." That's not what education is for. That's not what life is for.

I have so far been thinking of systematic crimes in the relatively remote past, but I cannot conclude without considering a tremendous crime that stares us in the face from a much more recent time. Indeed it continues in certain quarters, and I hope it will have become a very live issue—if not a resolved one—by the time this volume appears.

Not to put too fine a face on it, the United States has adopted torture as an official policy sanctioned by the highest office in the land. "We cannot move forward," writes David Cole in the *New York Review of Books*, "unless we are willing to account for what we did wrong in the past. . . . We may know many of the facts already, but absent a reckoning for those responsible for torture and cruel, inhumane, and degrading treatment—our own federal government—the healing cannot begin."[14]

With this I entirely agree. But as Cole himself implies, this reckoning would be only the essential beginning. Additionally, the healing must involve some kind of restitution for what we have done—"we" being slightly less than half of the voting population who voted for the George W. Bush administration, and the majority who let it take office and do its vile work in our name. Healing must include a deep examination of the prevailing American culture, which made all this possible. And most important, it must involve a sincere shift in attitude toward others and our role in the world with them.

There is a lot of evidence that this deep change would be accepted, gratefully and graciously, by our fellow inhabitants of the planet—in some cases even those who seem most intransigently wroth with us. It is hard to overestimate what a difference it would mean, this simple act of opening our minds and hearts to the reality of other people.

After extensive research done through his important peace-building organization TRANSCEND, Johan Galtung, probably the most distinguished peace researcher alive, was able to establish convincingly the real needs of the two great global antagonists, the United States and the Middle East. Very simple, really: we need oil; they need respect for their religion. How much grief we could have spared ourselves, not to mention the Iraqis and others, if we had had the generosity to give them what they need—the generosity of spirit. Imagine if we had heeded, for example, Gandhi's call for "reverential study of all world religions" throughout our educational and media world.

And we still can.

Notes

1. I have made a similar point about nonviolence in *The Search for a Nonviolent Future* (Novato, Calif.: New World Library, 2004), esp. pp. 166–172.
2. For my purposes, atonement sees the action from the viewpoint of the offender; reconciliation refers to the change of relationship between the offender and the victim. Individuals can make atonement regardless of the response from their victims (though I believe that on some level victims always do respond).
3. Elise Boulding, "A New Chance for Human Peaceableness?" *Peace and Conflict*, 2000, 6, 193–215.
4. For a grim message written by a prisoner on the wall of his cell, "I will act the way I am treated, so help me God," see my *Search for a Nonviolent Future*, p. 150.

5. Not that he didn't use moral vocabulary, but somehow moral vocabulary did not exclude scientific realities in that era.
6. Ted Nordhaus and Michael Schellenberger, *Break Through: From the Death of Environmentalism to the Politics of Possibility* (Boston: Houghton Mifflin, 2007).
7. From a lecture given in December 1900 in Los Angeles; see Marie Louise Burke, *Swami Vivekananda in the West: New Discoveries*, Vol. 3: *The World Teacher* (Mayavati, India: Advaita Ashrama, 1985), p. 359.
8. See Rachel Macnair, *Perpetration-Induced Traumatic Stress: The Psychological Consequences of Killing* (New York: Authors Choice Press, 2005).
9. This important form of war abatement through nonviolence developed from Gandhi's *Shanti Sena*, or "peace army," and was earlier called Third Party Nonviolent Intervention. Nonviolent Peaceforce is the organization doing this work today on the largest scale.
10. John P. Wilson, "Culture, Trauma, and the Treatment of Post-Traumatic Syndromes: A Global Perspective," in Anthony J. Marsella (ed.), *Ethnocultural Perspectives on Disasters and Trauma: Foundations, Issues, and Applications* (New York: Springer, 2008), p. 363.
11. "They became volunteer counselors at rape crisis centers, victim advocates in court, lobbyists for legislative reform." A. W. Burgess and L. L. Holmstrom, "Adaptive Strategies and Recovery from Rape," *American Journal of Psychiatry*, 1979, 136, 1278–1282, quoted in Judith Herman, *Trauma and Recovery* (New York : Basic Books, 1997), p. 73.
12. Laura Bushman, "Stolpersteine," *Berkeley Daily Planet*, Dec. 23, 2008, p. 4.
13. Communication from David Albert. Krishnammal and Jagannathan were awarded the Right Livelihood Award in 2008.
14. David Cole, "What to Do About the Torturers," *New York Review of Books*, Jan. 15, 2009, p. 24.

CHAPTER 4

at-one-ment

becoming whole

DIANE HENNACY POWELL

> The beginning of atonement is the sense of its
> necessity.
>
> —Lord Byron (1788–1842)

*As a neuroscientist and psychologist, Diane Hennacy Powell has
cultivated a practice of compassionate healing for her patients, many of
whom are the survivors and perpetrators of some of the most grievous
acts of hate and violence. The greatest hurdle she finds in the recovery
of deeply traumatized people is the instinctual desire for revenge and
retaliation, rather than forgiveness and atonement, and it is that
reflexive desire that must be overcome. Their recovery, she explains
here, is dependent on "the strength of the human spirit," as well as the
powers of empathy and compassion. For her, the task is to actually
shift their "worldview," to help her patients reach "a place of peace"
after their trauma by coming to realize that acts of atonement, the
making of amends, can set in motion truly long-lasting healing. When
terrible acts are committed by either politicians or war criminals, what
is most required for healing is atonement, "asking for forgiveness and
doing something meaningful to express one's contrition." Her work is
testimony to the resilience of the human spirit.*

Atonement requires asking for forgiveness and doing something meaningful to express one's contrition. Although
some religions instruct adherents to seek the forgiveness of those
wronged, many religions use the word *atonement* to refer only
to one's reconciliation with God. For example, when General
Norman Schwartzkopf was asked whether there was any room
for forgiveness toward the people who aided the 9/11 terrorists,
he answered, "I believe that forgiving them is God's function.
Our job is simply to arrange the meeting."

One of humankind's biggest problems is that people don't want to forgive. Instead, they want revenge. There is a pervasive lack of recognition of the benefits forgiveness can have on both our health and our spiritual development. As a result of this attitude, countless people have been killed or harmed. For this to stop, we need to embrace a perspective that lies at the roots of atonement.

Atonement's deeper meaning is hidden in its etymology. *Ment* refers to a state of mind, so *at-one-ment* refers to that state of mind in which we are "at one," at peace. The process of atonement enables us to become one, or whole again. In other words, when we feel shame, guilt, anger, or hurt; we need to come to peace with ourselves, with others, and with whatever we believe to be God. After bad things happen, atonement can lift the perceived veil separating us from God or the Divine. Even if we don't believe in God, we may still benefit from reconciliation with others and with life itself. Through atonement and forgiveness, we can pick up the pieces of our shattered lives. We won't regain our innocence, but we can become connected to a higher level of consciousness, as well as that within others.

The Growing Need for Atonement

People have spoken about atonement for millennia, yet the need for atonement has grown. Every day the news has at least one disturbing story. It might be about another corrupt member of Congress, a schoolteacher who sexually molested students, a financial planner who swindled people out of millions of dollars, a celebrity who got into a violent brawl, an attempted murder by an angry spouse, a bus driver high on methamphetamine, or acts of violence in the name of peace. Greed and lust seem to continue to drive human behavior, despite religious teachings and our brain's highly evolved capacity for knowing the potential consequences of our behaviors.

One reason for this discrepancy between our innate potential for good and our misbehaviors is that the same brain that enables us to think analytically also allows self-deception and rationalization. Our brain has made it too easy to disregard the need for atonement. That is why our actions, and those of our ancestors, have led us to this critical time in history. It is now essential for us to change our worldview, our paradigm. We need to switch from regarding ourselves as separate and recognize that we are all interconnected. As Chief Seattle said, "All things are connected, like the blood which unites one family. Whatever befalls the earth befalls the sons of the earth. Man did not weave the web of life; he is merely a strand in it. Whatever he does to the web he does to himself."

My experience as a psychiatrist has been that the majority of the people who seek therapy are not "mentally ill" but rather the members of society most aware of its problems and experiencing symptoms from them. Where I've seen the greatest ignorance of the need for atonement has ironically been in the "halls of justice." As an expert witness in court for patients who were physically or sexually assaulted, I've silently gasped when the perpetrators have lied while under oath or when their attorneys have found loopholes for a "get-out-of-jail card," even when they knew their clients were guilty.

I've come to the conclusion that many people believe their own lies and rationalizations or are convinced that they can simply do away with what they do not wish to believe. And survivors of crimes often do not want to forgive because they feel that doing so would be letting others get away with what they had done. By hanging onto those angry feelings, they perpetuate their own suffering. Getting them to realize this is often their first step toward forgiveness.

Another step is to look at the bigger picture. This may include understanding why persons have committed harmful acts. Perpetrators may have been coerced by their government; they may have been mentally ill, under the influence of drugs, or caught up in a vicious circle of revenge. For example, children of abusive alcoholic parents often come to the conclusion that their parents did the best that they could.

So far I've primarily discussed forgiveness. But how does one move beyond forgiveness and become whole? What constitutes an act of atonement? Often people want the opportunity to confront their perpetrator. They want to feel as though they have been heard and to receive a sincere apology. Most never get this chance. More important, even if they do get what they want, that alone is often not sufficient for them to feel whole again. This is where atonement requires a shift in worldview.

The Power of Compassion

A shift in worldview has been especially necessary for those patients of mine who have suffered the worst trauma imaginable. I've treated some of the Lost Boys from Sudan, whom experts have called the most badly war-traumatized children ever examined. Approximately twenty-seven thousand boys were displaced or orphaned during the Second Sudanese Civil War (1983–2005), when about two million people were killed. Their epic journeys lasted years. They walked across national borders to international relief camps in Ethiopia and Kenya. Many died along the way; others survived thirst, starvation, wild animals, insects, disease, and one of the bloodiest wars of the twentieth century.

Another group of my patients were survivors of the massive genocides in Rwanda and Burundi, where over one million people were slaughtered. I've also assisted the healing of women whose human rights activities in Islamic countries led to their arrest and who were then raped and mentally or physically tortured by government officers. Among my other severely traumatized patients have been survivors of incest at gunpoint and Iranian soldiers tortured by Saddam Hussein.

How have my patients come to a place of peace after being raped or having their children murdered or being betrayed by someone they trusted deeply? Some were forced to commit acts of violence against others, so they were also plagued by a guilty conscience. It might seem inconceivable that these survivors could ever get past their feelings of anger, rage, hurt, sadness, and despair. The most challenging were the Lost Boys, whose ordeals began at such young ages and had lasted for most of their lives. But the majority of my patients were able to heal. That is in large part due to the strength of the human spirit, but it is also a statement about the power of compassion and deep connection.

Sometimes I mention my patients' stories (anonymously) to people who feel hopeless about their capacity to overcome what has happened, because the stories show that even the most traumatized can learn to forgive others and even move beyond forgiveness. They can achieve a state where they are no longer conflicted within themselves, with others, or with their past. Part of healing comes from recognizing that suffering is part of the human condition, as stated in Buddhism. Suffering often entails a disruption of wholeness—a disruption of what is vital and sacred in someone's life. So it is not merely coincidence that the English words *health, heal, whole,* and *holy* all stem from the Old English word *hál.* Healing is the process of becoming whole.

Several of my patients were noticeably better at the end of a single session. I asked them what had helped them most. They all gave essentially the same answer. They saw in my eyes that they could tell me their story without feeling the need to protect me. They detected my compassion and felt that I personally understood their pain. Instead of shrinking back from their pain, I willingly joined them in it. They no longer felt so alone, which helped them release some of their pain. They appreciated that instead of feeling pity for them, I acknowledged their strength. Much of this work was done with the help of translators, but the patients' healing could not have occurred just through words. Healing comes from connection, which can be established through the powerful language of our eyes.

The patients of mine who had the easiest time finding forgiveness were those who had a deeply spiritual belief system in which forgiveness played a major role. Fortunately, this is true for all major spiritual teachings, including Islam. Many of my political torture patients were Muslim, and although the media portray Muslims as violent, their spiritual teachings state that it is better to forgive than to attack another. They state that true Muslims avoid gross sins and vice and that they forgive when angered.

But being told how good it is for one to forgive is often not enough. In a 1988 Gallup poll of Americans, 9 percent said that it was important to forgive, but 85 percent said they needed some outside help to be able to forgive. For many of my patients, spiritual experiences played a role. Many of them had come extremely close to death, during which time they had mystical or spiritual experiences. Mystical states of consciousness are powerful and life-altering. They universally include the sense that we are not separate from the rest of the physical world, including the other beings within it. The words *I*, *me*, and *mine* don't apply. Our sense of time is replaced by a sense of eternity. Another component of this state is the conviction that the "true reality" has been unmasked; separateness is the real illusion. I was able to validate the reality of these experiences and draw on them to help patients feel whole.

Zen and the Art of Atonement

Meditators from Eastern traditions regularly reach these mystical states of consciousness in which everything appears unified and there is no polarity. And if there is no polarity, there can't be an "us versus them." This perspective of reality no longer has a limited view of cause and effect, so engaging in "tit for tat" behaviors appears absurd. Seeking revenge cannot occur without harming oneself.

Prayaschitta is Sanskrit for "penance." Both *prayaschitta* and asking for forgiveness are a large part of the practice of

Hinduism. They are daily acts that stem from the Hindu belief in the law of karma. The literal meaning of *karma* is "deed" or "act," but *karma* is usually used in a broader sense to refer to a universal principle of cause and effect that governs all of life. Karma is the sum of all that an individual has done, is currently doing, and will do. One's deeds and their effects actively create present and future experiences, thus making one responsible for one's own life and the pain in others'.

Buddhism recognizes that feelings of hatred and ill will are self-destructive and have their own karmic consequences. Forgiveness is an essential practice that Buddhists cultivate to prevent harmful thoughts from wreaking havoc on their mental well-being. Buddhism encourages the cultivation of positive thoughts and the contemplation of the law of karma. Through these practices one realizes that the preferred reaction to being wronged is not to seek revenge but to practice loving-kindness and forgiveness. Buddhists consider the perpetrators of misdeeds the most unfortunate of all, because they have created very negative karma for themselves. This concept of karma has enabled the Dalai Lama to feel compassion toward the Chinese, despite their massive genocide of Tibetans.

None of this means that Buddhists never harbor resentments. When those feelings arise, Buddhists try to release them by questioning the reality of their causation. They see such feelings as products of their own consciousness and are therefore able to dismiss them. Through meditation they try to lose any attachment to the idea of the world being other than it is. They also realize that if they don't forgive, they will perpetuate an identity based around pain.

New Age reinterpretations of karma frequently cast it as a sort of luck associated with virtue: If one does good or spiritually valuable acts, one deserves and can expect good luck; conversely, if one does harmful things, one can expect bad luck or unfortunate happenings. People sum it up as "what goes around comes around."

The popular TV show *My Name Is Earl*, which ran from 2004 to 2009, portrayed the New Age view of karma. Earl is a beer-chugging, 7-Eleven-robbing, trailer park womanizer who wins the lottery—only to be run over while celebrating in the street. His lottery ticket flutters away, and he comes back to consciousness in the hospital, where he hears someone discussing karma on a television talk show. It is an epiphany for him. He realizes that bad things happen to him all the time because he is a bad person.

Earl writes a list of all of the wrongs he can remember having done to others and makes it his mission to make it up to them. He learns that this is never as simple as he had expected, and he almost always adds more things to the list before he's able to cross off an item. The show was a humorous treatment of the subject of atonement but one also full of lessons. Earl's desire to do good was initially merely to start having good things happen to him, such as getting his lottery ticket back. He does get it back, but he also learns that the main reward for doing good deeds for others is in the happiness that this brings to them.

Another New Age interpretation of karma can be found in the Course of Miracles, a metaphysical thought system. It essentially says that there is actually nothing to forgive. It says that because we are never really separate from God, we never lose our essential goodness. All creation is a loving and eternal thought of God, but we misperceive ourselves as separate from God. Forgiveness is waking up to the reality that the separation never occurred. Forgiveness removes the obstacles to seeing the eternal goodness in everyone and our unity with them.

A Story of Atonement

The story of my great uncle, Ammon Hennacy, provides an extraordinary example of atonement. He was someone who awoke to seeing the goodness in everyone. And he did so at a time very similar to the present. He was a passionate activist who wanted to "make things right" in a world where the rich were taking advantage of the poor, corruption was rampant, and the United States was engaged in wars that served the interests of the wealthy at the expense of others' tax money and the lives of young men.

Ammon came from a long line of Quakers. Consistent with his upbringing, he was an antiwar protester during World War I. However, unlike most people with a Quaker background, he believed that some wars were justified. For example, our ancestors were part of the Underground Railroad, and he believed that the Civil War was totally justified because it was "the war to free the slaves." World War I, in contrast, was a war tied to the interests of wealthy industrialists and was indefensible in his eyes. Despite his pacifist roots, Ammon developed the belief that it was morally correct to eliminate corrupt industrialists, especially those who severely mistreated their laborers. Alexander Berkman became a hero of Ammon's because he had attempted to murder an infamous industrialist whose hardworking laborers were barely surviving their harsh work conditions and paltry wages.

Ammon eventually met and befriended Berkman in the Atlanta penitentiary. The crime that landed Ammon in prison was protesting conscription during World War I. This was regarded as treason and put him alongside murderers like Berkman. The conditions at the prison were so poor that Ammon led a food strike and smuggled information about the guards' unethical practices to a reporter. Because of this leak to the press and his unwillingness to reveal who had assisted him, his life was threatened and he was thrown into solitary confinement for over a year and a half. During that time he had nothing to do but read the Bible. He read it repeatedly and was particularly captivated by Jesus' Sermon on the Mount.

The Sermon on the Mount is considered one of the main sources of Christian pacifism by many religious and moral thinkers, including Leo Tolstoy, Mohandas Gandhi, Dietrich

Bonhoeffer, and Martin Luther King Jr. The sermon led to Ammon's conversion. He realized that divinity was in everyone, including the guards whose atrocious behavior he had despised. He forgave them for their cruel tactics and lived the rest of his life as an absolute pacifist who no longer thought that any murder was justifiable. He fasted and picketed against capital punishment, against the building of the atomic bomb, against all of the wars during his lifetime (including the Vietnam War), and in favor of prison reform.

Ammon also refused to earn money because he didn't want to pay taxes that would support a war. Instead, he did farm work in exchange for food and shelter, lived in the Hopi Nation, and eventually came to live in the Salt Lake City homeless shelter he had started and run from donations. He also spent much of his time in jail because of his antiwar protests. He was frequently charged with disturbing the peace, to which he quipped, "No, I'm disturbing the war." He was one of those rare individuals who truly lived what he believed. He called himself a "one-man revolution" and believed that individuals could make a large difference. He sacrificed everything, including his health, toward his goal of world peace and atonement for the wrongs he saw committed by the rich and powerful. No matter what happened to him, he never gave up. A judge once asked him, "Hennacy, do you really think you can change the world?" He replied, "Maybe not. But it sure as hell isn't going to change me." Now that's about as close to feeling whole as one can get.

Recently, author Joan Borysenko wrote, "A mystic sees beyond the illusion of separateness into the intricate web of life in which all things are expressions of a single Whole. You can call this web God, the Tao, the Great Spirit, the Infinite Mystery, Mother or Father, but it can be known only as love."

The major theme that emerges from these stories and reflections is that atonement and forgiveness involve an *awakening to our oneness*—our interconnectedness—and to the divinity within us all.

burying the stone

rituals and ceremonies of atonement

KATE DAHLSTEDT

> And he shall make amends for the harm that he
> hath done in the holy thing, and shall add the
> fifth part thereto, and to give it unto the priest: and
> the priest shall make an atonement for him with
> the ram of the trespass offering, and it shall be
> forgiven him.
>
> —*Leviticus 5:16*

In her work as a clinical psychologist and codirector of Soldier's Heart, a veteran's healing initiative, Kate Dahlstedt has specialized in grief and loss, depression, trauma, and relationship issues for over twenty years. She uses a variety of dynamic approaches that draw on what is most meaningful in a person's life as a guide to healing, and that create a safe and comfortable environment to make changes. Together with her husband, Ed Tick, she leads retreats for veterans in which she uses various rituals and ceremonies to help them forgive themselves and atone for whatever harm they perpetrated during wartime. She has learned that for many veterans, as powerful and indispensable as forgiveness may be, it is not enough for complete reconciliation. What is critical in their healing process is for them to perform a concrete act of restitution or restoration, such as adopting orphans or building schools, if they are to complete their often painful reconciliation process.

L et he who is without sin cast the first stone," Jesus is said to have called out to the crowd. This passage is a reminder that it isn't possible to be human without doing harm. Whether by accident or mistake, by unconscious or calculated intent, it is our vulnerability as humans to sometimes do the wrong thing. Even those of us who strive to be morally honorable cannot avoid doing harmful things to others, to ourselves, and to the earth. It is our nature as humans.

"To err is human, to forgive divine," Alexander Pope reminds us. Much is written today about the important role of forgiveness and reconciliation in maintaining our well-being. Holding on to anger and bitterness toward those who have wronged us only festers the wound inside us and causes unhealthy stress. Whole fields are now devoted to the emotional freedom that comes from learning how to forgive. However, we seldom explore our own need to ask for forgiveness, to atone for our transgressions toward others, or to seek restitution. The result of avoiding our own culpability is that true healing and inner peace go unattended.

Reconciliation can only be successful if atonement, the missing piece, is part of the process. In my work with military veterans I have often heard the complaint that other posttraumatic stress disorder (PTSD) programs only explore the pain and horror of witnessing death and destruction, but not the pain of having perpetrated these on others. It's as if there is a cultural taboo about discussing the emotional and spiritual effects of having violated our own moral sensibilities, especially when the greater society is complicit in those violations.

If we don't discuss the damage to heart and soul, and face the reality of what we have done, we remain in denial and are likely to repeat our actions. Even when we accept responsibility for what has happened, something more than saying we are sorry is required for growth to occur. Making amends, a sacrifice, or an offering, that is, not just an apology but also a concrete restorative action, is what is needed.

Regardless of the reasons, the mitigating circumstances or external justifications that might exist, we all (except for psychopathic personalities) tend to hold on to self-blame. Even

when our own lives are at stake, we have an intuitive abhor-
rence of violating the moral dictate, "Thou shalt not kill."
We have such a deeply encoded moral code that we are mortified when we acknowledge that we have transgressed its dictates. We are anguished by the fact that we cannot go back and
change our behavior. It is a wound to the soul. We are tortured
by what we experience as the "black mark" that we must live
with forever.

Many religions attempt to cleanse and release the soul from
this anguish through particular ceremonies reserved for this purpose. Christian confession can be seen in this light. An individual tells the priest his sins and then atones by saying prayers to
satisfy God. Another example, the Jewish Day of Atonement,
is a day of honest self-reflection regarding our injuries to others
and asking forgiveness from the people we have wronged, rather
than from God. In either case, the belief is that you are made
pure again, that you are in *at-one-ment* with God.

Rituals such as these have been handed down from century to century, indicating that the impulse to be made clean
again, to undo the harm we have done to ourselves and our
souls when we have harmed others and the earth is an enduring
human longing. Even those who have no belief in God have an
internalized wish to clean the slate, to wipe away the burden of
knowing they have violated the moral dictates of civilized living, to remove the awful belief that they are somehow inhuman.

At the heart of such longing is the sense that our moral violations have upset the universal balance. We feel split away from
the good person we want to be, and we long to be reconnected.
We feel our souls condemned, doomed forever by the truth of
having done "evil" things. We wish to restore ourselves to goodness, to remove the stain from our souls, to be made whole and
pure again. Since we cannot turn back the clock, or retrieve our
words and deeds, or prevent the injury, we seek redemption.

Today, except among the orthodox, religious rituals have
become more like customs than serious meaningful rites.

Psychotherapy and counseling have become the arena for personal reflection but usually only focus on our own injuries rather than on those we have inflicted. Spirituality, moral and ethical concerns are usually left out of the process. When the soul's wound is not attended to, true healing cannot happen.

Atonement requires accepting who we are and all that has happened as our destiny. It means giving up the fantasy and the wish that past events could have been different. It requires a longing to make amends and a willingness to take action, beyond heartfelt words. It means doing something concrete that will rebalance the scale; creating in contrast to destroying. Finally, it necessitates an act of restitution.

When we are focused on our own guilt, we are essentially stuck in our own wound. The movement beyond guilt and shame requires connection to something outside of the self, something that gives shape and meaning to all that we have endured. Such connection is essentially spiritual. It puts us face to face with our authentic self in relation to something bigger than our individual lives.

Ritual is the conduit.

When done meaningfully, an atonement ceremony can provide what is necessary to transcend the ordinary self to reconnect with the higher self. Ceremony is what we *do* with symbols and metaphors; ceremony is the concrete structure we use. It sets the stage for the *ritual experience*, which is what occurs inside us. It sets to work the forces we want in our lives. Ritual is a rite of passage. It changes us. When we create a ritual atonement ceremony, we are balancing the scale; we are giving meaning to the harm we have caused. We change our actions and provide restitution. The ritual is the catalyst, the guiding force, the impetus. It is the transition point for a new identity, one that no longer includes shame and the heartache that shame carries.

Community offers the container for a ritual atonement ceremony. It provides enough safety to allow the freedom and permission to tell one's story honestly and openly. The community acts as witness, taking on the story as part of their shared legacy and their common destiny, and acknowledging that a change has taken place. The community then confers a new or renewed identity or relationship that no longer carries shame. In this arena, true forgiveness can be given and received. Individuals are "at one" with themselves and the community.

To be effective, ritual atonement ceremonies must contain symbols and metaphors that have meaning to the individual as well as the group. Being invested in the meaning behind the ceremonial activities allows for the experience of change and a new perception of the self and others. Using traditional objects or customs further deepens the experience as it connects the participants to their history, ancestors, and culture; this adds greater authority and reverence to the event.

An essential ingredient of atonement and forgiveness ceremonies is *storytelling*. I am reminded of the African proverb, "My enemy is one whose story I have not yet heard." In this sense reconciliation occurs when there is an understanding of the human experience of the one seeking atonement. We can forgive and even have compassion and empathy for those who have hurt us. But we must first hear their story. We can then find the human and universal aspects that touch our own heartstrings. Storytelling allows us to speak our truth, a confession of our humanness, even in the face of heinous actions. Words are a powerful healing tool. Telling our story, saying it out loud, enables us to begin to accept ourselves.

Restitution is another essential ingredient in the act of atonement. Making a sacrifice of some kind, a metaphoric gesture, seeks to repair, if only in miniature, that which has been lost. Restitution gives the individual the opportunity to create meaning from the original offense by offering to do something that he or she would not have done otherwise. It allows people to give when they have taken, to create when they have destroyed. Rebalancing the universal scales in this way is powerfully healing.

However, rather than viewing ritual atonement ceremonies intellectually, as a religious or philosophical ideal, I incorporate them into my work, especially with veterans and others for whom having done harm is a significant wound.

Traditional Atonement Ceremonies

While Western cultures have very limited vehicles for ritual atonement, tribal societies have long-standing traditions and ceremonies that address such issues. An example can be found in the documentary *Breaking Bows and Arrows: A Search for Reconciliation and Forgiveness.*[1] It explores the use of ceremonial forgiveness on Bougainville, an island that is today part of Papua New Guinea.

When Australian copper mining began on the island in the 1960s, landowners were paid very little and the environment suffered great degradation. The people rose up but were contained by the Papua New Guinea Defense Force. When Papua New Guinea gained its independence in 1975, many of the people of Bougainville wished to secede, and continued to fight the government forces. In response, the government offered financial incentives to those Bougainvilleans who would resist the uprising, thereby setting family members and friends against one another in a brutal civil war. They also set up a blockade that left the people of Bougainville without imported food, communications, or medical supplies. Fifteen to twenty thousand people died, and the island's infrastructure was virtually destroyed.

In 1998 a cease-fire was declared, but tensions remained high. Clans, communities, and families had been bitterly divided. But there was also much grief and remorse for the violence and bloodshed, and the people longed for peace. The only way to rebuild and reestablish unity was through a reconciliation ceremony.

After three years of talking to each other about what took place during what they call "the crisis," and discussing how best to go about creating reconciliation, people from both sides of the conflict come together at Hahon, on the northwest coast of the island, for a ceremony. The people live close to the land in meager circumstances. Many are uneducated, and most live in what we might consider impoverishment. Yet they can recall a time when they were at peace, when they were a close-knit community of family and friends and fellow clan members. They long for those days and wish to make amends with one another, to break down the barriers between them, and to rekindle their former relationships.

As they make preparations for this important day, their more recent negative attitudes toward one another begin to change. They have all shared in the sacrifices and horrors, and now they must carry that history together in love and respect. Special foods are harvested and prepared over open fires. Large, sweet-smelling flowers are cut in order to replace the negative thoughts the people have been harboring toward one another. When the day arrives, special garb, traditionally worn for making amends, is donned.

They begin by forming two lines and pointing their arrows at one another to symbolize what had taken place between them. Then each group pretends to row toward the other for the meeting. Across a metal platform the former enemies exchange betel nuts, a symbolic traditional gesture of peace. They then pass a pig, dressed for roasting, across the platform and back again. Once peace has been declared in this way, the ex-combatants apologize to one another and shake hands. They break apart their bows and arrows and throw them in a pile. Together they place their hands on a large ceremonial stone, a memorial to the peace pact and a reminder that the fighting is over. After they have lowered it into the ground together, they throw their broken weapons down over it. To these people the ritual has made the agreement irrevocable. No one would dare break it.

One of the ex-combatants, Frances Boisibere, had killed one of the clan chiefs during the war and buried his remains. The chief's wife had been pregnant and had several other children. Filled with remorse for what he had done, and to lift the heavy darkness from his heart, Frances asks for a personal atonement ceremony. He and other ex-combatants he had fought with carefully build a coffin and cover it with lovely cloth that they have selected themselves. They create something beautiful to atone for an act of violent destruction.

They carry the coffin out into the bush to the site where the chief was buried, and dig up the bones. Each one is removed from the earth, washed, and dried tenderly, then placed in the coffin. Frances surrenders to this experience. He is saddened as he covers the coffin. With each bone that is cleaned, he feels the impact of what he did ever more deeply and cannot hold back his tears. It is as if with each tear, with each bone wiped clean, Frances is also purified and cleansed. With his gentle, caring movements, he has restored his humanity.

The coffin is carried to the chief's wife and mother, where a ceremonial funeral "house" has been created and decorated traditionally. Frances apologizes to the family in front of the whole community and offers the wife a financial gift. They all exchange betel nuts to open their hearts and then place the coffin into its final grave. Although they are all still saddened by the loss, they have peace in their hearts toward one another. Frances has atoned. His heart is light.

Rites of Atonement

In our healing work with veterans, my partner and I create ritual intensives, which include veterans and their family members, helping professionals, clergy, students, and other interested community members. Over the three days we are together, we incorporate the components that are most essential to healing from the war experience. These are similar to the elements we have seen in Frances's ritual experience.

In June 2009 we had the joy of conducting such an intensive at a retreat center nestled in the foothills of the Berkshire Mountains. We began by calling out to our higher selves and creating an altar made up of military memorabilia and other special objects. One by one, our participants introduced themselves by telling the group about the special meaning behind what they were placing on the altar. Telling each other such personal information, however brief, brought a group of mostly strangers together in a special way, thus creating our retreat "community." We then broke for the evening, allowing the words and images to mingle with our dreams.

The next morning we began with a guided meditation, taking participants to their own inner "safe place," which they could return to if need be. In this way, combined with building the altar the night before, we had created a safe and sacred container to hold the healing work we were about to embark on.

Our next task was to create a circle, together holding a rope that symbolized our unity as a group, as well as our unity as a nation. Again, we were reinforcing a sense of at-one-ment with one another. Slowly, one by one, we peeled off those who had gone to war and sent them away from the circle to surround us in a way that represented their place of service and their distance from us in battle. Those who had served but remained stateside stood in the middle, separate from the group, but not overseas.

As the rope began to slacken and holes formed in our circle, everyone began to feel a powerful sense of loss. Those who were "off to war" shared their feelings of fear, anger, isolation, guilt, envy, and grief. They were slogging it out in the jungle or the rice paddies, or in the desert, while many of the others were at home, getting on with life, fearing for loved ones overseas in the military, or protesting the war.

Many of the country's most prominent factions were represented in this fine and courageous group. Everyone had an opportunity to share how he or she felt as we reenacted our own histories regarding war. This kind of exercise is very powerful; it is never the same twice, and each time is enlightening. The important ingredient is the act of storytelling in a sacred environment that invites our hearts to open and implies that we all have a piece of the larger "Story"—that is, we are all culpable and injured in one way or another. Like it or not, in the truest sense we are all in this together, veterans and civilians alike. Until we acknowledge this reality and reach out to each other, we will not heal as a nation.

To finish our ceremony and bring our veterans back, the civilians formed two lines to create a pathway, and drummed and rattled and sang as one of the civilians brought each veteran, one at a time, back in among us all. We shouted their names and welcomed each one of them home. We then proceeded to our lunch, where each veteran was attended to and waited on by a civilian of his choice.

After lunch we discussed the meaning of destiny, and each veteran spoke to the group about his relationship to his own destiny and place in history. They each then shared the nature of their suffering since their war experience, as did others in the group.

In the evening we made a fire and shared words of gratitude for our coming together, and a vow to keep our hearts open. We each fed the fire with kindling as we vowed to let go of something we no longer needed to carry—bitterness, despair, victimhood, and so on. Some people threw memorabilia, letters, or photographs into the flames. More stories seeped out as we gazed into the fire under the clear night sky, purging ourselves by sharing our wounds with the rest of the group. An intimacy and trust had formed between us as we shared tears and laughter.

We devoted our last full day to storytelling. All of the veterans took turns holding the talking stick, which symbolized the right to talk without interruption. They each told the group about an experience they had had in the military that had been weighing on their souls. Telling their stories to this community, which had bonded in love, trust, and absence of judgment, opened the way for them to understand and forgive themselves, and to feel at home for the first time.

We finished the day with a ceremony of community forgiveness and a vow to carry each other's stories. Our Soldier's Heart organization distributes T-shirts that read, "Caring Means Sharing the Burden." This is how healing happens.

The last morning together was a time for what we call Warriorhood Vows. After a memorial service and a blessing ceremony, the veterans in the group each vowed one thing they were going to do as an act of restoration and restitution. The circle was complete. Everyone was changed.

In this ceremonial way, together as veterans and nonveterans, addressing the ethical and moral dilemmas that war inevitably forces on us makes healing from war possible for all of us. It helps us gain the larger perspective that war touches each of us and that we must all heal together. In this way, veterans are welcomed home and reintegration becomes possible.

Vietnamese Buddhism teaches that if you feel bad about something you have done, then open your heart, do good works, and love everyone. This is how we counteract the negative karma of our actions. In other words, we make up for our transgressions by atoning, by devoting our life to purposeful, life-affirming action that does as little harm as possible. Perhaps it is as simple as that. It is not just people like Frances or military veterans who need this advice. Who among us is without sin?

My healing work with veterans in the ceremonies I have described here always amazes me. Something unpredictable and beautiful always happens. Beyond all of the particulars—the threads of the cloth—the ritual never fails to bring about an exquisite and unique pattern and hue. As I watch the changes that occur in people as our weekends unfold—the coming together, the at-one-ment—my hope for a future of peace is always renewed.

Note

1. Ellenor Cox (prod.) and Liz Thompson (dir.), *Breaking Bows and Arrows: A Search for Reconciliation and Forgiveness* (Firelight Productions & Tiger Eye Productions, 2001).

taking the crucial step
forgiving the other and forgiving yourself

KATHARINE DEVER

> If you want others to be happy, practice
> compassion; if you want to be happy, practice
> compassion.
>
> —His Holiness, the Dalai Lama

In this essay, which ranges from England to Australia and from the Amazon to Ecuador, writer, lecturer, and therapist Katharine Dever takes us from a probing story of sexual abuse to reports on abuse of the earth itself. With avidity, she asks the difficult question, What does it take to break the cycle of abuse, whether on the personal or the collective level? Her answer goes to the heart of this book. For Dever, true reconciliation, whether on the personal or the collective level, requires two crucial steps. First, the victim offers forgiveness to whoever has harmed them, then offers the violator the chance to atone. Together, the steps allow both victim and violator an opportunity to "get their lives back." This must be our focus, she writes, because it is a "universal truth" that not only are we connected to one another, but "we are, in truth, all one."

Alison Redwood lives on the North Island of New Zealand in a beautiful house just a short distance from the beach. Alison has shoulder-length strawberry blonde hair and a warm, inviting smile that is fresh and breezy. She is funny and warm with a wonderful sense of humor. She is many things: a mother, a photographer, a writer, a trainee counselor, a health professional, and a good friend.

Alison is also the daughter of a father who sexually abused her for most of her childhood and into her adult life. She was eight years old when the abuse began and twenty when it finally stopped. It took another seventeen years for her to fully realize what had happened to her throughout her youth. Her abuse and her suffering occurred during the very years that are supposed to be the most carefree days of our lives. Only now does she realize was robbed of her childhood.

As a friend, I look at Alison and see a joyous, loving, and accomplished woman. Despite what happened to her she is still open and generous. I find myself wondering how she has possibly achieved so much peace over the abuse in her past and then gone on to accomplish so much as an adult.

Her courage has compelled me to ask questions: How does anyone overcome the crippling mistrust, fear, and anger that are felt after one has been taken advantage of by the one man who was supposed to protect her? How does a teenager reconcile her thoughts and feelings about sex and love after that? How did that little girl grow up to be such a dynamic, loving, accomplished, funny, and successful woman—despite what she has endured?

I believe the answer is at once simple and complex, elegant and painful. She managed to forgive, and then courageously managed to take one more crucial step. She allowed herself and her father to atone in such a way that gave her her life back.

Whenever I consider the subject of forgiveness and atonement, Alison is the first person I call. She lives and breathes it. Forgiveness is what has enabled Alison to be who she is; atonement has given her a new life.

When she and I talk about forgiveness, she shares with me that it wasn't easy. When her daughters were in high school, she realized how angry she had become; she was prone to outbursts and had a deep rage inside her that needed to come out. Fortunately, a wise friend suggested she take ten days to go on a course that would enable her to safely release her anger, before she damaged her girls. The course worked wonders, as did regular counseling and her church group. Ten years later Alison is now counseling abused girls, and even abusive fathers.

I'm slightly surprised that Alison sees these actions as a form of atonement. That's what makes this story so complex. Although Alison was the victim of abuse, she admits that she also made choices that she needed to atone for. She says, "The circumstances I experienced as a child were beyond my control, but the choices I had made as a grown woman were not. I realized that the ripples that came out of my past were making my behavior toward my children unhealthy and damaging. The realization made me want to seek a way to change my life, and make amends."

A pivotal moment in Alison's atonement came when a man stood up in front of the entire congregation of her church and admitted to sexually abusing his niece. Alison approached the man afterward in private and acknowledged his courage. In turn, he admitted to her that he was seeking counseling, and asked if she knew someone who could help him.

This incident inspired Alison both in her private life and in her training and fruition as a compassionate and experienced counselor helping the victims and the perpetrators of abuse.

What's so poignant in Alison's case is that the abuser is at the same time a victim, while the victim, Alison herself, became an abuser. Fortunately, Alison realized this terrible development and made adjustments in time. She admits that if she had not taken her personal path of healing, forgiveness, and atonement, with the support of her church and counseling, she would by now be in a very different situation, at best on medication to ease her suffering or at worst institutionalized.

What a different story this could have been.

The fact that Alison can find compassion for her father, and other sexual offenders, is remarkable. She has found a perspective that makes this possible, which is that she sees him as both abuser and abused. When she confronted her father, she was horrified to learn that he had been touched inappropriately as a child. He was also a scarred victim. Worse, he never found a way to understand his own abuse, and so, tragically, he not only failed to stop the circle of violence, but he passed it on to his own daughter.

As Alison later discovered, over 90 percent of abusers have themselves been abused. Slowly, she came to understand that the roots of her father's intolerable abuse of her were a result of his own abuse.

Alison's view is that no one is just "born bad." She doesn't believe in the "bad seed" theory—that there are evil people who wake up every morning thinking, "Who can I abuse today?"

She says, "No one *wants* to abuse. . . . It's just that life gets messed up, and people make poor choices as a result . . . that's why the work we do on forgiveness and atonement is so important; it breaks the cycle and enables us to allow something good to come from it."

For Alison the path of atonement was a long journey, and a spiritual process inspired by her faith as a Christian. Recently, she told me: "My atonement journey and subsequent healing cannot be separated from the power of God working in my life. I didn't do it with my strength alone. I reached out to God and came into a personal relationship with God. Within this relationship I was able to ask God for forgiveness for not forgiving my father earlier, and eventually forgive myself. From there I could make amends to myself to find peace, and eventually forgive my father."

From my point of view as a therapist, Alison was able to break the cycle of abuse only when she realized that holding on to her abuse hurt herself and others. I believe she was able to move "beyond forgiveness" by forgiving her father and then forgiving herself for some of her own abusive behavior when she was a child. Although what she did was not as grievous as what had been done to her, she needed to acknowledge what happened. Then she needed to forgive herself for the anger and fear that she had allowed to control much of her life.

Furthermore, she strongly believes that by forging a strong bond with her Creator, she was able to make peace with herself, make things right in her own life and family, and spread that love and peace out to her wider community through her work as a counselor.

Through the choices she has made and the journey beyond forgiveness she has walked, Alison has been able to transmute the cycle of abuse into a cycle of compassion, in her work as an extraordinary healer and counselor at her local church. If she had *not* broken the cycle through her own courageous choices, her anger and fear and shame would have continued to control her life. In this way, the abused becomes the abuser, over and over again.

Alison could have continued living her life as a victim, but she chose to forgive her father no matter what the response from him would be. She realized it didn't matter whether her dad ever truly admitted it to himself or freed himself from it, only that she fully free herself, repent for her past thoughts and actions, and go on to take the necessary steps of atonement that would turn her life around, and help others to heal also.

Once she had fully forgiven herself and her father, Alison realized two important things. First, she had to confront her father and give him an opportunity to atone; and second, she knew she had to speak out about what had happened, and make her life an example of the power of atonement. She wanted others to know that it is possible to live a fulfilled life even after such extreme abuse and mistreatment. Her father at that time was almost seventy years old, and she could have had him imprisoned if she had wished. Instead she made a request that she knew was what she really needed from him. It may seem insignificant to one who has never suffered at the hands of an oppressor, but Alison's simple request was to be respected and spoken to nicely by her father.

Respect and kindness were what she needed from her father in order to have a relationship with him again. He agreed and apologized for upsetting her, but he failed to fully own up to what he'd done. Nevertheless, for the last two years of his life they had a repaired relationship. He kept his promise and changed his actions, treating her with the respect she had gone without for her entire life—and she looks back on that gratefully. They agreed to be honest, to speak their feelings. On his deathbed he entrusted Alison, over his son and wife, to manage his affairs and carry out his last wishes. Because of his reluctance to fully admit to his actions, she could never really trust him to be alone with her two daughters. That was the one area that was never fully repaired between them because of his unwillingness to fully accept what he had done. Yet his tangible change in behavior toward Alison was enough for her to know that he was sorry, and that on some level he did know that what he had done was wrong. He wanted forgiveness from his daughter and to atone for his past.

You can see how this is almost a perfect picture of atonement on both sides, the victim and the abused, but for her father's lack of real remorse, which made it impossible for her to trust him fully. She believes that he just didn't know how, that he didn't have the tools to accept what he had done. This story affirms the importance of examples of real-life atonement, which provide a framework for us to follow, and it sheds light on a course of action we can take to redeem our wrongs. Whether we are the ones granting or seeking atonement, we must recognize the three crucially important parts of the process: forgiveness, repentance, and atonement. Otherwise, one or both parties may resent the forgiveness or, as in Alison's case, never fully trust the other again.

Alison gave her father a chance; she told him he was forgiven and that it didn't depend on him. She was doing it for herself to take her life back. At first Alison felt a desire for revenge; she was filled with rage and would plan ways to murder her father. It's amazing to me how far the process of forgiveness, repentance, and atonement that she has been through has carried her. Through atonement, Alison tells me, "I am at peace with myself now . . . or I have a sense of peace, and the anger that once fed my revengeful, murderous thoughts subsides and leaves me with a sense of well-being. I know that I have transformed my past into something that benefits me, my family, and others in my community."

To move forward, Alison learned to love, forgive, and accept herself, but crucially, she had to take action. It was freeing for Alison that she had forgiven, but what she really needed was something tangible. She needed a practice that would rebalance her life. After she found the courage to release and to let go of the desire for revenge or retaliation, she was able to do something that would honor her journey and help her continue to heal, while also healing others, joining the ranks of what anthropologists call "wounded healers."

For me, the ideal analogy is electrical circuitry. Forgiveness is the "circuit-breaker" that ceases the ongoing flow of pain; it's like a switch that stops a current of electricity. Once that switch is turned, atonement can pave the way to a new set of circumstances that prevent a reoccurrence and that create peace. Atonement is a kind of rewiring or rebuilding that heals wrongs and prevents their repetition, but it works only when there is an *action*. Atonement is deep, active, and powerful in its tangibility; it is not just a philosophy, theory, or perspective but a verb, a "doing word." It is only the action, restitution, or required gesture that fully rights a wrong, and Alison has dedicated her life to being an ongoing and lasting example of that.

As human beings, we all make mistakes. Without the choice of atonement we would be stuck—held back by guilt and shame. By following a consistent practice that links compassion for the self with forgiveness, we can break the bonds of resentment, shame, and retribution. When we choose the conscious and unconditional act to atone for the past, we go beyond the hurt, beyond the wrong, and make amends, no matter what. No one is saying this is easy, but it's absolutely necessary if we want to break the cycle and make a situation better. This is why compassion and forgiveness are the essence of virtually every religion in the world, and the message of every spiritual teacher who has ever walked on earth, including Jesus as he prayed, "Father, forgive them, for they know not what they do," as he was crucified.

Collectively and individually, we have a choice. We can live in an attitude of revenge and hatred, or one of compassion and forgiveness. If we choose the former, we are forever severed and separated; if we choose the latter, we become "at one." We make our peace with inner pain, and we release those who have harmed us, by allowing them the opportunity for their atonement—as well as our own.

From Apologies to Atonement in Australia

On February 13, 2008, the prime minister of Australia, Kevin Rudd, stood up and apologized to the Aborigines. I was deeply inspired by this act, seemingly a promising indication that the full reconciliation process had begun.

The prime minister and his government acknowledged the need to confront mistakes of the past to unite the country and move forward collectively, despite some parties' resistance. In meeting that resistance he told parliament a powerful story of a wonderful, elegant woman in her eighties named Nanna Nungala Fejo. Nanna remembers her earliest childhood days living with her family and her community in a bush camp just outside Tennant Creek. She remembers the love and the warmth and the kinship of those days, such as the traditional dancing around the campfire at night. She loved the dancing.

Sometime around 1932, when Nanna was about four, she remembers the men from the Children's Welfare Office coming with a truck, along with two white men and an Aboriginal stockman on horseback cracking his stock whip to round up the Aboriginal children—for "protection." The children were herded and piled onto the back of the truck. Tears flowing, Nanna's mother clung to the sides of the truck as her children were taken away to the Bungalow in Alice. A few years later

Nanna was also separated from her brothers and sister. She never saw her mum again, and found out from her brother years later that she had died years before, a broken woman fretting for the children who had literally been ripped away from her.

Prime Minister Rudd asked this eloquent lady what she would like him to say about her story. He says, "She thought for a few moments, then said that what I should say today was that all mothers are important." She added: "Families—keeping them together is very important. It's a good thing that you are surrounded by love and that love is passed down the generations. That's what gives you happiness."

What Rudd found truly amazing was that as he left, Nanna Fejo took one of his staff aside to make sure that he would not be too hard on the Aboriginal stockman who had hunted her and the other children down all those years ago. Rudd said, "The stockman had found her again decades later, this time himself to say, 'Sorry.' And remarkably, extraordinarily, she had forgiven him." He ends his reflections with these words:

> This is not, as some would argue, a black-armband view of history; it is just the truth: the cold, confronting, uncomfortable truth, facing it, dealing with it, moving on from it. . . . Until we fully confront that truth there will always be a shadow hanging over us and our future as a fully united and fully reconciled people. It is time to reconcile. It is time to recognize the injustices of the past. It is time to say sorry. It is time to move forward together.

Rudd's words of repentance were strong, repeating the word *sorry* three times in his speech.

But as history teaches time and time again, words are not enough. One year later—to the very day—Aboriginal people protested at the foot of Parliament Hill that more had not been done to back up these words. This is exactly the point: an apology may be noble, but it will be empty, incomplete, and disappointing to those who have been harmed if it is not accompanied by action.

It's true that many Aboriginal people hold prominent positions in Australia today, that they can receive an education denied their forebears and take posts at the state and federal levels of government. Sadly, however, this is just not enough; the actions necessary for genuine atonement of the wrongdoings done to the Aborigines in Australia are yet to be truly felt or seen.

By asking for forgiveness, the foundation for healing is put in place. But mere words will not be sufficient for the people who have had their families, communities, and identities irreparably damaged. "Sorry" without action is empty. As we have seen, without the change in behavior to back it up, the word is meaningless. For atonement to be complete, the wrongdoer must seek not just forgiveness, not just repentance, but also restitution, unless the wronged party waives it. This making of amends usually comes in the form of halting one type of behavior to replace it with another that is requested by the injured party.

The real tragedy is that it seems the resentment felt by the Aboriginal communities has gone even deeper since their witnessing the apology, for it was followed by an overt lack of prioritizing the needs of indigenous Australians. After a moment of hope they are furious that more has not changed since the apology, and that Rudd even extended elements of the previous government's Northern Territory intervention (which restricts how welfare payments are spent) into Queensland.

Pat Turner, former chief executive officer of the Aboriginal and Torres Strait Islander Commission, notes, "You do the symbolic things, that's what governments and white Australia is comfortable with, but when it comes to putting money on the table, it's not going to happen."

To me this portrays a sad, poignant example of the unrealized power of atonement. Atonement is the missing piece of the puzzle; it's the committed action, compensation, and demonstration of repentance, and it can go some distance to right wrongs. I believe that it's obvious that saying "sorry" is not enough in some cases. When you look at photos of the Aboriginal Australians involved in the forced relocations, you can see the emotional wounds expressed in the faces of these families, even in the young children. It's devastating. Today the needs of the Aboriginal communities are still being sidelined; their communities are still being stereotyped. And on average they are still expected to live seventeen years less than a white man. At some point there has to be a true recognition that this is by no means good enough. Rudd and his government must go the distance to heal the past by going beyond their apology and leading the practical actions necessary for atonement.

Australia is a modern example of how the ugliness of the past catches up with the present when it is not addressed and dealt with. The injustices are not going to disappear; they are in living memory, and we have to be accountable for what happens in the world. At this time in history, with our advancements of technology and world travel, we can't claim ignorance. What affects one people in one part of the world affects the entire human family. Justice and equality are rights for all. We have to consider how we would feel in others' shoes. It's uncomfortable but necessary to take suffering in any part of the world seriously and personally. These are problems we can't keep at arm's length.

Mistreatment of children, mothers, fathers, families, and our environment is catching up with us, and that is no more evident than in the destruction of the world's rainforests. Atonement is being called for from the heart of Mother Earth to the global human family; soon there will be nowhere to hide from this realization. The sooner we acknowledge the places where we are in disharmony with our environment, the sooner we can begin the work of atoning for the destruction our way of life has caused. As in the prime minister's moving injunction, it is time to acknowledge our collective wrongs, admit the consequences we are now witnessing in the world, discover what needs to be done to heal the destruction, and take action without delay. To fully appreciate this, let's travel to one of the remotest places on earth, the heart of the Amazon rainforest and the lungs of our planet.

Amazonian Atonement

In August 2008, I visited the Amazonian rainforest of Ecuador with Bill and Lynne Twist, cofounders of the Pachamama Alliance. They act as partners with indigenous tribes in the region to preserve and protect their land, their communities, and their way of life. What I experienced and learned on this journey affected me deeply. I was shocked that so much of this pristine virgin rainforest had been destroyed. Here, however, children played happily in the river. The men were strong and healthy, and the women sang their sweet songs for us and shared ancient ceremonies and rituals with our group. Every morning we awoke to an orchestra, a cacophony of sounds from the raucous grunt of the mating howler monkeys to the tireless chirruping of the cicadas. I felt privileged and humbled. Can you imagine how it feels to be in the midst of five million acres of untouched rainforest? The indigenous people living where I visited are called the Achuar. They have a relationship with nature that many of us have forgotten. The rainforest provides the Achuar with everything they need to survive, including shelter, food, and drink—and medicine.

One day our small group was walking through the forest with an indigenous man named Ruben. He led us to a tree. He stuck his machete into the bark, folded a leaf into a cup, and collected a large drop of the red sap that oozed out of the wound. He passed us the cup, and we dipped our finger in; he showed us how to rub the sap onto our skin, where it turned into a white, creamy substance. Ruben told us that this sap is applied to wounds, cuts, and bites and has many other uses. As he was sharing this with us, I was struck that, at the same time, he was closing up the tree's wound with a small amount of clay he had picked up from the ground.

It was no big deal. He didn't draw attention to the respectful way he treated the tree. In the middle of the Amazon jungle this man was living in harmony with nature. These communities and individuals have a sophisticated understanding of their impact on the environment and of the interconnectedness of all life. Ruben had to wound the tree in order to obtain the balm that would heal his wounds, but in return he was sure to heal the wound of the tree in an act of atonement. For me this is a small but poignant example, an object lesson in living in the natural world as a guardian, a protector, and a caring father of the environment.

When we recognize that we have this role as guardians and that we are but a single thread in the web of creation, how do our behaviors change? If we could see and feel the impact that some of our actions have, how would we change? Could we begin to atone by living in harmony with nature, rather than fighting her? Could we actively seek to be of service to nature, finding ways to help with reparations such as preventing damage, preserving life, or cleaning up our oceans and other environments we have allowed to become polluted on our watch? We, as guardians, have a sacred position, a "response-ability" to our planet. What must we give in our individual and collective atonement if we are all to survive in harmony on this earth?

These are questions we must ask in order to begin to atone and transform our relationship to our planetary home. The condition of the planet affects each one of us. For example, each of us has a critical stake in the wellness of the rainforest, which are the lungs of our planet; and the oceans, which are a crucial part of our life-support system. All of us, in big and small ways, consciously and unconsciously, have perpetrated damage to the earth. I believe this means that all of us are being asked to atone, to adopt new behaviors that will be better aligned with Mother Nature.

Beyond Healing to Reparations in Ecuador

In northern Ecuador, billions of gallons of toxic wastewater have been left behind by Chevron Texaco. The rainforest in this part of Ecuador is not the forest I discovered on my trip. Over one hundred million gallons of wastewater fill 627 open pits in an area three times the size of Manhattan. Thirty thousand people drink this water, which is as much as 250 times the limit for safe drinking water. The indigenous communities in this toxic environment are ravaged with cancer, birth defects, and a 150 percent increase in miscarriages since the oil companies moved in. The people who have lived peacefully here for thousands of years suffer the consequences of wholesale destruction in the name of profit and progress. Where the indigenous people whom I met were guardians of the richness of the Amazon, the people here are "guardians" of contamination, sickness, and poverty.

In a small house in this contaminated area lives an indigenous man named Pablo Fajardo. Pablo grew up in this part of Ecuador. As a boy of just fourteen he went to work for "the company"; he quickly realized that what they were doing would hurt and poison his community, so he and his brother voiced their concerns. They were promptly fired. Pablo and his brother decided to create an organization in order to stop the oil companies. Shortly thereafter, Pablo's brother died mysteriously, possibly murdered. Recognizing that education was crucial in his fight, Pablo attended high school. He graduated from law school three years ago. Today he is the head lawyer on the case against Chevron Texaco. He and a group of lawyers are pursuing their case against the giant oil companies and Chevron Texaco's team of over two hundred lawyers for environmental damage to the tune of sixteen billion dollars. This giant American firm is being brought to a small South American courthouse to atone for deliberately dumping over eighteen billion gallons of toxic wastewater in the Ecuadoran Amazon. If Pablo and his team are successful, the case has the potential to set a judicial precedent that will benefit millions of people around the world who suffer from living where oil companies drill. In Texas, when oil was drilled, the waste product was put back in the ground, but here in the pristine Amazon rainforest, to save a few dollars per barrel, the waste oil was, and still is, left behind. Their neglect has damaged the community and culture of the indigenous people, and violated their philosophy and cosmology. I can't help but juxtapose the actions of Ruben sealing a tree after a small nick to its bark, with the utter failure of the oil companies to make amends for the damage their oil exploration has caused.

What amazes me above all is that when asked, Pablo says that he is trying this case for the peace of the spirits and souls of the executives and the people of Chevron and Texaco. The indigenous people have not forgotten the universal truth of who they really are, of who we all are, oil companies, corrupt governments, and economic hit men included. Most of the oil from the Amazon basin feeds our energy needs in North America and the rest of the so-called developed world. But the Amazon is suffering. The issue goes deeper than oil. The Achuar don't see it as merely oil; they see it as the blood of their mother, the life force of their land. We have lost this level of connection, or have lessened it, to make our everyday consumption justifiable, but deep inside we know we can't continue this way. We have to change. We have to atone. If we live in Europe, America, Australia, or any other developed nation, we have work to do and an atonement to make to the earth.

Atonement is not just saying sorry. It is a process of acknowledging and then healing the damage that has been done on our behalf, of going an extra mile to take action—to make a move, a reparation of some kind—in order to make amends. Atonement is being humble enough, and brave enough, to recognize our part and take responsibility for it in a tangible way so that people can see it and feel it.

Beyond the Cycles of Abuse

Our planet has been at the mercy of an unsustainable world-view, under which perhaps many of us have been unconsciously operating. In telling the story of Alison and the stories of indigenous peoples, a parallel emerges, which we can choose to view with some hope. Our abuse of the earth could be seen in some ways as similar to the daughter who suffered at the hands of her abusive father, the person who was supposed to love and protect her. It might threaten to overwhelm us to look at the damage caused, the pain incurred, and the scale of destruction, and yet there is a facet of the human spirit that makes it possible to change, to heal the past and recover. This is our power. Our ability to transform ourselves is living proof that our lives can be examples of atonement—of restitution and inspired action. Whether we consider the necessity for atonement on a personal scale, that is, in our own lives, or on a global scale within and among our countries, in view of our creeds, gender, race, or environment, what matters is that we put the energy and action behind the words. If we act, we can begin the reconciliation we need to make for the sake of our relationships, families, nations, and environment.

To accomplish this, we can practice atonement. It is the vehicle we can use to bring us back to the present, release and forgive the past, and restore our relationship with the earth to one of guardianship. It might seem daunting to us to change our ways and make amends for our way of life, but we can see signs of transformation everywhere.

As global citizens we must quickly recognize that what affects one, affects all. It is high time for us to make amends and take the steps we know we must take before it's too late.

Our deepest atonement lies in our service to the people around us. The combined powers of atonement and forgiveness, along with the compassion that lives in the heart of each of us, may overcome many of the world's critical problems. No matter the circumstances of the situation—whether between a huge oil company and a poisoned community; a government and its indigenous people; or a father and his daughter—universal truth may be expressed in the word *at-one-ment*. We are not simply connected; we are, in truth, all one.

The words of Lila Watson, an Australian Aboriginal woman, highlight the nature of this oneness: "If you have come to help me, you are wasting your time, but if you have come because your liberation is bound up with mine, then let's work together."

The author thanks Alison Redwood, Olivia Boyce Abel, the Pachamama Alliance, and the Achuar tribe for their help in informing this essay.

CHAPTER 7

a twelve–step approach to atonement

ANONYMOUS

> AA is no success story in the ordinary sense of the
> word. It is a story of suffering transmuted, under
> grace, into spiritual progress.
> —Bill Wilson, cofounder, Alcoholics Anonymous

When asked to write about my experience in applying the twelve-step method to atonement, I was surprised to discover that nine of the twelve steps deal directly or indirectly with atonement, the act of making amends for the harm we have done to ourselves or to others. I learned this method as a result of my activities in Alcoholics Anonymous (AA). In this essay I will refer to the twelve-step philosophy in more general terms because many organizations now use these steps.

To begin, in my fellowship we rarely think of ourselves as atoning, because for active members atonement is such a natural part of our lives. It's as if we were fish that have been told that we swim in the ocean, and only then do we come to discover that we are swimming in water. Similarly, atonement is such a daily part of our lives that we rarely think about it. We don't even use the word, probably because the word itself can create a barrier to appreciating the underlying essence of atonement. I'd say that the last thing we are looking for when we come to the twelve-step program is spiritual awareness and ways to atone for our mistakes.

As with any spiritual tradition, those who are active in twelve-step methods are probably unable to communicate the full essence of our tradition in "pill form" or in brief. In fact, we are usually very reluctant to write about the methodology. We believe that in doing so, we would be in danger of diluting the message of the twelve-step way of life. True spiritual insight within any tradition can only come from an accumulation of ongoing experiences.

The twelve-step program was developed in the mid-1930s by the founders of Alcoholics Anonymous and consisted of two or three groups of fewer than one hundred individuals who had adapted principles from religions and other philosophies for their specific needs. These steps were first published in 1939. I often think of AA and the members of its family as a spiritual democracy because there are no authority figures and the philosophy is able to evolve to meet the needs of its members through democratic methods. Since AA's formation, many groups, usually recovery-oriented, have adapted these same principles to their respective communities. These organizations include Al-Anon (primarily for friends and family of AA members), Overeaters Anonymous, Gamblers Anonymous, Nicotine Anonymous, and many more. My learning experience has not been limited to one organization. I contribute this essay anonymously to honor all twelve-step traditions, as all place principles before personalities. I acknowledge that my comments are my opinion only, and are not endorsed by any twelve-step group. My goal is simply to communicate some of the essence of the twelve-step way of living with a special focus on atonement.

Within the method, the first specific connection to atonement comes at Steps 8 and 9, which read as follows: "8. Made a list of all people we had harmed and became willing to make amends to them all." "9. Made direct amends to such people wherever possible, except when to do so would injure them or others."

Before going on, I need to provide insight into the steps that precede these two, as the earlier steps prepare us for atonement.

I will intentionally deviate from the wording of the AA-adopted steps in this discussion to better address the subject of atonement for the general public, even if this will water down the original statements.

The first three steps are what I call foundation steps in making real changes in my life. In Step 1, I make an admission that my current way of living hasn't been working to my satisfaction and that I have become powerless in changing some (or many) aspects of it. This surrender step is often a gut-wrenching experience. Only after I admit that my approach to life hasn't been working too well am I able, in Step 2, to find a power greater than myself to help reestablish a more centered life. This power can be the "God" of my chosen religion, but to avoid the potential polarization among the great number of spiritual traditions (more than thirty-six thousand denominations within Christianity alone), we simply refer to a "Higher Power." Step 2 is so important because I am preparing myself to become teachable, or open-minded. In Step 3, I make a decision to follow a spiritual way of living and follow the guidance of my newly found Higher Power as it is revealed in the remaining steps and by my fellow travelers.

Step 4 is where the hard work begins. Here I take a personal inventory. My first actual experience with this task was that I could access only some of the more glaring mistakes from my memory. We often use the metaphor of an iceberg, since we can only ever see the top 10 percent of an iceberg, as we can observe only a small portion of our life. Once we clear off that top layer and dump it into the ocean, 10 percent of the remainder will surface. This metaphor is a gentle clue for us to be patient with ourselves and know that our journey is deep and continuous.

Let's say that my personal inventory revealed that I had once stolen money from my friend, Bob. As we uncover our various mistakes and traits within Step 4, which might suggest a need for atonement, we move on to Step 5, in which we share this information with another person. Typically this person is what some traditions call "a partner in believing." We might also call him or her a spiritual coach or sponsor. By first sharing our wrong thinking and actions with someone who is supportive of us, and not a victim of our misdoing, we obtain insight into the issues at hand. This is invaluable support as we march toward the atonement climax with our direct amends, in Step 9. But first we need to embody Steps 6 and 7.

In Step 6 we are introduced to another preparation for atonement. We must become ready to have our defects removed by a God of our understanding. Next, in Step 7, we ask our Creator to remove our shortcomings. I have come to believe that few of us can develop a mental state of atonement without an internal readiness and a change of heart. The essence of this change of heart may be the single most important aspect of the atonement process. For what is atonement if the heart is not there? Everyone will sense the hollowness.

Moving on to Step 8, we list the people we have harmed. In my simple example, Bob is listed. Step 9 gives me the opportunity to meet with Bob. When we do meet, I tell him what I stole. I admit to him that I was wrong, and I ask for forgiveness. This is what I would call the forgiveness phase of my atonement. The next phase of this step would be to make amends, which might sound like this: "Bob, I want to repay you, and I can do so over the next few months. In addition, I will not do it again. Furthermore," I tell him, "God willing, I will amend my life and not steal from anyone else ever again." This simple format can be used for much more complex issues such as marital problems, slander, hidden debts, neighborhood disputes, business misunderstandings, and so on. As a matter of fact, a simple atonement with a friend can provide good practice for the more complex and darker issues of our lives.

Years ago I owned an apartment project with my investors. A tenant had withheld rent, claiming that the water flow in her apartment was insufficient. I had inspected her apartment and concluded that the water flow was fine. Subsequently I filed a lawsuit against her—her father was her attorney. I won the suit; she appealed. I then tried to avoid service. My insurance company then administered the case because it had elements of malicious prosecution on her part. Although I was convinced that she had been totally wrong, I had become "too clever by half" in avoiding service and by not being sensitive to bringing harmony to the conclusion.

This drama totally consumed me. Finally, against my lawyer's advice, I called her to apologize for my role in the drama. I explained that I was doing so for my benefit, following my understanding of the tenets of the twelve-step philosophy. To my great surprise she said that she understood, because her brother was active in a similar program. She expressed compassion toward me, yet she held me accountable. My never calling anything she may have done inappropriate allowed the discussion to be fruitful, I believe.

The fear, anger, and resentment that had gripped my life for some time dissolved instantly. We settled the case. We even became casual friends and talked from time to time.

I learned a variety of lessons from this episode. First, be sincere and courteous regarding issues that seem minor, for they may be major to the other person. Second, in victory, allow the opposition to maintain a sense of dignity even if the issue appears to be frivolous. Atonement still needs to be completed after a judge rules. And third, don't bend the rules, cut corners, or use trickery, for these can easily create an environment of disharmony, which itself might someday need atonement.

On another occasion my efforts at atonement were received with great resistance. A close friend and I had gotten together for a social hour and had run up quite a tab. In the past, he had consistently claimed that he was short of funds. Too often, I felt, I ended up having to pay the bill. It was somehow implied. This particular night I decided, then and there, to teach him a lesson. I walked out of the lounge, leaving him to pay the bill, though I knew he didn't have the cash. This was in the days when the term *passive-aggressive* was a new concept. Unfortunately, my sudden departure damaged his business reputation. When I went to him to apologize, my efforts were definitely not well received. His words were not enlightening. And yet I felt an inner strength for having done my part to make amends. I had apologized. Later, we became cordial again and respectful. We even referred business leads to one another. My fear of using the atonement technique diminished with each encounter. I benefited in that I learned that I was human and fallible. Even more, I learned that I had to humble myself, to submit myself to the mercy of others.

I've learned from the practice of atonement that when disharmony exists, the other person may likewise have wronged us. The natural tendency is to focus on the wrongs done to us. But for those of my ilk, that doesn't work. In theory, atonement should happen in both directions. I admire those who have accomplished such a thing. However, my approach is to focus on my own mistakes. I believe this can provide leadership by example. With time, the other might join in to complete any unfinished process of reconciliation.

Some might say that Steps 8 and 9 are merely practice runs for a life of atonement. This is because in Step 10 we are asked to continue to look for errors in our thoughts, words, and deeds. Then we are asked to make appropriate amends immediately. While in Step 11, which is about prayer and meditation, we are encouraged to review and monitor the more subtle aspects of our thoughts and feelings, which might need an overhaul.

In my spiritual twelve-step community, most of us feel extremely fortunate in that we share our "street smarts," our insights from real living, continuously. One day I walked into a social club that attracted fellowship members, and a friend greeted me, asking, "How are you?"

"I'm mad as hell," I said.

"Oh," he said slowly, "you mean you didn't get your way."

I mumbled for a moment, then went on, explaining, "She didn't do this . . . and she did that . . ."

He retorted, "Yes, you mean you didn't get your own way."

Then I was really mad. He had struck a nerve. I knew it but had no idea how to respond.

A few weeks later, I mentioned the episode to another friend. He said, "Oh, sure. *Anger* is 'I didn't get my own way today.' *Resentment* is 'I didn't get my own way yesterday.'"

I thought, "He's struck another nerve."

"And by the way," he continued, "*fear* is 'I may not get my own way tomorrow.'"

Bingo!

I spent the next ten years concentrating on the relationship between these three spiritual roadblocks or obstacles—anger/resentment, fear, desire—and I've come to accept the fact that I will probably focus on them for the rest of my life.

But in the spirit of Step 10, I continue to take a personal inventory as presented in the literature of my fellowship. It has taken me twenty years of diligent work to develop an expanded understanding of this step. It has become an adventure of self-discovery. In broad terms, in addition to looking at our gross mistakes, Steps 4 and 10 ask us to look at three aspects of our lives: anger/resentment, fear, and excessive or inappropriate desires. I believe that these aspects of the inevitably difficult reconciliation process are addressed directly and powerfully in the wisdom traditions of Buddhism, Taoism, and Hinduism, while working more obliquely in Judaism, Islam, and Christianity. But I think the twelve-step technique is unique.

Those ten years were a very difficult time in my life, including as they did a divorce and financial problems. Had someone asked me whether I had resentments, I would have responded that I did not—probably with teeth clenched. But my closest friends would say things like, "What's playing in your mind?"

"Are those people and events in your mind getting free rent?" "Resentments are 're-sensing and re-feeling.' If the story is playing in your mind, it's probably resentment."

I have to admit that I had many stories playing in my mind. Ten, as I recall. Most or all of these resentments were more imagined than real. It was probably a survival technique, because I had to blame others for my problems. It couldn't have been me. Or could it? I had been taught by the lay members of my group that if I held some resentment, it was my problem. No matter who was at fault. As has often been said, "Resentments are like a poison; I drink the poison hoping the other person will get sick."

So in those days I had chosen to be a victim. My denial techniques had been so powerful that I was able to keep my iceberg submerged. But eventually the forces of resentment overpowered my denial, and the resentments popped up to the surface. I became debilitated as a result of the dramas playing in my mind.

My minister taught me a great technique. She said that I should write out a statement like "I forgive X, and X forgives me." She said that there was always a two-way connection. Then I was to write a statement each morning: one for every situation that was playing in my mind. I was to read it aloud while visualizing the other person and me smiling and shaking hands. I did this. To my great amazement, five of the resentments lifted the very first day. Over the next ten days, the remaining five dissolved. One might say that this process only included the forgiveness half of the reconciliation process. I would agree. However, in most of these situations there was no victim other than me. I was the victim of my own thinking. In reality, then, I was making restitution with myself. In doing so, I hope to have done more good than harm to the world around me.

Eventually I learned to bless and give thanks for these resentments because they were the harbinger of an expanded awareness. Acknowledging these resentments allowed me to circumvent the path of denial. The resentments were like a weather vane showing me where the wind was coming from. In the past, I had tried to turn the weather vane in another direction. Now, I was no longer a victim, perceived or real.

Recently a new friend of mine described a process that she uses to stay calm and centered when others have offended or hurt her. She told me that when someone "flips her off" on the freeway, she thinks of the person as having a bad day at home or at work. Other times she thinks of the road-raging driver as someone living at a low level of enlightenment who is doing the best he or she can. As impressive as those examples were to me, what really caught my ear was that she was able to depersonalize the experience by saying to herself that it's not about her, that it would have happened to anyone who happened to be in the path of that troubled driver. My friend concluded by telling me that the depersonalization technique can be used with more grievous offenses, such as burglary and even sexual abuse. I had to tell her, I thought it was a wonderful way to avoid the trap of victimhood that permeates our culture.

In my twelve-step group, we are encouraged to follow a similar tack. We view an offender as a sick person. Then we pray for his or her well-being. Finally, we ask in prayer how we might be helpful to the offender.

Our truest and most complete atonement comes in the last phase, Step 12. There, we try to practice our new way of living in all dimensions of our lives. This can be a cure-all for any amends that were impractical to complete, such as when a person has died or can't be located, or when we fudged the numbers on our tax return. As an example, suppose I had stolen ten dollars from my grandmother, who has passed on. I could leave a ten-dollar bill on her grave, or I might look for regular opportunities to do something nice for grandmothers who touch my life today. Most of us would agree that this is a good form of reconciliation.

Thus, with time and continuous awareness, we change. Our desire to help others is a wonderful "curtain call" for the drama of atonement. I have learned firsthand the power of this process.

The twelve-step program includes a bonus of twelve *traditions* and twelve *Concepts of Service* that can serve as effective guidance for how we might best interface with the world. Tradition 11 says, "Our public relations policy is based on attraction rather than promotion; we need always maintain personal anonymity at the level of press, radio, and films." Similarly, Tradition 12 says, "Anonymity is the spiritual foundation of all our traditions, ever reminding us to place principles before personalities." Many in my community take these traditions very seriously, and rightly so.

In my own life, the most illuminating example of this came when someone whom I didn't know well broke two of the traditions many of us consider to be sacred. This person, in the opinion of many of us in the fellowship, had broken both of these traditions by advertising AA on television in a neighboring country. What could I do to rectify the situation? After reflection, I had to conclude that enforcement was impossible. Finally, I became reconciled to the fact that I could work on myself only: I could practice the tradition, as I understand it, with the hope that others would follow. This powerful incident reminded me of Gandhi's challenge: "Be the change you want to see in the world." This is sage advice, but for me the alpha and omega of true atonement is revealed in the story that Bill W. revealed in his book *Alcoholics Anonymous*:

"My schoolmate visited me," he wrote, "and I fully acquainted him with my problems and deficiencies. We made a list of people I had hurt or toward whom I felt resentment. I expressed my entire willingness to approach those individuals, admitting my wrong. Never was I to be critical of them. I was to right all such matters to the utmost of my ability."

PART TWO

stories of
atonement

There is no greater agony
than bearing an untold story inside
of you.

—Maya Angelou

memories of my grandfather
atonement the gandhi way

ARUN GANDHI

> Anger and intolerance are the enemies of correct
> understanding.
>
> —*Mohandas Gandhi*

*As the fifth grandson of Mohandas Gandhi, the sociopolitical activist
Arun Gandhi has followed in his grandfather's footsteps by dedicating his
life to teaching the virtues of nonviolence. This essay reveals the roots
of his grandfather's belief in the twin pillars of satyagraha—forgiveness
and atonement—and illustrates the power that stories can have in
promoting nonviolent conflict resolution, from generation to generation,
and from culture to culture. Here, Arun Gandhi reveals for publication
for the first time the strange background to the story of his grandfather's
assassination and the remarkable lesson that he gleaned from it: namely,
that "forgiveness must always be unconditional" and that we need to
practice atonement by clearing our own hearts of hate. He concludes
with a moving testimony to the lifelong influence his grandfather has
had on his own life mission, which is to transform the world by helping
society better understand "the futility of hate and prejudice."*

During his teen years my grandfather was influenced by
a youthful Muslim friend from school who appeared to
have answers to all questions, including the independence of
India and why the British were able to colonize the country.
One day he said to Grandfather, "If you seriously want to drive
the British out of India you will have to eat meat like I do and
become tall and strong as I am."

This friend was athletic and Grandfather was suitably
impressed by his prowess on the track and field at school. He
was a fast runner, and no one at school ever dared confront him.

This was more than Grandfather could say of his own physical attributes. He was small and weak and constantly plagued by real and imaginary fears. Grandfather was mortally afraid of darkness, while everyone else, including his teenage wife, walked into dark rooms without any concern. All of these problems, his friend insisted, were the result of a vegetarian diet.

Eating meat was taboo, not only in the Gandhi household but in the homes of many Hindus in the state of Gujarat who were then influenced by the teachings of Vaishnavism and Jainism; both religious sects abhorred meat and eggs. Grandfather was old enough to understand that meat eating would have to be done clandestinely, but he did not know how low they would have to stoop to achieve their goals. Grandfather's older brother, Tulsidas, had already succumbed to this friend's dietary experiment, though not for the same reasons. Tulsidas was physically bigger and stronger and had none of the fears that assailed Grandfather. This I think convinced Grandfather that there might be some truth to the power of meat eating. He readily agreed to participate in the experiment.

Grandfather's compulsive desire to become physically strong and fearless compelled him to defy the family injunctions against eating meat and smoking cigarettes, although he was aware how mortified his parents would be if they learned what the two brothers were doing.

In his autobiography, *My Experiments with Truth*, Grandfather writes that he never did acquire a taste for meat, although he persisted with it for over a year. Meat was tasteless and rubbery, and he heard goats bleating in his stomach at night.

Over time he realized he was having to sink lower and lower into the depths of conspiracy and lies. To buy meat and have it cooked, he had to steal money from home. One day when he found no money, he stole a small piece of jewelry and sold it. In addition, he had to lie to his mother about not eating at home. But he just could not come to terms with deceit.

Not many teenagers are smitten by morals and ethics, as ours is an age when most young people indulge in all forms of experiments. So it is interesting to note the widely differing reactions of the two brothers who were guilty of the same crime. Lies and deceit did not seem to bother Tulsidas as much as they did Mohandas, my grandfather. Mohandas found that instead of curing him of his fears and making him stronger, this experiment was leading him deeper into the depths of "hell," as he put it.

In his autobiography, Grandfather titles the chapter in which he describes this incident as "Atonement." One day when Grandfather could stand it no longer, he decided to unburden his guilt by confessing to his father; but he lacked the courage to do it verbally, so he wrote a long, remorseful letter telling him about all the bad things he had done. In his confession he made no mention of Tulsidas. He decided that was not his business. Then, after sitting over this confession for a day, he plucked the courage the next afternoon to take the letter to his father, and stood next to the chair while his father read it slowly and deliberately.

Grandfather expected to be severely reprimanded, if not thrashed, so he was surprised when he saw tears streaming down his father's cheeks. The father put the letter aside and embraced his son, and the tears of "both mingled together to wash away the sins." In his letter, Grandfather had promised never to do any wrong ever again.

It was the magnanimous response of an anguished father that taught Grandfather the importance of atonement and the charity of unconditional forgiving. Atonement and forgiving are two sides of the same coin. It is important here that we dwell on other possible responses considered normal in today's relationships. Had his father punished him or played on his son's guilt at every opportune moment, it is possible that my Grandfather would not have had the cleansing experience that mingled the tears of father and son.

If forgiveness and atonement are two sides of the same coin, then forgiveness without atonement is worthless just as atonement without forgiving means very little. But equally, atonement has a double meaning—changing one's self, and changing the issues created by others that create the conflict. All his life my grandfather was involved in self-improvement and in improving society by making us aware how each of us contributes to conflict. While it is easier to improve the self, it is not always easy to change others, which should not mean that we do neither.

The man who assassinated my grandfather, Nathuram Vinayak Godse, had made eight previous attempts on his life before he succeeded in accomplishing his task, in 1948. After the third attempt, in the mid-1930s, Godse was caught by some volunteers and brought before Grandfather, who welcomed him warmly and invited him to sit down and discuss the issues as sane adults should. For several hours Grandfather tried to have an intelligent dialogue with the assailant, but in the end, when he realized that there was nothing he could say that would convince the man of the futility of his attempts, he let his future assassin go with a blessing. Grandfather believed that we each must do what we have to do. The man was not handed over to the police, nor was a complaint lodged. The moral of the story is that sometimes atonement cannot be wholly accomplished, but that should not mean that forgiveness should also be denied. Forgiveness must always be unconditional.

My own fear is that punishment seldom brings about reformation of a character; I fear it only shames the person deeper into the hole of shame. Many is the time I have heard prisoners in my work as a counselor for our Gandhi for Children program ask me, "We are willing to atone for our sins, but is society willing to forgive us?"

This incident taught Grandfather two important lessons: first, that it is important to confess your guilt sincerely; and second, that it is just as important, if not more so, that atonement is followed by an act of unconditional forgiving. Atonement and forgiving not only played an important role in Grandfather's personal life; they became the pillars of his philosophy of nonviolence.

Throughout his life he deliberated intensely over every action, and if it still resulted in a mistake, he had no qualms about confessing sincerely to his "Himalayan blunders." It was this transparency that marked his leadership and earned him the implicit trust, not only of the people who followed him but also of the opponents he fought against.

In the late 1930s, the British launched a smear campaign to tarnish Grandfather's image. They published lies and innuendoes and cast aspersions on his moral integrity. All this was done with Churchill's blessings. Significantly, the person who publicly defended Grandfather and castigated the British government was none other than the prime minister of South Africa, Gen. J. C. Smuts, against whom Grandfather fought for twenty-one years. General Smuts said he did not agree with Grandfather on many political issues, but on the question of ethics and morality he had not seen anyone stand as tall as Gandhi. Smuts snubbed the British prime minister to uphold the moral integrity of a man whom he had once considered a lesser human for being black.

Another lesson that is directly linked with atonement and forgiveness but is almost totally neglected by scholars who have interpreted Gandhi's life and philosophy is the lesson of "anger management." Grandfather firmly believed that without the ability to manage one's anger and use that energy intelligently, atonement and forgiveness would be virtually impossible to achieve. It is possible that Gandhi's father was moved to anger by the infraction his son had committed. Consider the humiliation the family would have to endure if word got out that Grandfather had become a meat-eater. However, instead of lashing out in a moment of madness, his father channeled the energy intelligently and reacted positively to his son's confession.

Around the same time as the meat-eating incident, Grandfather learned through his wife, my Grandmother Kastur, what he described as "a very important lesson in nonviolent conflict resolution." Kastur had never gone to school, and could neither read nor write; yet, she taught him a profound lesson. They were both thirteen when they were married but did not start living together until the age of fifteen. Grandfather was young and impulsive and resented the fact that she was not assailed by the fears he had but could bravely face darkness. Male chauvinism erupted, and he was going to show her who was boss. He went to the local library and checked out books on the husband-wife relationship. The more he read, the more he realized that even Western authors believed that a husband must be the master and that he must lay down the rules in his own home and enforce them strictly.

After reading about male dominance, Grandfather came home one evening, and in the privacy of their bedroom he told Grandmother very sternly: "From tomorrow you will not step out of this house without my permission. This is the law, and you will obey it strictly."

Grandmother did not retort or throw tantrums. Calmly, she turned away from him and went to sleep. The next morning, life continued as though nothing had happened. She went out of the house with the wives of other brothers who were all living under the same roof as a "joint family."

Now one must understand that in traditional India, under joint family circumstances, during the day the men and women lived in different parts of the house. If my Grandmother Kastur had to get permission from her husband every time she needed to go out, she would have had to invade the male section of the house, and in the presence of everyone else would have had to ask for her husband's permission. She did not see anyone else doing this and concluded that the new law was too ridiculous to be obeyed.

So she totally ignored the rule.

Grandfather was aware of the goings-on in the house. One night he confronted her again: "How dare you disobey me?" he said, seething with anger.

This outburst did not impress Grandmother one bit. In a soft and calm voice she asked Grandfather: "I was taught from childhood to always respect the elders in the house, and I believe in this house your parents are the oldest. Are you suggesting that I should not obey your mother but obey you? If that be so, should I tell your mother tomorrow that I will no longer obey her but obey you instead?"

This could not happen.

Grandfather could never tell Grandmother to disobey his mother, and so the matter was settled calmly and peacefully. Grandfather claimed in his autobiography that this incident was the first and most profound lesson in nonviolent conflict resolution that he learned. When later he developed his philosophy of nonviolence, learning to use anger intelligently and positively became an important requirement.

It is only when one is able to use anger positively that one finds ways of forgiving an oppressor. The early examples in Grandfather's life stood him in good stead when he arrived in South Africa as a young lawyer determined to do well in his legal practice but who instead became a victim of vicious prejudice. He was physically and emotionally abused, and his pride cried out for vengeance, while common sense nudged him away from the prevailing notion of an eye for an eye toward a more sane form of justice—a change of heart.

Grandfather suffered the ignominy of the first physical abuse without retaliation, but the second time, when he was almost killed by a white mob, he decided to put his philosophy into action. On this occasion the police in Durban (South Africa) had arrested a few white assailants. Grandfather was invited to the police station to file charges; he went but refused to

charge them. He told the group, as well as the police, that punishing them would not teach them the lesson that prejudice and
discrimination are not normal civilized behavior. "I forgive you,"
he said. "But I hope you will reflect on the incident and see how
hate can destroy you more than your victim."

"If you don't charge them, we will have to let them go free,"
the police warned.

Grandfather did not change his mind. The men walked
free. At least one of these four men became a lifelong friend
of Grandfather's, and one of his followers. Throughout his life
Grandfather forgave those who attempted to harm him, convinced that that was the right thing to do.

When I went to live with my grandfather as a twelve-year-
old boy, I was angry because I had suffered the same kind of violent prejudice in South Africa that my grandfather experienced
there more than thirty years before me. But I did not have the
wisdom that he had. I was determined to fight back when necessary. Grandfather taught me that nonviolence is much more
than a strategy for resolving conflicts peacefully. Nonviolence is
not a weapon; it is a lifestyle.

The lessons he taught me during the eighteen months I was
with him, and the parenting I got at home in South Africa from
Manilal, Gandhi's second son, and Sushila, helped me realize that Grandfather was trying to teach people that they must
enlarge their concept of violence. We assume that violence is
only in the physical form, that as long as we don't fight and kill
people we are basically nonviolent. Grandfather said we have
created a whole culture of violence, which is so deeply rooted
it has taken over every aspect of human life. Our language,
relationships, behavior, attitude—in fact, everything about us—
are violent.

As a way of introspection, he taught me to build a genealog-
ical tree of violence having two branches, physical and passive.
Every day, as part of my learning experience, I had to analyze
all the events of the day and put them in their appropriate

places on the tree. Physical violence was easy to define. It was all forms of violence in which physical force is used: slapping, murders, rapes, killings, wars, beatings, and so on. What was difficult was defining passive violence. What is passive violence? I had to use a simple yardstick. If the action—whether committed by me or someone else—caused someone anguish or emotional injury, or made someone unhappy, then that would be passive violence. It could be anything such as wasting global resources; wasting food or other valuables at home; overconsuming, as we do in the United States and other affluent countries; discrimination, oppression, name-calling, or teasing. All are acts of passive violence.

After a few months, I filled up a whole wall in my room with lists of acts of passive violence. That is when my grandfather explained the connection between the two. We commit passive violence every day, consciously and unconsciously, and that causes anger in the victim, who resorts to physical violence either to get justice or to seek revenge. Therefore, it can be said that passive violence is the fuel that ignites physical violence. If we wish to put out the fire of physical violence, we need to cut off the fuel supply. Since we all contribute to the fuel, "We must become the change we wish to see in the world," as Grandfather was fond of saying. Unless we change our habits, the habits of the world will not change.

If peace seems elusive today, it is because we attempt to douse the fire with the one hand while continuing to pour fuel onto the fire with the other. The conflagration subsides, giving the illusion of peace, and then fires back up like a spark caught in a raging wind.

Nonviolence may be used as a tool to achieve immediate goals, but those goals will not be long-lasting, just as peace attained through the barrel of a gun is illusory. What happens today in India, South Africa, and other countries that attained freedom through nonviolent action is sad, because these places continue to suffer internecine violence almost incessantly.

The inconclusive debate today is, "Which came first, the culture of violence or the culture of materialism?" Indeed, they are interconnected and feed on each other. The culture of violence seeks control through fear, while the culture of nonviolence seeks it through love. Fear spawns negativity, such as greed, hate, prejudice, and lack of understanding and respect. Negativity also leads to violence.

Love, on the other hand, evokes positive thoughts and feelings, like respect, understanding, and compassion. In a Native American tradition there is an appropriate story that illustrates this point. Sitting in the wild under a tree, a grandfather tells his grandson that inside every human being are two wolves who are at war with each other.

The grandson asks, "Which one wins?"

The grandfather explains, "The one you feed."

In a selfish, materialistic society, we tend to feed the violent, arrogant wolf until it attacks us and we are disturbed. My grandfather once said that the world can produce enough "for everyone's need, but not for everyone's greed." In today's world we have become greedy, and each one of us is attempting to grab as much of the pie as we can for ourselves. This has led to gross imbalances in the distribution of wealth and basic needs. Some of us have an abundance of everything we need, while others, even in affluent countries, have nothing or very little. In our arrogance we pity the poor, and often derisively describe them as "worthless bums." Pity is the result of material arrogance. Instead of showing pity to the poor and giving them on a platter what we think they need, Grandfather said it is much more constructive to show compassion and, working together, help them rebuild their self-respect and self-confidence. Pity is easy. One can write out a check and mail it and be happy that one has done a good deed for the day. Compassion needs a good deal more commitment and dedication to work with the poor as equal partners.

An integral part of the philosophy of nonviolence is the concept of "trusteeship," which as defined by my grandfather means that we don't "own" the talents we possess but rather are "trustees" of those talents. Viewing ourselves as owners of the talent, we become selfish and exploit the talent for our personal gain with virtually no concern for others; as trustees, we help those less fortunate find solutions to their problems using our expertise.

The philosophy of nonviolence is not about protesting injustice alone; it is equally about doing constructive work to help rebuild a just and equitable society for all.

Clearly I learned many valuable lessons from my grandfather. Among them were two he taught me as a thirteen-year-old living with him. These lessons, on forgiveness and atonement, put life into perspective for me and transformed me. I grew up in South Africa, where like Grandfather I was subjected to physical violence because of the dark color of my skin. It filled me with rage, and typically I was obsessed with the desire for revenge, an eye-for-an-eye form of justice.

Grandfather told me that if we respond to hate with more hate, we only increase hate in the world. He said that we need to transform those who hate us by showing them unconditional love. To be able to love those who hate me, I had to forgive them and practice atonement, first by getting rid of hate within myself and then by helping society see the futility of hate and prejudice. Since that time with Grandfather, this has been my mission in life.

CHAPTER 9

healing the wounds of war

atonement practices for veterans

EDWARD TICK

> Strange thing about *war wounds*—the older you get,
> the less proud of them you become.
> —Col. *Werner Visser in* Hart's War

Edward Tick, Ph.D., began counseling Vietnam War veterans in the
1970s and has since treated veterans of numerous conflicts, from
the Spanish Civil War to the Iraq War. His healing methods for those
suffering the long-term effects of combat are based on his study of
spiritual, mythological, and psychological traditions from around the
world. In this essay, Tick reveals his ardent belief that the human race
shares an essential oneness, a unity that is shattered by the violence of
war but which can be restored. He has discovered that the healing
of veterans in those conflicts often begins with the veterans' telling of
their stories, which in turn carries the potential of leading them to self-
forgiveness and, crucially, to the next stage, making amends. "Acts of
atonement," he writes, "simultaneously repair and restore the outer world
as they heal the inner. War shatters worlds. Atonement reconstitutes
them—within and without." Tick's work brings to mind the poetic lines of
Pierre Teilhard de Chardin: "We are one, after all, you and I. Together
we suffer, together exist, and forever will recreate each other."

War breaks, fragments, incinerates, ravages, shoots, shreds, smashes, stabs, and destroys. It is a violent act of division and deconstruction waged with cosmic powers on a cosmic scale. Our world exists in an essential unity; war is its opposite. War obliterates Oneness.

When we go to war, we declare that we are not and cannot be at one with the other. We now label the other "enemy"— a word that in its origins means "not friend"—and we treat them as foes. We no longer cooperate or try to get along. We have been unable to convince or persuade the other of the legitimacy of our point of view, our needs, our rights, our beliefs, or even our lands and belongings. We no longer accept theirs. All channels of communication, through which we usually maintain a shared community, have failed. We believe that the other has become a threat of such magnitude that we must resort to violence to neutralize it and make ourselves safe again. We have become so alien to one another that we believe the other must be broken, vanquished, or destroyed. To kill, we must render this alienated other as something less than ourselves, less than human. War destroys Oneness in every aspect of our existence, and its aftermath can be so fraught with pain, suffering, loss, anger, failure, betrayal, hunger for vengeance, brokenness, confusion, grief, shame, or guilt that it can seem impossible that we will ever again become reconciled with our former enemy—or ourselves.

Fortunately, human communities throughout history have developed practices to heal what war has torn asunder. Atonement is one of the practices.

The root of *atonement* is "oneness," "becoming one with." In essence, atonement entails not just awakening or exchanging feelings of empathy, friendship, or forgiveness but *performing acts of repair that bring what was separated, divided, or broken back into union*. Restoring what was broken, uniting what was divided, re-creating oneness within and between peoples and nations from the shattered bits of their worlds that are left in the aftermath of war's carnage—these are the agonizing but essential goals of healing and repair that are available through atonement. Atonement is necessary for soldiers and nations to return home and to heal from war. Without atonement after war, our survivors and their world remain broken within and without. But with atonement, amends are made, relationships are restored, and what war has sundered may become one again.

As a psychotherapist who has worked with veterans for over thirty years, I have seen atonement work time and time again with combat veterans and other war survivors who could find no other path to healing.

Transformations of Oneness and Intimacy During Warfare

In 1936, William Herrick joined the Abraham Lincoln Brigade to fight against fascism in the Spanish Civil War, which he tells in his semiautobiographical novel of that war, *Hermanos!*

Jake Starr, the novel's protagonist, is an idealistic young American Communist whom party leaders thought might make a good official. He is pulled off the front lines during the siege of Madrid to be tested for the Party's elite. Escorted into a prison dungeon, Jake watches as, one by one, enemies are brought into the room and shot to death.

When the last prisoner is escorted in, Jake is appalled to see that the man is a front-line ally, the leader of a peasant party. Wanting to consolidate power, the Communists have branded anyone with a competing ideology as "the enemy." Because this peasant leader had been an honorable and courageous comrade on the battlefield, his captors grant his final wish—to choose his own executioner.

The peasant leader looks deeply into the eyes of each captor. He indicates the idealistic young American and says, "I prefer him to marry me."[1]

Not just in this example, but also throughout history, the word *marry* has had widespread use as a slang term for acts such as handcuffing, torture, and execution that join people through violence rather than love. This may indicate that those perpetrating violence are, on some level, aware of the profound intimacy and irrevocability of their acts.

More than three decades later, during the mid-1960s, in another war, Wilbert Michel, a Native American of the Kootenai tribe serving as an army infantryman, killed his first enemy combatant in Viet Nam's Central Highlands. He reports seeing the enemy's face, then shooting him, and for the rest of his life remembering that face and feeling that the enemy soldier had given him a chance to live.

Traditional cultures from around the world teach that, whether in war, crime, hunting or accidents, we are responsible for the souls we release to death. I heard a traditional Lakota elder declare this belief regarding warriors: "When you kill an enemy warrior you become responsible for his soul." Veterans from any ethnic background may sense this responsibility, wish to fulfill it immediately after a death, and be unable to because of modern military practices or battlefield conditions.

As a child growing up on a Montana reservation, Wil had been taught by his elders that after an act of killing, whether in hunting or war, he must appease and support the spirits of the slain by explaining why he had to take their lives. He had done this as a hunter at home. But Native combatants such as Wil later suffered decades of anguish because they could not find any words or thoughts to justify this wartime killing of other young men from a traditional people much like their own.

Generally, we think of war and violence as inherently destructive. We think of killing as the opposite of intimacy. Yet as these stories indicate, and as veterans have confessed to me for decades, the act of taking a life is profoundly intimate, one that engenders a lifelong bonding to the other. Some survivors of war feel closer to those they killed during warfare or to the wounded men or corpses they tended than to anyone living with whom they have been intimate before or since. Some feel that they are bonded forever through the act of taking a life to those whose life they have taken or through the sacrifices comrades made for each other on the battlefield. But these survivors rarely have the means by which to turn such bonding into positive or life-affirming relationships. They may then feel haunted and incomplete for the rest of their lives. And because their acts led to destruction and death, many survivors no longer trust themselves with intimacy. They replicate war's brutality in their intimate relationships or feel that loving will only lead to destruction. Further, killing, like loving, is penetration. But it is unwelcome, uninvited, forced, done with brutality rather than tenderness, performed in order to take rather than create or restore life. Killing is thus an intimate and ultimate act that defines and determines the shape of one's life and that forever bonds survivors and slain. For all these reasons, war fosters a *reverse intimacy*, a union that is neither "at one" nor at peace.[2]

On the political level, too, war is a nationalistic unifying force even as it breaks apart world unity. War reinforces the belief in "one nation" by opposing it to oneness with the other or to the outer world. As war correspondent Chris Hedges wrote, "War is a force that gives us meaning," uniting people of shared nationality who might otherwise be in crisis or internal conflict into a common mythos and cause. The culture perceives a common threat and unites to repel it, whether or not the threat is real or truthful.[3]

Thus combatants, whether individuals or nations, are "married." Ironically, war creates a oneness of shared destiny born of the hellfire of combat. But this marriage of souls, cultures, and histories is a negative, fearful, and pained relationship. It is a marriage that leads not to a joyful oneness but to incompletion and enduring pain. This marriage of individual and collective souls through war and violence must somehow be transformed from a destructive to a creative and life-affirming intimacy.

The new marriage must tend to every aspect of oneness that was harmed during warfare. Listening closely to the agony in the wound we call posttraumatic stress disorder (PTSD), we hear that the survivor laments the loss of unity, harmony, and peacefulness with self, significant others, and his or her own culture and nation; with the people, culture, and nation of the enemy against whom we warred; with the great principles of morality, history, and destiny; with the dead of all sides; and with life and death themselves. In response to this loss and his or her culpability in it, the survivor is often crippled with overwhelming guilt. The harm experienced or caused in each of these arenas must be not only recognized, grieved, and forgiven but also addressed and redressed through a particular form of action—making amends in direct or symbolic response to the wounds one has caused.

Atonement makes this possible.

Recall that upon witnessing the first atomic bomb test, Robert Oppenheimer recited from the *Bhagavad Gita:* "I am become Death, the destroyer of worlds." With today's advances in technological weaponry, a tragic amount of innocent life is lost in battles across the world, and a soldier all too often feels like a "destroyer of worlds," one who has harmed the cosmic order. So great is the destruction caused by war that afterward the cosmos itself must be tended. Through the principles, rituals, and acts of atonement, we can indeed make what was broken one again. I know from experience that this healing work is more than a platitude; it heals the wounds that can't be seen—in individuals and between former foes and nations.

Let us see how it works.

Atonement After the Viet Nam War

Several years ago, in an effort to assist healing from war's aftermath, I helped conduct a public reconciliation ceremony in my community of Albany, New York, for all Americans hurt by the Viet Nam War. Veterans, family members, and survivors, and antiwar activists gathered to set aside old differences and discover what they had in common. A married couple opened the event. The husband was a combat veteran; the wife, a protester. Their marriage, they declared, proved that as a generation and nation, we could find unity after dissolution.

They began our conference by lighting a candle to the Viet Nam War, hailing it as "our great teacher." Hung over our dais was a banner that read, "You were never my enemy."

The event brought significant resolution to our local community. Through public witness, forgiveness, storytelling, and ceremony, we sought to transform our relationship to the pain of war and reconcile with and honor each other no matter what our experiences or politics during the war.

After decades of serving as a psychotherapist for veterans, I came to appreciate the limitations of treating war wounds solely within the traditional consulting-room relationship. Resolving feelings about having participated in massive destruction and death helped, but it was not enough to heal veterans' traumatic wounding.

Seeking far greater healing and reconciliation than can normally be accomplished in the traditional psychotherapy setting or in public events at home, I began leading annual journeys to Viet Nam in 2000. On these trips I arrange for my veteran and civilian travelers to meet with former allies and foes, view war's long-term aftermath, participate in Buddhist and other traditional spiritual practices, bond with and help Vietnamese wounded during the war and youth born since the war, and carry through philanthropic restoration projects. All the while, our travelers engage in storytelling and soul-searching with each other and the Vietnamese to uncover their contributions to or complicity in the war and to search to correct and heal it.

John Fisher was a forward observer during most of the war, three times the only survivor emerging from exploding jungles, before finally ending his tour on artillery teams. He suffered for decades from being unable to accept or find peace for the destruction and death he had helped cause. He says:

> I never wanted to hurt anyone. Not even in the war. My nature is to give service for health and healing. I wasn't qualified for that during the conflict, so I was given a rifle and the training in how to use it. Then I used it—a lot. Many enemies died, and I came home remorseful and tainted. Now I'm a good chiropractor, but deep down inside I've always been in despair over the

killing I did. Offering patients an opportunity for a new life is rewarding, but I've taken life away as well.

Fisher made great efforts to achieve healing through therapy, writing,[4] and returning to Viet Nam several times, first with an all-veterans group, then with me in order to address the wounding to his soul, and now leading healing journeys there for our organization, Soldier's Heart. He finally realized that healing himself was not enough; his efforts had to include acts of atonement, which would help repair the world he had helped break apart. In early 2009, he led his first trip back to the very countryside where he had fought, so that he and other veterans and healers could offer his healing services as a chiropractor to the Vietnamese, with the intention of relieving some of their pain.

I went back to the land of my nightmares; my healing tools were included with my baggage. What would it be like to work on those people? What if a former enemy climbed onto my table? I wanted it, even craved it. Would it equalize the damage done? Then it happened—a man missing an arm, later another without legs.

Fisher realized that healing "the other," the former foe, was a way to heal himself:

Hundreds of patients were arriving at my clinic, much more than I ever see in a day at home. It was surreal, like being in a time warp. My humanitarian work became the reason for my mission. I could atone for my participation in the war's destruction by offering to heal them, not me! The past wasn't even an issue for the Vietnamese. But what about my former adversaries? Was their presence lost while working among the multitudes? When I finished, I walked out of the clinic room and saw them. The men whose bodies I had just manipulated for healing on my chiropractic table were waiting in line for lunch. They had indeed been in the war—fought against the Americans.

Viewing those long lines of elderly and disabled Vietnamese veterans against whom he had fought brought Fisher a vision of reconciliation and his part in making amends and restoring the world:

I looked at the men that I had at one time tried to kill, but I had also adjusted their vertebrae. These are both extremely intimate experiences. It didn't matter if I was adjusting a carpenter at home or a former NVA regular in my Viet Nam clinic. While adjusting I never think whether the patient once tried to kill me or I them. We came together for a purpose—both times that we met. Our meeting this time became an opportunity for me to forgive—but not what one would think. It became a time for me to forgive myself for being involved in the inhumanity of war. My patients that day, my former foes, allowed me to marinate my love of chiropractic into their spines. Forgiveness was never a question in their hearts, nor in mine. They let me off the hook. If I had killed their brother, they released me from carrying the burden of his soul. The graves in the center of my heart filled in. After all the treatments, it appears to be hard to tell who received the greatest healing after all—the patient or the doctor.

And then a North Vietnamese Army veteran took his former foe's hand and kissed it.

Through acts of atonement after war, as we help heal our former adversaries' bodies and land, they help heal our souls. Many war veterans seek to make amends in such ways in order to make peace with themselves, rehumanize and reconcile with the other, and restore the broken world order. Veterans' groups around the world work to clear old mines and bombs, build medical clinics, and restore vital services in places where they fought. On every trip I lead to Viet Nam, we engage in projects that bring not just feelings of forgiveness but that make amends through acts that right the wrongs done, restore the broken world, re-create combatants' former identities, and bring our alienated peoples into oneness. Here are a few examples:

Marine veteran Bob Reiter, a helicopter door gunner during the war, has traveled back to Viet Nam with me twice. On his first return journey, he purchased a water buffalo cow and calf and donated them to a poor farming family in the very region he had sprayed with machine-gun fire during the war. During our presentation ceremony, he confessed that he had killed many such creatures during the war, and he directly asked forgiveness of the Vietnamese peasants. His request to be forgiven had not felt complete without the act of restoration. The Vietnamese farmer blessed him, told him to forgive himself for former mistakes, and invited him to return in the future as his American cousin. On his second return journey, Bob and other vets wandered Viet Nam's streets, practicing "random acts of kindness" with huge smiles as they distributed American dollar bills to any poor people they met.

Perhaps atonement is the secret twin of forgiveness. We tend to think of forgiveness, the opening of the heart, accepting the horrors we have seen and done, accepting what was done to us, blessing all survivors and encouraging them to live and go on, as enough to restore wholeness. But it is not. In the minds and hearts of survivors, the bombs still fall, the countryside still burns, souls still scream, and we are responsible. Moral trauma is an unacknowledged germ in the core of the wound we call PTSD that must be directly addressed.

Atonement—making amends—goes beyond forgiveness to actually repair the damage done. It restores life-giving forward movement, transforms the relationships between aggressor and victim into a positive bond, and transforms the identity of the aggressor into one who protects, preserves, and repairs—a guardian and a healer. Making amends heals moral trauma.

After thirty-seven years, Bob Reiter was able to say about his wartime killings, "It wasn't me who did that." Finally, he is able to accept the inevitable horrific transformations that happen during wartime and affirm his new positive identity.

Art Myers served in the First Military Police Battalion in Da Nang during the war. He had been willing to protect the airfield of a large safe base rather than slog through the bush in combat. But during the Tet Offensive, in a base emergency, he had to raise his gun and kill. Though later a successful electrician and family man, Art suffered from PTSD. He had to keep his "war stuff" quiet because of the unpopularity of the war. He felt like a man without a country.

Art and his wife, Linda, returned with me to Viet Nam. By the time we arrived in Da Nang, midway through the trip, Art felt comfortable enough to explore his old base without the group. He hired a motorbike driver as a guide. At the end of the day, Art returned, beaming. His driver had been Viet Cong. He took Art to a Viet Cong memorial, located on the site of the old PX, and together they lit incense and mourned the dead of both sides. Then he took Art to a makeshift roadside restaurant used by memorial workers, where they had a conversation. Though the guide wrote in perfect English, he could not speak it. Still, Art felt they understood each other.

That year our group donated a Compassion House, a single-family weatherproof home for the war-wounded, widowed, orphaned, disabled, or destitute. We gave the house in a poor village on the outskirts of Art's old base. We invited Art to present the new home to the poor family of a disabled Vietnamese veteran. Art made a speech to the villagers, declaring his joy at making this gift in a place where he had harmed and taken life. He concluded, "Since returning from war, I have not been able to come home in America. But here today in your Vietnamese village and community, I finally come home again." Then Linda declared that their family would support two young children of this Vietnamese family through their secondary education.

The following Christmas, instead of giving gifts to their eight grown children, Art and Linda provided the money to build a second Compassion House in Viet Nam. The couple wrote notes to their offspring telling them the gift was being given in their names. The plaque on the wall of the Compassion House bears this inscription: "From Arthur and Linda Myers, Washington State, USA, and their children Melissa and Scott, Jason, Karl, Russell, Laura, James, Peter and Gregory. From our family to yours, in the spirit of friendship and peace."

In this way, not only our veteran but also the entire Myers family made amends for Art's participation in the war, achieving oneness as brother veterans and as extended family with all the Vietnamese. They are remembered in their Vietnamese village as beloved benefactors and American relatives.

Daniel Martin, a Marine veteran of the Viet Nam War, did not have children of his own—another frequent and uncounted war loss for many vets. But he made several trips back to Viet Nam, the first in 1999 in the company of a World War II vet who told him he was not responsible for all the death and destruction of war. Daniel returned again in 2001 and decided to adopt a Vietnamese infant girl from a Da Nang orphanage. He met his daughter-to-be, Jessie An Joli, on Father's Day 2002 and brought her home that August. He has been raising her, but not just as his daughter. Reminiscent of Gandhi's admonition to a rioter to raise a foe's child in its own religion, the religion of his enemy, Daniel has been raising Jessie as Vietnamese. Daniel returned to Viet Nam again, once with me and again with a veterans' group. He returned yet again to the country he calls "my second home" in 2009 with his wife and daughter "so that Jessie could meet her birth mom, two half-brothers, grandmother and great-grandmother. I guess we have what is called an 'open-adoption.' Jessie has already stated that she would like to go back again, so we shall return in a few years." Daniel had been in prolonged grief about his participation in the destructive war. He now accepts the entire birth family as his own extended American-Vietnamese family and helps support them. In an act of atonement that helps unite us all, the Martins and the Vietnamese have become one family.

Stephen Priesthoff was only fifteen when his older brother and best friend, John, was killed in combat in Viet Nam. Stephen's family fell into deep and chronic grief. "I felt as if something inside had been broken and could not be mended."

In 2008 Stephen returned with us to Viet Nam. With the help of old maps, his brother's surviving comrades, and Vietnamese locals, we found his brother's death site and performed a memorial and atonement ceremony there. But even that was not enough to bring Stephen peace over his brother's death in war. In response to both his and the Vietnamese people's needs, we decided to build a medical infirmary for the Da Nang Street Children's Center and dedicate it to his fallen brother John's memory. ARVN and Viet Cong veterans who staff the center welcomed the memorial to the slain American, promising to build an altar in his memory and perform a monthly Buddhist ceremony for his soul. Stephen declares, "My brother went to fight and kill, but in his memory children will be healed. This project has completed the broken circle in my and my family's life." As an act of atonement, it brings an end to the family's decades of unresolved grief, gives his brother's death meaning, makes the family one with the Vietnamese, and helps some of his brother's surviving comrades find resolution.

The Vietnamese understand the need to make amends and the peace such actions can bring. They quote the Buddhist teaching, "Donation is the best consolation," suggesting that by giving back what we took, by creating where we destroyed, we can heal. Further, they teach the Buddhist lesson, based on the laws of karma, that if we feel bad about actions we have taken in the past, we do not have to suffer or collapse in disability or despair. Rather, their monks tell our veterans, "Open your hearts and do good. Change your karma through compassionate action."

Vietnamese veterans testify to this possibility of returning to oneness after war. They understand that war indeed fosters intimacy and that survivors become responsible for one another and for witnessing together. Ninety-year-old O Tam Ho, known as Mr. Tiger, is a veteran of twenty-five years of warfare against three different invading nations. He says to my groups of visiting American vets, "Vietnamese and American veterans are brothers and sisters who have survived the same hell." Tam Tien, a Viet Cong veteran who was severely wounded during the war, joyously welcomes our group of visiting vets and civilians to his Mekong Delta home. With a laugh, he insists on hearing their stories, "in case we met before under different circumstances," and he compares scars with his counterparts. Says Tam, "For the rest of our lives, American and Vietnamese veterans must be the lips and tongues of the same mouth telling the world the same story."

On such healing journeys in Viet Nam today, we discover that it is possible to achieve oneness and peace again even after brutal and sustained warfare that has destroyed these very principles. In Viet Nam we practice confession, witnessing, storytelling, and forgiveness with former foes, blessing and honoring each other's wounds, and acts of restoration. Atonement is one of our guiding principles and goals, as it has the power to bring profound healing to war-tortured souls.

Atonement with History and Truth

We can and must extend the principles of atonement to all wars and to the great forces that shape our lives: to history, destiny, and cosmos. War makes us fall out of history into a zone of endless horror. As Aeschylus told us twenty-five hundred years ago, "The first casualty of war is truth." We must become one again with history and with truth. That means we must find the means to affirm our destinies, no matter what we had to do during warfare. And we can perform right actions at home and in our own society, as well as in places we fought, in order to make amends.

Recall the story of Wilbert, the Native American combatant who judged his first killing to be unjustifiable. This veteran's story was locked inside him in silence for forty years. He was tortured by grief, guilt, rage, loneliness, and a sense that he had betrayed the traditional warrior path his people had taught him. Finally, in 2008, he attended a veterans' healing retreat that I conducted. We sat in a talking circle with Lee, an anguished young Iraq combat Marine, who was about the same age Wil was when in Viet Nam. Lee declared that he was not only a trained professional killer, as the military had made him, but also a murderer. He wondered if there could be any hope or redemption for someone like him. He believed that he was the only one who carried such anguish and that no one else could understand.

Wil felt profound sympathy and concern for this Marine's suffering. To help a new young vet, he broke four decades of silent shame. The elder vet said to the new returnee: "Don't keep your stories locked up. Tell me. Trust me. I kept mine locked away and have suffered endless loneliness and heartache. I see myself in you. I don't want you to suffer the same way."

Then Wil told his story in great detail.

The Iraq vet responded that day by telling some of his war tales to our entire group for the first time. Following our retreat, Lee put his trust in elder vets, gave up substance abuse, and attended a veterans' group on a regular basis in the hope that he could finally overcome his self-condemnation.

Wil's courage to speak was an act of atonement that accomplished several things. He gave meaning to his acts of killing, which had been incomprehensible to him, by using his experience as a teaching story for a new vet. And he declared his brotherhood with, and devotion to, the next generation of veterans and his willingness to serve as elder warrior. In essence, he was finally able to respond to the spirit of his slain foe with the message, "I'm sorry I took your life, but I have finally given the deed some purpose. Together we will help bring healing, peace, and understanding to the newly wounded." Wil accepted his history and became one with his victims, as well as with Lee and the new generation of veterans, all in one act of sacred storytelling at a retreat in the homeland four decades after his service.

As a young Marine during World War II, Ed Bloch fought at Okinawa, where he was wounded. When the war ended, he was not sent home but rather to China during the cultural uprisings that eventually led to Communist rule.

A young lieutenant and rifle platoon leader, Ed was ordered to turn his unit's guns on an innocent village. He says:

> When I gave the order to fire on a Chinese village in North China—together with a unit of the Japanese Kwantung army (with Nambu machine guns) and their Chinese puppets—the guys in my platoon cursed me out for my insanity. It had only been a few weeks since the Japanese and we Americans had been killing each other, and Chinese villagers were supposed to be our friends. It took several months before I finally asked myself what the hell we were doing in China that would warrant committing atrocities against Chinese civilians.

This incident has haunted Bloch his entire life, shaping his psychology and defining his relationship to history. "Everybody has a conscience," he says. "But when a transgression is played out on a world stage—with possible consequences for the planet—that's different. When fully recognized, it has a deadly numbing effect on the perpetrator. The first instinct, of course, is to keep the terrifying secret under wraps."

Bloch did keep the secret for years while questions regarding the morality of war itself and each citizen's culpability and responsibility became his passionate concerns. "Was I alone at fault?" he asks. "The answer of course is no. But then the whole First Marine Division operation in the Chinese civil war was hushed up except in the official history of the U.S. Marine

Corps in World War II—an admission of general criminal guilt if ever there was one."

Now in his mid-eighties, Ed Bloch is an active member of Veterans for Peace and a leader in New York State's veterans' organizations. He says:

> My North China atrocity became my catalyst for change. I do not forgive myself and I should have been tried at the United Nations Criminal Court. But absent that, I can take myself off the hook *on one condition:* I'm compelled to leave no stone unturned in letting the whole world know what we did sixty-four years ago and the circumstances under which we committed atrocities in this turn in evolutionary history.

Ed Bloch declares that he will not be able to rest in peace until he has successfully seen this atrocity find its rightful place in history. He continues his solo crusade to record this event, writing and talking about the unknown massacre in China as often as he can.[5] Taking one's rightful place in history and witnessing the truth of historical events rather than allowing them to be distorted, whitewashed, or to remain secret amounts to atonement, not only with the wronged other and the self but also with history and truth. War's first casualty is truth, and restoring truth sets us free. In his relentless quest to record his and our Marines' wartime atrocity, Ed is making amends for the harm done, not only to the innocent Chinese victims but also to the forces of history and truth.

Conclusion: Atonement with the Cosmos

Often combatants feel like they are "destroyers of worlds." As we have seen, service as a combatant transforms one's identity into that of killer, destroyer, and life-taker. Atonement restores identity as creator, preserver, builder, and healer. Yet combatants have harmed not only people, infrastructure, and land but also life itself. "I have conspired to blow up the world," veterans of the Cold War have said to me. Veterans must move from disorder to the reestablishment of a positive, creative, affirming, and intimate connection and order, not just in themselves but with all of life.

We can experience the wartime disorder of the cosmos caused by war being corrected and replaced with a vision of cosmic restoration and inclusion.

Michael Broas, who has returned with me twice to Viet Nam, served as a front-line radio and telephone operator during the war. He was often alone in a bunker ahead of the front, calling in warnings of enemy action and artillery and air strikes on the foe. From his first battle, three days after arriving, until our return together to Viet Nam in 2007, Michael felt alone, alienated, and broken off from other veterans, as well as civilians. His war became a secret, and life itself felt incomplete and disordered.

During the war, Michael formed a deep bond with the Montagnards, the collective name for all indigenous peoples of Viet Nam. "In a world gone mad," he explained, "they were the only ones offering love, hope, and hospitality. During the war, I would have lost all faith in humanity—except for the Montagnards." It became critical that he return. Together we visited their traditional villages in the Central Highlands. "One evening in Pleiku," he says, "while sitting around a fire under the full moon in a Montagnard village, I was swept away into another world by the enchanting gong music and rhythmical, magical dancing of young maidens."

In response to the welcoming ceremony the Montagnards gave us, Michael made a speech to their community, thanking and honoring them for sustaining him during the war. Then he called forth the village chief and presented him with an American buffalo tooth necklace. "The buffalo is sacred to both our peoples," he told the chief. "It is my honor to initiate you into the American buffalo clan."

After the ceremony, Michael and I and a few others walked into the night-darkened jungle awash in the light of the full moon. In Vietnamese mythology, the moon is Hang Ngha, the goddess of love and beauty. It was Michael's first time in the jungle without a gun. He continues:

> We looked up to witness the heavens and stars in a mystical alignment. There was the radiant beauty of the full moon, caressing her benevolent light on us all with soft blessings of peace and forgiveness. The constellation Orion appeared, yet somehow looking different from this side of the planet—with his sword pointed toward the earth! And then Mars, the planet and god of war, appeared, nestled in the middle of the path we had just walked. I understood in that deeply magical and mystical moment that the entire universe aligns itself and supports any soul's intentions of peace and healing. Many years ago in those very mountains, my heart was so wounded and fractured that I never thought it would be possible to recapture any sense of innocence, order, or meaning. Finally, in the deepest recesses of my soul, I understood that what the Vietnamese had been telling me was true—there was truly no forgiveness necessary. I understood that the true meaning of atonement is not to "atone for my sins" but to open my heart and soul to the experience of being at one with all of life. Only from this place can Grace come alive and bring peace to a ravaged soul.

Michael left that jungle this second time feeling like the cosmos had aligned in perfect order and harmony "for me!" and that homecoming and the healing of the entire world order after warfare was were indeed possible.

War breaks essential unity into disparate and conflicting pieces within the individual and between peoples, within a society and between conflicting cultures and nations. Atonement—making one again—is necessary for healing the self and reconciling with the other and for healing within a nation, between nations, and with the entire cosmos. Acts of atonement achieve this reunification by actually repairing, replacing, or healing what was broken or harmed in the physical world. And when the one who repairs is the same as the one who first harmed, then moral trauma is reversed, the identity is re-created, and the soul heals. In such cases, PTSD symptoms very often evaporate; veterans once tortured by nightmares sleep in peace again. Thus acts of atonement simultaneously repair and restore the outer world as they heal the inner. War shatters worlds; atonement reconstitutes them—within and without.

Jesus said that we should love our enemies. Shall we love those who have tried to slaughter us? Whom we have tried to slaughter? Those whom we have dehumanized and demonized or who have done so to us? Those against whom we have spent untold resources and have sacrificed the lives of our loved ones?

The Master was correct. After war, we can achieve such love. It is a love as deep as the cosmos and is the ultimate atonement.

Notes

1. William Herrick, *Hermanos!* (New York: Simon & Schuster, 1969), p. 255.
2. For a complete exploration of the forms of intimacy resulting from partici-pation in combat, see Edward Tick, *War and the Soul* (Wheaton, Ill.: Quest Books, 2005), pp. 119–133.
3. Chris Hedges, *War Is a Force That Gives Us Meaning* (New York: Public Affairs, 2002).
4. John Wesley Fisher, *Angels in Vietnam* (2002) and *Not Welcome Home* (2006), both available from the author at http://www.johnwesleyfisher.com.
5. Ed Bloch, "An Unknown Side of the 'Greatest Generation's' War," *Veterans for Peace Newsletter*, 7; Kate Gurnett, "A Call for War-Crime Justice," *Times Union*, Sept. 15, 2000, pp. D1 and D3; Paul Grondahl, "A Vet Seeks Atonement," *Times Union*, Apr. 25, 2005, pp. A1 and A4; Bob Conner, "Veteran for Peace Unloads His Secret, *Schenectady Gazette*, Nov. 21, 2005, p. B1; and Nick Reisman, "Fighting for Peace," *Post Star*, Oct. 22, 2007, pp. A1 and A7.

The author is grateful to all the veterans mentioned herein for their love, courage, service, devotion, and trust in sharing these stories. Names, stories, and quotations are used with permission.

Viet Nam and other Vietnamese names are spelled in the traditional Vietnamese way as two words throughout, rather than in the Westernized version as one word.

CHAPTER 10

after the death of my son

my journey of forgiveness and atonement

AZIM NOORDIN KHAMISA

When the heart weeps for what it has lost,
the soul laughs for what it has found.

—*Sufi aphorism*

*Since the murder of his twenty-year-old son, Tariq, in 1995, Azim
Noordin Khamisa has become an ardent social activist, dedicating his
life to helping break the cycle of children's violence through a series of
lectures, workshops, seminars, books, and interviews with the media.
By founding the Tariq Khamisa Foundation, in honor of his slain son,
he has been able to spread the gospel of nonviolence to people around
the world, often with Ples Feliz, the grandfather of Tony Hicks, the
fourteen-year-old boy who murdered his son. Azim's message combines
the virtues and morality of forgiveness with the compassion and humility
of atonement, which includes reaching out to others who have also lost
loved ones to violence. Beyond his teaching and writing, his website
posts thousands of stories written by students and others whose lives
have been stricken by violence. For Azim, the telling of one's story at
any age is where long-lasting reconciliation begins. As described in this
interview, the forgiveness and opportunity for making amends that he
offered to his son's killer is similar to the deeper reconciliation that is
possible for those whose lives have likewise been shattered. Never one
to underestimate how difficult the task is, he has dedicated his life
to offering hope to victims and perpetrators alike. "We humans
continuously confront defining moments in our lives," he has written
elsewhere. "At these moments it's important to make the right
choices. When we do, we're able to manifest miracles and produce
transformation in ourselves and others."*

On January 21, 1995, my one and only son, Tariq Khamisa, was murdered while delivering a pizza in San Diego. Tariq was only twenty years old. He was engaged to be married. His killer was a fourteen-year-old gang recruit named Tony Hicks, who had become estranged from his mother and was being raised by his grandfather.

I was devastated. I was suicidal. Essentially, I lost my son at twenty. Tariq was a very important part of my family. He wasn't a child who died at birth, or in his fifties. He'd just gotten engaged, and he planned to have children with Jennifer, his fiancée. He was a great kid, very charismatic, generous and kind, with a great sense of humor.

When Tariq died, the rug was pulled out from underneath me because it was so sudden, so random, so meaningless. Although meaning has come out of it, at that point I didn't know how to live without my son. I was in my forties, and suddenly I became a toddler again. I had to relearn how to live. So I kept asking myself, "How do I move forward?"

What I did was move forward, step by step, from grief to forgiveness to atonement. I believe I was able to do this because my spiritual practice as a Muslim helped me deal with the tragedy. A very important part of our funeral ritual is that I had to climb down into the grave and actually hold my son's body. This taught me a powerful lesson about forgiveness, about letting go.

The Sufi tradition teaches that when you are in the grave holding the body of your son—as in my case—or another family member, there can be no denial. When you throw the first spade of dirt on the body, it is a visceral reminder that your loved one is gone. What often happens for parents is that they don't have that deeply physical realization and they stay in denial about the deaths of their children. One man I recently met told me that it took twenty years for him to admit that his son had died.

I was helped by wisdom given to me by my spiritual mentor. He told me that during the forty-day period after death, the soul or spirit of the person stays in close proximity to their loved ones and their families. These days are supposed to be allocated for grieving and prayer. We have prayers to say every day, but we have special prayers on the tenth and the thirtieth days, while the most significant prayers are meant to be said on the fortieth day after the death.

But forty days was not enough time to get over my son's murder. Quite frankly, I was very alone. I didn't have a social life. I wrote my book, *Azim's Bardo: From Murder to Forgiveness—a Father's Journey*. I started the Tariq Khamisa Foundation, in honor of my son. I walked the beach, morning and night. I worked out in my gym. Finally, after three and a half years, the clouds did part. One night in Washington, D.C., I had my first date, with my friend Rene. When I actually cracked a joke, I had to put my hands over my mouth in shock. She even asked, "Are you OK?" I said, "I'm fine—but I haven't laughed for years and it felt funny."

That was the moment I knew I wasn't grieving anymore.

Of course, it's important to grieve. Through grieving you can expand the faculty that you feel joy with. But Sufis believe that *excessive grieving* after the forty days impedes the soul's journey. I was taught that instead of grieving I should do good deeds. This is because good deeds are "spiritual currency" that you can transfer to the departed soul, which then provides "high octane fuel" for its long forward journey.

So while it is important to grieve, it's also very important to eventually stop grieving. You have to stop going through life as a victim. If you live like a victim, there is no quality of life. If you remain stuck there, you are essentially living on crutches. You have to leave them behind. I know I didn't want to go through life saying, "I lost my only son. Feel sorry for me."

The way you move on with your life is by moving through both forgiveness and atonement. The way to move beyond grief is by *making amends*, or as my spiritual teacher told me, by giving back to society. That is the power of atonement.

Atonement from my perspective was about dealing with guilt. I wish I could have protected my son. I wish I could have been there with him. If I had, I would have put my body between him and the shooter.

Although I had a very full life when my son was alive, I lead a much fuller life now. I was an international investment banker. Today my work is very different: I work with kids and adults, and I am an activist who promotes peace and forgiveness.

The Journey of Reconciliation

The night Tariq died I had an out-of-body experience. It was like a bomb going off inside me. It was so painful, I couldn't really stay in my body. So I left it. Since then I've heard about a lot of people in trauma, like rape victims, who left their bodies. I went further than that: I went straight into the loving embrace of God. He held me for the longest time. When the explosions subsided, He sent me back into my body with the wisdom that *there were victims at both ends of the gun.* That realization wasn't something that came from my head or even my heart; it was something that came from my God.

For this piece of the process of reconciliation and healing, you have to transcend your head and your heart. Your head is where your intellect lives, and your heart is where your emotions live, and neither one is a very reliable faculty. You have to go beyond them. That's what I did; I went beyond the head to the *soul.* The soul is a far more powerful faculty than the head and the heart. The soul is where you meditate *from,* and I had spent years meditating, which is a sort of preparation for hard times. A blessing is when preparation meets grace. In some ways, forgiveness *is* a blessing. With Tariq's death, I was given a kind of gift or blessing, of learning how to practice an ultimate form of forgiveness. When you have that much capacity to hold the divine spirit, you can do much more good in the world.

Surprisingly, I met great resistance to any ideas about forgiveness. An hour and a half after I found out about Tariq, my best friend arrived at my side and said, "Whoever those kids are who killed Tariq—I hope they fry in hell."

Suddenly I was back in my body.

I told him, "I see victims at both ends of the gun."

Now I was speaking the kind of wisdom that I had learned in my out-of-body experience, which led me to forgiveness and atonement.

After Tariq died, people from the mosque visited me for forty days. In our grief tradition you are not supposed to cook or perform any other chores. You are simply supposed to grieve. Knowing this, they came and sat in my living room, bringing me food at breakfast, lunch, and dinner. I had so much food in the house that I had to give some away. They prayed with me. But because Tariq was tragically murdered, they wanted all the details. I could tell the story; I could say the word *Tariq*, but I couldn't say the word *died*. His name was a 2,000-volt current running through my entire torso. But the people from the mosque waited, and encouraged me to tell the story, even though I was thinking, *I can't tell the story one more time*.

When I look back at that time, I see that I told the whole story of Tariq's death each time, with each visitor. It was non-stop storytelling, and it was painful. Each time I retold the story, it was like picking the scab off a wound; yet each time the scab reformed, the wound was a little smaller.

In retrospect, I think that what I was really doing was trying to forgive the killer of my son—for *myself*—because I didn't want to go through life as a victim. I wanted the full life I had had while my son was alive *back* again, which was essentially selfish because I didn't want to have to live in resentment. I'm reminded of a quote from Nelson Mandela, which he didn't write but did make famous: "Resentment is like drinking poison and waiting for your enemy to die." If you are stuck in anger and resentment or victimhood, you are hurting yourself first. It's really self-abuse. You might as well take a whip to your body. Why have that important real estate of your psyche occupied by someone who has hurt you? Why not forgive and free that real estate so that love and joy can live there?

But forgiveness is only one third of the journey of reconciliation; repentance is another third. And reconciliation is not complete until you go past the forgiveness and the repentance to *atonement*.

There is a beautiful story in *The Prophet*, by Kahlil Gibran, which is about joy and sorrow. Gibran says that when joy is sleeping on your bed, you're feeling sorrow; when sorrow is sleeping on your bed, you're feeling joy. It's the same thing. He gives the example of a potter who is making a masterpiece with clay. First he wets the clay with his tears. Then, to radiate the beauty of the clay, he has to put his masterpiece into an 800-degree oven for eighteen hours. I know what it feels like to be there. If you look at pain that way—that it is helping you radiate your beauty, that it is like the potter helping the clay become porcelain—then it's possible to see pain helping you expand your joy. There are always rewards. Even a painful process can be a process of learning.

So I forgave the killer of my son, and later made it possible for him to atone for what he had done.

Three Steps

The steps I took to move through forgiveness and atonement were essentially a *process* and not an event. You don't get to say, "I forgive," and then it's all over. *It's a daily practice.* This is what I teach. I tell my students that you go through three milestones, three steps, which I learned from my journey and which were inspired by my Sufi faith.

The *first* milestone or step is a hard one. You need to acknowledge that you have been wronged, which leads to a painful grieving process.

The *second* step is to give up all the resulting resentment. This is also a difficult step. If you've taken my son, I want one of yours! This is the eye-for-an-eye mentality. But that doesn't bring a son back. It doesn't stop the grief and the pain. The second step takes you through *intention* and through *empathy*. I do it through meditation. I used to meditate one hour a day, but when Tariq died I couldn't eat or sleep—my biological functions changed. Everything changed when he died. I wasn't the same person.

In this regard, I believe that even my DNA changed and is different now. The book *The Biology of Belief* explains that DNA can shift. I've coined the word *soulular* to explain what happens when we shift at the level of the soul, which is deeper than the cellular level. We have trillions of cells, but when we shift at the soulular level it creates a shift in our DNA, which rearranges itself. Through the process of meditation and the process of intention, we can give up all the resulting resentment.

The process of giving up all the resentment requires *empathy*. The empathy in my son's story comes from my belief that there were victims at both ends of the gun. I was able to see the humanity in the kid who killed my son. I did not demonize Tony Hicks, my son's murderer. I saw him as another human being, who made a huge mistake. If you look at every incident of violence, you will see that there will always be two victims. Since my son's death, I've met gang members who are caught up in five generations of the cycle of violence, and it's essentially the same story. People ask me all the time how I was able to forgive Tony, and I tell them that it was not easy but that it was necessary for a full reconciliation with what had happened.

Five months after Tariq died, I met Ples Felix, the grandfather of the kid who killed my son. This meeting led to my meeting Tony five years later. I sat near him in prison and looked into his eyes for a very long time. I saw him with my "real eyes," and I remember trying to see if there was a murderer there. I didn't find one; I didn't find a murderer. I saw another soul, much like mine; I found my own soul in him. I didn't see any difference between us. Through his eyes, I was able to touch his soul and feel his humanity. That's because, I believe, when you see with your *real eyes* you realize that empathy is important. You understand that you and the other are one at the soulular level. So the second piece of the puzzle of reconciliation is giving up all the resentment.

The *third* step is to go beyond forgiveness and *reach out to the offender in love and compassion* in order to create "spiritual currency" for the departed.

Atonement lives in these actions. It means that you have taken something that is meaningless, random, tragic, unwanted, and dark, and you've transformed it into light. You've reached out, and you've realized that you're no different from the person who harmed you—that we're all human beings. You realize that the person has made a big mistake, but that doesn't mean he isn't human.

And yet, to have empathy, you have to know him.

In Tony's case, I had to learn about all the challenges he had endured while growing up. He was born to a fifteen-year-old girl. His father didn't want him and beat him up; his favorite cousin was shot. Finally, when he was eight, his mother gave him up and sent him to live with his grandfather, although she is now in his life again.

By the time Tony was eleven, he was an angry kid. So he joined a gang. One night when he was high on alcohol and drugs, somebody gave him a gun. His hormones were raging. What he did that night almost anyone would have done in his shoes. Most people would have made the same decision if they were on the slippery slope he was on.

I've been talking about forgiving somebody else, but there is more. For me to forgive, and stop there, was not enough.

My Own Atonement

It is in the doing where the healing gets to atonement. And what is that doing? I reached out in the third step—to Ples, Tony's grandfather—and I explained to him that we had both lost a child: "My son died, and your son went into the prison system.

There's nothing I can do to get him back from the dead, though I wish I could. There's just nothing you can do to get your grandson out of adult prison. He joined the gang at age eleven, and now he's locked away for twenty-five years to life. But what you and I can do is keep other kids from making the same mistake. You're tied to this tragedy because your grandson took my son's life. It behooves both of us to be responsible here. We have to do something. I have started the Tariq Khamisa Foundation, which is intended to 'help stop kids from killing kids' through a program that can help break the cycle of youth violence. By empowering kids to make the right choices, they won't join gangs for the wrong reasons. I have come to invite you to join me. We save lives, we teach peace, we teach forgiveness."

Ples and I have been working together like brothers for fifteen years. Our foundation has now reached eight million kids, and I have established another intervention program that is now operating in eight cities around the country. Through it all, I can honestly say that I've never met an offender who was not a victim. I've found that the worse the crime, the more heinous the victimization. We have a cultural issue here. Empathy is important to have in your heart—not revenge. Taking that last step happens when you've gone beyond forgiveness to an act of restitution, which is atonement.

I helped Ples by creating an opportunity for him to save face. I told him, "I'm not looking at this with revenge, and anger, and resentment. I'm not taking the position that your grandson took my one and only son so let's hang him from the highest pole. That won't do anything to improve society. I've come to you in forgiveness and in empathy. Beyond all these challenges we are having, and through our story, we can try to make sure that no other kid makes the same mistake as your grandson did. I'm about that now. I can't bring my son back; you can't get your grandson out of prison. How about saving other kids? Will you help me?"

Ples was very quick to take my offer of forgiveness and for us to take action together.

For me, it is through this work that I have been able to atone—and he's been able to atone—for somehow failing the young men we were trying to raise. Sometimes I feel that Ples carries a greater load. Tariq is dead; he can't be harmed. But Tony, who is a young, good-looking, charismatic kid, is in adult prison. He is in danger every single day. His grandfather, Ples, wakes up every morning and worries about that.

From my perspective, atonement is about working through your guilt, whether you were responsible or not for certain actions. I wish I could have protected Tariq. I wish I could have been there that night. I wish I had known he shouldn't have been a pizza deliveryman. I wish I had spent more time with him, because I was divorced at that time and he had to come down to San Diego from Seattle where he had been living with his mother. I suffered through all those issues about not being there. If I *had* been there, I would have put myself between him and Tony when the gun was pulled out.

The good thing is that there was nothing unfinished between us. I saw him twelve days before he died. I had just come back from India. He told me he wanted a green rug. He loved the color bottle-green, so I went to about twenty stores looking for a bottle-green rug and took my time to find the right one. I learned the history of how the rug was made. When I gave the rug to him, over dinner, I knew that he loved it. That was the last meal we ever had together.

After he died, one of my aunts had a dream where she felt Tariq's presence and heard him tell her that if his girlfriend, Jennifer, wanted to connect with him she should meditate on that rug. That was a powerful dream.

All told, when we're talking about atonement, we're talking about forgiveness. Essentially we're dealing with two factors. We're dealing with resentment for what has been done to us, or we're dealing with guilt for something we have done—or haven't done.

When I was able to reach out in love and compassion and establish the foundation with Ples, which will eventually include Tony, who is going to join us when he is out of prison, I was first honoring my son. His name is on the banner of the foundation. We do the work in his name, and because of that I feel that I have atoned. The guilt I had about being away and being divorced has gone away. I'm spending much more time with him now than I ever would have done, because he is helping me from the other side. He's here, as we speak.

I'm reminded of a touching story about Yoko Ono and John Lennon. After John Lennon was shot and killed, a journalist asked Yoko Ono, "This must be hard for you because you and John were together 90 percent of the time." They had been inseparable. Her response was, "Now we're together 100 percent of the time." That's how I feel about my son, Tariq. Now we work together 100 percent of the time.

Tony's Atonement

At some point, we all have to take our grief and transform it into "spiritual currency," which means doing good deeds in the name of the departed. I try to do that every day. That's the work that inspires me, that particular advice I got on the forty days of prayer after my son died.

When I started the foundation, my inspiration came from being a father. I wanted to do something for my son. When you go on vacation, you buy a gift for your kid before you buy one for yourself. When I get up every morning, I know I have to go out and create spiritual currency for Tariq, which consists of good, compassionate deeds, because I feel he's not dead; he's in a spiritual form. I feel his presence and believe that eventually we will be together. My work now is a journey. I want to create millions and millions of "dollars" of this spiritual currency so that he can finish his life journey in a kind of rocket ship. My intention when I started was to create it for him, but it's helping me, too.

These acts create the atonement that is beyond forgiveness. If I had just forgiven Tony and gone on with my life, the atonement would not have occurred. But I think that the combination of forgiveness and atonement—putting our words into action—and then taking that third step of reaching out to connect with the rest of humanity helps both sides. When I forgave Tony, I had no clue I would have the kind of impact I did on my son's killer and his family.

Now let's talk about Tony, and atonement from his perspective. I did forgive Tony, but I soon discovered that it was hard for him to forgive himself.

There are five steps in this process. As the offender, the *first* step is that you must take responsibility for your actions. Most of us usually don't do that, although all of us do wrong; all of us make mistakes. But we rarely take responsibility for our actions.

Nine months after I started the foundation, I forgave Tony and I also reached out to his grandfather. But Tony's trial did not happen for another year because they were trying to figure out if he should be tried as a juvenile or as an adult. As a juvenile, they could release him at twenty-five; as an adult, they would just put him away and throw away the key. On January 1, 1995, the state of California reduced the cutoff age from sixteen to fourteen; Tony had committed murder on January 21. He became the first fourteen-year-old to be tried under the new law, and our case was covered by newspapers around the world.

Now I had already forgiven Tony and already started the foundation by the time his court hearing came around. I had also worked closely with a man named Mike Reynolds, who met with Tony twenty-two times to explain to him that the case wasn't going to be about anger and resentment, that I had already forgiven him and was now working with his grandfather. But that wasn't on Tony's radar screen, because he didn't even understand forgiveness. He came from a world of revenge: "You take one of mine; well, I'll take one of yours."

The day before the hearing Tony shifted, at the soulular level.

In the courtroom, Tony said, "I shot and killed Tariq Khamisa, a person I did not know who was not doing anything wrong to me." Those are his exact words. He didn't say, "Not guilty." "Not guilty" is what the accused parties say ninety-nine times out of a hundred. The judge was surprised. There was no trial because Tony said, "I did it." When you get a murder conviction, you automatically get a new trial. But there was no reason for a new trial. Tony waived his right. That saved millions of dollars of taxpayers' money.

Today ours is considered a classic case in law schools all over the country, simply because Tony, at his hearing, took responsibility and confessed. In his powerful and remorseful speech, he said, "I shot and killed Tariq Khamisa, a person I did not know who was not doing anything wrong to me."

This is what we teach at the foundation created in my son's name: you have to take responsibility for your actions.

The *second* step for an offender is to ask forgiveness of the people you have hurt. Whether you get it or not, you have to ask. You have to create the apology; it's part of the forgiveness *and* the atonement process.

In his courtroom speech, Tony also said, "I pray to God that Mr. Khamisa will forgive me for the pain that I have caused him." He knew that I had already forgiven him, but asking me directly for forgiveness was very significant and authentic. I teach that now. If you forgive *inauthentically*, as in "I'll forgive him *if* . . . ," that's not forgiveness. There can be no strings attached. If it is authentic, if there is sincerity, if there is integrity, then the atonement process can work.

There's no way you can do dirt, commit a terrible act, and not chip off a piece of your own humanity. No way you can harm somebody and not harm yourself. Remorse is a big piece of the puzzle of reconciliation. The speech Tony gave at his trial was full of remorse. I agree with Michael Nagler (Chapter Three) that atonement *dissolves* resentment in both the victim and the offender. But again it is in the doing, in the action; in this example, in the expression of remorse.

I get certain questions when I teach my course on forgiveness: "What if you forgive in your head, but not in your heart?

Are you then still forgiving? And what if the other person doesn't change their behavior?" I answer that if the other person, the person who has harmed you, is not changed, then you need to look at the quality of your forgiveness. It's probably not real. If it's authentic and real, *you will change the person!* If you don't, then there's still something that's not authentic or real in your consciousness; there is a bottleneck.

The moral is, do the right thing. It's not so important who goes first, who apologizes, or who makes amends. If you're waiting, you're not forgiving. That's not authentic reconciliation.

The *third* step is for offenders to forgive themselves. Self-forgiveness is the tough part.

The *fourth* step is atonement. I have no scientific proof, but I believe that *atonement can shift something in the offender*, what I've called a *soulular shift*. In reaching beyond forgiveness, it can change a person's behavior.

When I met Tony, five years after the murder of my son, I had a connection through our eye-to-eye contact, but I also wanted to fill in some gaps in the events of Tariq's last night, because Tony was the last person to see my son. He helped me fill in the gaps of my son's final moments. He told me exactly what happened between him and Tariq the night of the murder.

Then I told him, "Not only do I forgive you, but I want you to know that you can come to us and join the foundation when you come out of prison. OK?"

To that end, I am working with the governor's office to get Tony out of prison early so that he can come and work at my foundation. By doing this, I created space that will allow Tony to redeem himself. That's atonement. When I told him that he could come join the foundation, that was a huge shift for him. By then he was nineteen. For those first five years of incarceration, as Ples will admit, Tony would tell him, "Daddy, I'm going to die in prison." So it has been very difficult for him to be in prison. I gave him hope by saying, "You'll have a job waiting for you at the Tariq Khamisa Foundation. You can come and work with your grandfather and me." That gave Tony the hope that helped his consciousness to shift.

After that meeting, he started to study. He passed his GED; he educated himself. Now he's reading five books a month, even though he used to hate to read; and now he's a good writer. He has even gone on to college-level courses. I told him, "Now you have enough time to do two Ph.D.s in prison." Since then, the sheriff arranged for me to interview him in prison. We have him on camera for two and a half hours. It's brilliant stuff, which we use in classrooms. We teach that Tony is not the same person; he's not violent; he's not a gang member. He's never going to be an offender again. In the film footage of him at fourteen, you can see the gang member in him, with all the clothing, the signs, the speech. Now he comes across as a monk!

So what happened? I think it's an example of soulular shift.

The *fifth* step is redemption, which is an important part of making amends for something you've done. Tony will be able to redeem himself by working at the foundation. He'll be able to look at these kids while on stage with his grandfather and me, and tell them straight: "When I was eleven I joined a gang, and when I was fourteen I took Mr. Khamisa's son's life. I've spent the last umpteen years in prison, and I'm here to tell you it's not worth it."

See the power of that! Tony's shift will transform other kids, because his *intonation* will have the quality of the person who pulled the trigger. When Tony describes the consequences of his actions, the power of his words will help him atone. He will be able to say, "I'm doing something to redeem myself." This is a significant piece of the puzzle of forgiveness and atonement.

Starting with Empathy

You don't shift or rebalance when two *like* powers meet. It's no big deal when Mohandas Gandhi and Martin Luther King Jr. meet. But when two *opposing* forces meet, you shift the universe. Ultimately, this story is about my meeting Ples: two opposing forces meeting in hopes of making things right again. Such meetings can create a huge shift. Believing this, I tell people: "Notice something here. I'm an investment banker, which means I have a Ph.D. in avarice and greed. Ples was a Green Beret, Special Forces, a trained killer, who did two tours in Vietnam." I tell them that this is not about Gandhi meeting King to talk about forgiveness. This is the story of an investment banker meeting a Green Beret in the spirit of forgiveness. Ours is a story of opposing forces that collide to create a monumental shift in order to help rebalance the world.

There's no reconciliation without a complete healing process. I teach that *empathy leads to compassion, compassion leads to forgiveness, forgiveness leads to atonement.* These qualities are prerequisites for real reconciliation. You can't have empathy for someone you don't know, so you have to meet, look at the history, and have that spiritual, physical connection. The way we teach in the school is that *empathy* is a big word. You don't know me until you've walked a mile in my shoes; I don't know you until I've walked a mile in your shoes. Then I get it. If I walk a mile in your shoes, I get to know you and you get to know me. That's empathy.

Here's an example from a class we teach on empathy. There was a Hispanic kid in the class, a seventh-grader, who in his walk, in his mannerisms, was a wannabe gang member. But when we taught about empathy, the stories got to him. We had told the students, "Now practice empathy. Get to know somebody you don't know now by walking a mile in their shoes. Then next week, when you get to your class on compassion, you share your homework."

When they came back to class, the teacher we were working with, who is also my daughter, Tasreen, asked them, "Who wants to share their homework on empathy?"

The Hispanic kid put his hand up. This was the most disruptive kid in the class! I hesitated, wondering if I wanted to risk his ruining the lesson, but I called him anyway. But what he said was that the rules are very simple; it was brilliant.

"I was walking in the hood last week," he said, "and this kid gave me a dirty, angry look. A seventh-grader! He was African American; I am Hispanic. If a kid gives you a dirty, angry look, you go beat him up. But since you taught me 'You don't know me until you walk a mile in my shoes, and I don't know you until I walk a mile in your shoes,' I walked right up to him and said, 'Why are you giving me a dirty, angry look?' The kid said to me, 'I'm not giving *you* a dirty, angry look. *I'm* angry, because my brother was shot and killed last night.' So I reached out to him and I held his hand, and we cried together. I told him, 'I know how you feel because my uncle was shot and killed six months ago.'"

Do you see the power of this?

Think about it. This is empathy. What could have become a violent act was transformed into a compassionate act. He took the time to say to this kid, "I want to know who you are." Once you have that connection, you can empathize; and you can't commit violence. Each kid knows how the other feels. A connection has been made. And this boy walks the road every weekend.

The Journey of Atonement

Atonement is in the doing. I want to emphasize this point. If I weren't doing this work, my own journey of grief and reconciliation would be very incomplete, very vague. I believe we all have a spiritual purpose. The gift my son gave me was my spiritual purpose, which was not to be an investment banker. My spiritual purpose was doing *this*, working with kids. I have a full life now. I love this work. It doesn't make as much money, but it saves lives. It's much more purposeful, much more meaningful. I feel I'm now on my spiritual path. The universe is giving us clues all the time.

The gift Tariq gave me was a new purpose in my life. Is it tragic, or is it spiritually meaningful? Well, it's both. I'd have him back in a minute—but his death also inspired this work. We started with eight thousand dollars in the bank. Now we have fifty employees, and we are moving to Escondido. We have six programs and plan to franchise nationally. In one of the most violent schools in the country we have helped to drive down violence in the first year by about 25 percent in an area where 3 percent is statistically relevant. We are teaching the principles of nonviolence, peacemaking, empathy, forgiveness, and atonement. We're teaching it in a very real way. It's in the *doing* that you find the most meaning in your life. Without the doing, you are a little bit doomed; the journey from forgiveness to repentance is incomplete. You've got to take action, do something that creates spiritual currency for the departed or something better for the social environment.

I believe the work I'm doing is going to make a better world. So *I'm* a better person now as a result of my choice to forgive and to atone, and to help others atone. The Tariq Khamisa Foundation has done well. When we go into the schools, the programs begin with someone saying to the students, "This man's grandson murdered this man's son." How often do these kids see or hear this? How often do they hear that the desire for revenge can become forgiveness; that people can atone? This is so powerful that even when we speak in middle schools—which is the hardest lot to speak to because the students' hormones are raging—there is pin-drop silence. They see something very different from what they are used to seeing. Our message is authentic; our programs would not be as impactful if we didn't walk our talk, or talk our walk. I'm not teaching forgiveness using concepts that are in the Bible, the Koran, or the Torah. I'm role-modeling forgiveness. I've traveled this journey. I'm saying that I forgave the killer of my son and here is the grandfather of his killer. I met him, and I did it. In Western cultures and in most Eastern cultures most of us don't make that choice;

instead, 99 percent make the other choice, the "eye-for-an-eye" choice. And soon, as Gandhi said, the whole world is blind.

Fourteen years after my son's violent death, I can look back and say with crystal clarity that *I made the right choice*. If I had gone the other way, where would I be? But because of my choice, I don't come across as a victim. The work I'm doing is meaningful, powerful, and purposeful. It has helped me on my path, which came from a hard choice not to seek revenge but to offer Tony a chance for atonement.

My story makes sense because it's a win for me, and it's a win for Tony; it's a win for Ples; it's a win for Tariq; it's a win for society. It makes sense and feels good because it's about atonement and forgiveness coming together to heal lives. The atonement that Ples and I have performed helps him carry his load, and he helps me carry mine. Ples always tells me, "I'm here to support you. Ask anything." We are water-bearers for each other. And he's now an important part of my family, my life. Without Ples, my life would not be complete. This is an important example of the old quote, "There's no holier ground than when an ancient hatred becomes a present love."

Atonement as Restorative Justice

At the Tariq Khamisa Foundation, we teach six key messages:

1. Violence is real and hurts everyone.
2. Actions have consequences.
3. We can all make good and nonviolent choices.
4. Choose forgiveness instead of revenge.
5. Everyone, including you, deserves to be treated well.
6. From conflict you can create love and unity.

These are the principles of nonviolence, compassion, and peacemaking. That's all I want to do: teach these six key messages to every kid in the world so that they will have peace, love, and unity. Out of these teachings comes the equation, *Forgiveness plus action (making amends) equals atonement.*

We are now involved in a criminal case: the State of California vs. Tony Hicks. Our criminal code is from our mother countries, like those in Europe, most of which were monarchies where the king or queen owned most of the land, and the people. When a crime was committed, it was always against the king or the queen. Of course, in America we don't have royalty, so the crime is against the state. But what does the state have to do with this crime? In a crime, there are three parties: the victim, the offender, and the community. But things are changing. Now there is the restorative justice system, which actually came out of the Aboriginal communities of New Zealand and Australia, where the formula for justice is very different. The state is the facilitator; it's not a party to the actual justice process. *The goal is to make the victim whole.* They can't bring my son back. Tony wishes he could turn the clock back, but he can't. But eventually, working with Ples will bring some restoration to me. If Ples had become angry, it would have been far more difficult. But he immediately said, "I will help you." Then he added, "I will *prove* my cooperation by joining you. I will support you." Tony did the same thing. I think it was because they could both see that my forgiveness was authentic.

That's restorative justice. First you have to make the victim whole. Second you must return the perpetrator to society as a functioning, contributing member. When a youth offends in Australia or New Zealand, the whole village shows up and says something positive. They then sit him in a circle and ask him to make amends. They don't lecture him. Here, we lock him up and throw away the key. When youth are connected to society, they're less likely to reoffend. When you separate them out, you have a problem. But the prison population keeps growing— that's not a very holistic way to go. The third step is that you have to heal the community. When a child dies, everyone is diminished. They're all your children. It blows my mind that our criminal justice system came from the sophisticated, advanced culture of the Europeans, and the restorative justice system came out of aboriginal cultures that speak like this: *click, click, click.* Which is more civilized? You be the judge.

But for true reconciliation to occur, there has to be a change of behavior, that is, redemption. You can't just say, "I'm sorry," and then walk away. What are you going to do to redeem yourself? How are you going to show me that you're not going to do this thing again? How are you going to help others? There has to be that soulular shift. Again, it comes back to taking some kind of action. The healing is in the doing, and that's really profound. Of course, there's healing in the philosophical sense in saying, "I forgive you," but when you start to take action, then the healing is really profound.

The last step toward complete reconciliation is taking all your grief, which is essentially energy, and transforming it into positive action. I don't think revenge is in our DNA; I think atonement is in our DNA. When you are in a state of compassion, forgiveness, or empathy, these are very high vibratory emotions.

My son's tragedy was random. If it hadn't been Tariq, it would have been any of ten other pizza deliverymen. It was a totally random, meaningless, bizarre, and brutal act. And yet, look at the meaning that came out of it. The Lord works in mysterious ways, and encourages us to atone for our misdeeds. The act of atonement creates reconciliation between two opposing forces, which is something true and powerful. I see it working in my relationship with Ples. We're very tight; we hang out together. He's going to Australia with me this year; he travels with me more. We travel to schools together every week. We have met each other's families. We went to a play this week about two fathers, one who lost a child and one whose son did the shooting. It was inspired by our story, though it was a little different. We spoke to the audience and worked with the students on the mess that came out of this story.

There are two journeys in any tragedy: the victim's journey and the offender's journey. Where then does all the hatred come from? I think it comes from our being brought up in a punitive system. In that system there's a lack of spirituality, which is an important part of who we are; it's an interweaving. Spirituality is about having high morals and about teaching the concepts of friendship, empathy, compassion, forgiveness, and atonement. In my practice I try to be free of judgment, anger, resentment, jealousy, greed, and avarice. That's not where happiness lives. It lives in this higher vibratory emotion that we've all felt. But the challenge is to be there all the time. This is what we have to teach our children if we are to survive.

This essay is based on Phil Cousineau's interview with Azim Noordin Khamisa in La Jolla, California, on January 19, 2009.

ten days of atonement

RABBI MICHAEL LERNER

> The Day of Atonement atones not for sins of man
> against man, until the sinner makes his peace with
> his victim.
>
> —*Talmud, "Yoma"*

*Michael Lerner is an American rabbi, political activist, prolific author,
and editor of the progressive Jewish interfaith magazine* Tikkun, *a
word that refers to the healing of the broken world. In this interview,
Rabbi Lerner advocates the strategies of atonement and generosity,
forgiveness and compassion, rather than revenge and retaliation. At the
heart of Jewish atonement, he explains, is a practice that goes beyond
forgiveness: A change of heart is required for long-lasting reconciliation
between individuals, communities, and nations. For him, the genius of
atonement practice in Judaism is its urgency, which he says works like
"intensive, short-term psychotherapy" and is "brilliant as a spiritual
process." Speaking out against the popular misconception that apology
and atonement are acts of weakness, he concludes by affirming the
age-old belief that they actually strengthen relationships. Together, they
can create the spiritual and political transformations that make caring
communities possible. His remarks here are a bold echo of one of the
oldest reminders in Judaism, the ancient proverb that says, "God wants
the heart."*

A tonement is a big theme in the Jewish world. It's a recognition of the inevitable fallibility of human beings. It realizes the ways in which we are not fully embodied in our being,
as created in the image of God, and as the manifestation of
the holy. Unlike religions that see human beings as essentially
flawed, as coming from some form of original sin—whether
that be a metaphysical sin, a sin of the selfish gene, or an
inherent tendency toward domination, evil, hurtfulness, or male

power—Judaism doesn't have ultimately negative psychological, biological, or metaphysical claims about the human condition.

Instead, Judaism's view is that human beings have a fundamental *theotropic* element—that is, we turn toward God; we turn toward the love and the kindness of the universe. Consequently, the actual manifestations of evil and hurtfulness are a distortion of who we truly are. But that doesn't mean that those manifestations aren't real and terrible or that they don't need to be combated. They do need to be combated.

To do so, Judaism has built in a practice of atonement. The practice is that once a year we dedicate ten days exclusively to a process of repenting for the ways we have gone off course, and we try to reset our spiritual course. In these ten days of repentance we say, "OK, we have gone off course, and we need to get back on to connect to our higher being."

This practice is not meant to be confined to the ten days of repentance. Three times a day, every day except on the Sabbath and holidays, the Amida prayer said by religious Jews contains a call to God: "Forgive us and help us to do *teshuva*." That is the Hebrew word for returning to our highest self. The ten days of *teshuva*, or repentance, are only one part of what is a year-long practice, but they are meant to focus our full attention on the process of inner transformation and to give ourselves over to it totally.

The Process

The Talmud makes clear that the ten days of repentance (the last one of which is called Yom Kippur, the Day of Atonement), are meant to provide us with a way of atoning for our sins. But this process only works for our sins in relationship to God. It doesn't work in regard to our sins in our relationships with human beings. Jewish religious law requires us to use those ten days to actually and directly make amends to people we have hurt. It is a requirement that we go to everyone whom we may have intentionally or unintentionally harmed and ask them for forgiveness. That is one of the elements of the ten days.

As part of the Jewish Renewal Movement, I worked with *Tikkun* magazine to develop a process in which we show people how to focus on exactly what one should be doing. We explore the issues one should be raising in one's life: one's relationships with other human beings, with God, with social healing and transformation, and with one's own body. These are the important issues that need to be raised. The task is not to just beat one's heart and say, "Oh, I've sinned." The task is to work out a concrete plan for how to change.

I find this ten-day process, in which you are directed to reflect on the difference between who you are—your essence—and who you've become in your practice, that is, what you've *actually lived* over the previous year, to be very powerful. You are then directed to develop recognition for the ways in which you have gone astray or sinned.

The word in Hebrew that is translated as "sin"—*cheyt*—actually means "missing the mark." The idea is that we are like an arrow heading toward a bull's-eye—and then somehow the arrow goes off course, and doesn't quite hit the bull's-eye. The ten days of repentance are meant to get the arrow back on course, that is, get ourselves back on course, until we understand that our essence is goodness and generosity and caring, and that we have just gone astray. For this reason, the ten days can be an extremely powerful process, a spiritual transformation.

Precisely because the process has the built-in notion that the tenth day of atonement is really the moment in which your fate is going to be sealed—your karma is ready to be set in stone for the next year—atonement creates an urgency that makes it like intensive, short-term psychotherapy. It is not meant to be a ten-year analysis. Instead, atonement in Judaism is meant to be a ten-*day* process of "Get it together *now.*"

I find this notion of atonement to be immensely helpful and brilliant as a spiritual process. It is the step that helps us get back to who we most deeply are and reconnect with our truest selves as embodiments of the holy, in the image of God.

The *Teshuva* Tradition

I have a small congregation, only a hundred families. But that is still a lot to take on in those ten days. I try to meet with the families of the congregation in this period. But our main work is with the individual. Now, if I see someone going seriously astray, I might say something about the person getting back on track. Although I was also trained as a psychotherapist and had a therapy practice before becoming a rabbi, most rabbis are not formally trained to be spiritual counselors, which requires many skills not taught in the kind of program in which I received my doctorate. But religious clergy should receive training in spiritual counseling because it is a skill that people generally expect when they come to talk to us. Luckily for us in the clergy, most people we encounter already have an intuitive understanding of how to get back on track, but they turn to us for help.

In our congregation we have developed a different system from the spiritual counseling you find in other traditions: we have "*teshuva* buddies." We ask people to buddy up with somebody they don't know, or whom they barely know, or at least with whom they don't have a relationship that's going to make it hard for them to talk honestly about what's going on in their lives.

What we ask is that everyone check in with his or her *teshuva* buddy every day during the ten days of repentance to find out how the *teshuva* process—the repentance process—is actually going, to determine whether the person is ready to make atonement. You can't really make atonement unless you have rectified your relationship with the people that you have hurt. Beyond that, we also ask whether you have worked up a plan for what you are going to do *differently* in your relationships next year.

For the *teshuva* buddies the task is not to provide counseling in the sense of giving direction or telling people, "Hey, what about doing this, that, or the other thing?" Their task is not to give judgments or advice but just to be a sympathetic ear, on one hand, and on the other, to repeat back to the other person what they've heard in order to describe what they think the person is dealing with. Each *teshuva* buddy provides this sympathetic ear for the other through this process of active listening.

This ten-day spiritual process has great impact. It encourages people to take the whole process seriously rather than to simply go to the synagogue and say, "Oh, I've sinned"—and then simply go back into their life and fail to take the process to the next level, which is to do what they can to make peace and seek forgiveness from those they've offended. The process also encourages people to develop a concrete plan for how they are going to be different in the coming year. The notion is that when you finally do the atonement on Yom Kippur, you are *committing* yourself to a plan you have already developed.

Repentance and Atonement

There are distinctions to be made between repentance and atonement. Repentance is a process of saying and planning how you'll be different. In the Jewish world atonement originally was offering something to God to buy off God's anger. But we have developed far beyond that conception of God. There was a time when Jews thought that what God really wanted was a good lamb chop or sweet-smelling this or that. But the destruction of the Second Temple, in 70 CE, led to a new development in Judaism in which, for one thing, there is a notion that what God really wants is a change of heart.

Atonement at that point became a practice of offering one's soul and one's heart to God in a full way. That is what the atonement process really became in the Jewish world—a full offering of one's soul and one's heart to God. If you're carrying within you all the anger, upset, and hurts from the past year, the atonement can't be done. The atonement and repentance process is trying to get past all those hurts and distortions of the past year so that you're able to offer yourself to God and make a real commitment to renew your soul as a pure embodiment of the spirit of God.

In the atonement process, without the burden of the distortions that have screwed us up over the past year, we are offering up our heart and soul to God fully and purely. Now the offering doesn't mean throwing oneself onto a pyre and being burned to death. It doesn't mean that one is going to stop one's life and become a rabbi or a full-time religious person. What it does mean is that one is offering the intentionality to be fully alive to what God wants from us, and being present to Her in one's life.

So Yom Kippur is meant to be the beginning of a new lifestyle. The new lifestyle is one in which you are more and more present to the spiritual reality of the universe. So atonement is *at-one-ment*. The process is about moving to the moment of being at one with God in a way that helps us sustain that experience and consciousness throughout the whole year.

But Judaism recognizes that we are living in a world that continually reinforces that which is most negative and hurtful. Living in that kind of a world, we can't expect to be able to be totally what we want to be. We will need tune-ups. That's why we need to go through the process every year.

Of course, at one level, we're always at one with God because there is nothing else *but* God. God is the totality, the spiritual reality of the universe of which we are a part. But while that's true at the metaphysical level, it's not always true at the level of consciousness. Atonement and repentance bring us to a point where the truth about that oneness is very conscious, and the tradition encourages us to hold on to that realization. The ten days of repentance are meant to be a reminder that atonement should be practiced 365 days of the year. One of the ways that we address this in our congregation, and a practice that others in the Jewish Renewal Movement have adopted, is the notion of the Forgiveness Prayer. This is a little prayer that we say every night, a kind of spiritual exercise, in which we try to bring into consciousness anybody whom we may have offended and to try and repair that relationship. We also try to bring into consciousness anybody who may have made us angry, who has hurt us in any way. We ask God to forgive that person.

The practices in the accompanying box appeared in *Tikkun*. You don't have to be Jewish to use these practices to seek forgiveness and to forgive others. They can be used by anyone—including atheists and people from any and every religion—at any time in the year that works best for you.

PRACTICE 1: Repentance

Carefully review your life, acknowledging to yourself the people whom you have hurt and where your life has gone astray from your own highest ideals. Find a place where you can be safely alone, and then say out loud the names of the people whom you've hurt and how you've hurt them and yourself. In the case of others, go to them and say clearly what you've done, and ask for forgiveness. Do not mitigate or "explain"—just acknowledge and sincerely ask for forgiveness. We do not start from the assumption that anyone has become evil. Rather, we envision any "sins" as "missing the mark." We are born pure and with the best of intentions to be the highest possible spiritual being we can be. It is as though we were an arrow being shot straight toward God to connect more fully, yet at various points in our lives the arrow has gone slightly off track and has missed its mark. Repentance is really about a midcourse adjustment to get back on track.

PRACTICE 2: Forgiveness

Every night before going to sleep, or every morning before engaging in your various tasks, projects, and interactions with

(continued)

others, review your life: Recall to mind the people whom you feel have hurt or betrayed you and toward whom you are still holding resentment or anger. Then find a place to say out loud a prayer of forgiveness.

Rabbi Michael Lerner, "A Spiritual Practice of Forgiving and Repentance," *Tikkun*, November 2008. Adapted and used by permission of Michael Lerner and *Tikkun* magazine.

Atonement Is a Spiritual Practice

Atonement is definitely a spiritual *practice*. It requires energy and effort and attentiveness; it takes being present to oneself, to the other, and to God.

Atonement is certainly the essence of the Jewish notion that there needs to be reconciliation between people. The goal is not to end up castigating one another for how evil we are but to transform each other and ourselves in ways that make it possible for us to live together as a loving community. The central part of this process is to connect ourselves to one another, to be more loving and generous, more caring in spirit.

To say that we're making atonement with God is to say that we are doing our part to be more of the God-energy of the universe. It means being more conscious of that energy, more present to that aspect of our potential selves.

Today in the Jewish Renewal Movement, our model of God is a loving energy that pervades the universe and makes possible transformation and healing. We believe it's our task to embody that energy in our individual and collective lives, and to create a social order that reinforces rather than undermines that capacity we have for love.

That's a big task.

The reality is that we need to make as many changes as we can in ourselves, through either the Day of Atonement process or the repentance process that starts on Rosh Hashanah and continues to Yom Kippur. This is also possible in our daily practice of forgiving other people when we review our day each evening.

All of these processes are important. But they are in continual danger of being undermined because we live in a society that encourages selfishness and materialism. Furthermore, our society sees retribution as the primary means for dealing with people who have gone astray; instead of loving, caring, and accepting those people to help them transform into being the people they really want to be. This is reflected in our entire penal system as well as in the so-called war on terrorism. Instead of recognizing that it is possible to transform people with love and caring and a spirit of generosity, our society acts as though our only option is to make those who have gone astray suffer as much as possible. The idea of loving a person into wholeness and transformation is simply not a part of the acceptable discourse of our society. Yet this is precisely what God offers us for those who are willing to open to that love and then take the steps necessary to do a full repentance, an inner *tikkun* (healing and transformation) of our deepest selves.

Collective Atonement

Yom Kippur also has the element of *collective* atonement. It carries the idea that "*we* have sinned." The liturgy for Yom Kippur is entirely about "*we* have sinned." Collective atonement is something Jewish people believe we as a people need to do, but we also believe that the idea should be adopted by the rest of the world. The underlying view is this: we each and all together have collective responsibility for all of the pain and hurt in the world.

Yes, of course, individuals should take responsibility for any harm they have done. But we as the whole community have created or have inherited a world that generates pain and distortion. We have not done enough to transform that

world so that it no longer generates people who are materialistic, selfish, insensitive, or hurtful toward others. We see
ourselves as intrinsically connected to one another, and communally connected as well. We should then take communal
responsibility for those distortions, embedded in social, economic, and political institutions, which in turn help shape
the personality structures and behaviors of others. Instead
of seeing people as peculiarly or specially evil, we see them
as reflections of a distorted world, the same world that has
helped distort us as well. We take responsibility for them,
because from a spiritual perspective, they are us and we are
they. We are all one.

At *Tikkun* magazine, we advocate for this consciousness
becoming an American or a global consciousness. We would
like to encourage all people, Jews and non-Jews alike, to take
ten days of repentance each year, which culminate in a day of
atonement. We'd like to see our country take dramatic steps to
collectively atone for racism, the slave trade, the genocide of
Native Americans, and for more recent acts like the genocide
of the Vietnamese and the slaughter that we helped precipitate
in Iraq. And for the suffering our global capitalist order generates around the world by holding in place economic arrangements whose outcome is that over 2.5 billion people live on less
than two dollars a day and 1.5 billion people live on less than
one dollar a day, and the UN estimates that on any given day,
approximately ten thousand to twenty-five thousand children
die from starvation or from diseases that feed on malnutrition or
that could have been cured had there been an adequate health
care system in place.

And so we in the Jewish Renewal Movement would very
much like to see public events, public amends, public atonement, and public process that would happen each year. During
this time we would collectively acknowledge that all the benefits we enjoy in this country were built on the back of pain,
cruelty, slavery, and racism.

As Jews, we should also be atoning for what we have done to the Palestinian people. We should create an International Jewish Peace Force to go to the West Bank, Gaza, and Lebanon and to other places in which Israeli power has been used in a destructive way. We should rebuild those countries economically and connect with them through a process of repentance and atonement. To do that, we need to reconnect to the humanity of the Palestinian people, and to Arabs and Muslims more generally. We need to say we are sorry; we are sorry not just in our words, for we have come here to act that sorrow out in our deeds.

I would like to see the same kind of apology and atonement in the United States. First of all, we could establish a Global Marshall Plan. That global plan would take between 2 and 5 percent of the gross domestic product of the United States each year for the next twenty years. Using these resources, we could once and for all end global poverty, homelessness, hunger, inadequate education, and inadequate health care, and we could repair the global environment. But our plan, which I've detailed at http://www.spiritualprogressives.org/GMP, doesn't depend solely on money—it requires a changed heart, so that the advanced industrial countries of the world approach those whom we have wronged in a spirit of repentance and an openhearted desire for reconciliation. And the key is to implement this program from a spirit of generosity, recognizing that homeland security is far more likely to be achieved through generosity and genuine caring for others than through military domination and power over others.

This concrete way of atonement goes much deeper than saying, "We're sorry."

Rectifying the Past

In May 2009, in a speech delivered in Cairo, Egypt, President Obama apologized to the Arab world. But that didn't go very far, because his words didn't reflect a consciousness within the United States that what the president was apologizing for was true. Obama's speech reflected only *his* consciousness. Unfortunately, he hasn't engaged in any activity to help Americans understand the role of global capitalism, as supported through corporate and media domination in much of the world, or to understand the role we have played in creating the suffering that goes on in other countries.

Until that happens, we don't have a genuine repentance or atonement. We have a leader with an advanced consciousness who is slipping through an apology, rather than having an apology that is a genuine reflection of the understanding in American society as a whole.

That has to happen.

Then there has to be a Global Marshall Plan, which would be a step toward people in advanced industrial societies of the West saying, "We want to rectify the consequences of our bad behavior in the past by transforming your countries. Or at least provide the possibility of transforming your countries so that all countries are relatively economically sound and on a strong footing."

That's a dimension of what we can do.

Now one of the elements of such a Marshall Plan is to change the conditions of trade between the United States and the rest of the world. Unfortunately, we (not just the United States but Western countries) have succeeded in imposing an economic system on the rest of the world that disadvantages them systematically while advantaging us.

We need to transform the trade agreements, and all of the economic arrangements. We need to have our army become a massive peace corps. Instead of training people to kill, we need to train people to build. We need to train them to be caring—and more than that, to actually involve themselves in the rebuilding of the political and social lives of the rest of the world.

However, we have to do that in the spirit of humility, in which we acknowledge that just because we have more material well-being doesn't mean that we have greater spiritual well-being. On the contrary, the most impoverished countries tend to be deepest in their spiritual understanding. We have a huge amount to learn from the rest of the world.

For us in the United States our process of atonement has to be one that integrates giving what we have to give with being receptive and learning from others who have a lot to teach us. I have heard that the Dalai Lama once described America as a third-world country spiritually and a first-world country economically. The problem from my perspective is that those who do understand the need for repentance and atonement have not confronted the issue of the far right who view any apology from America as a sign of weakness.

I would love to have had President Obama return to the United States after his speech in Cairo and talk to the American people about how the path to strength is the path of love, caring, and generosity—and that that requires atonement. It requires acknowledging first what we've done to Native Americans; second, what we've done to African Americans; and third, what we've done by participating in a global system that has oppressed other people.

No, atonement is *not* a sign of weakness. It's a sign of strength when one is able to apologize. Apology does not undermine America; it strengthens us in the world. Apology strengthens *any* human relationship by acknowledging that you have hurt the other person, that you have been wrong. It does not undermine your ability to be strong in the relationship. On the contrary, apology and atonement strengthen the relationship, making it much more likely that the relationship will last, that you will overcome whatever weakness you have by virtue of your pretense of always being right. That pretense actually weakens the capacity of relationships to be strong, and to last.

Those who think that apology and atonement are wimpy need to go to a church, synagogue, mosque, or some other spiritual place and get themselves straight on what the right values are—because they've got the wrong values. In other words, we need to challenge on the *values* level, and not allow to go unchallenged that discourse from the right that repentance or atonement somehow weaken us as a society.

Phil Cousineau conducted this interview with Rabbi Michael Lerner in Berkeley, California, on June 23, 2009.

CHAPTER 12

the iroquois great law of peace

atonement among the haudenosaunee

DOUGLAS M. GEORGE-KANENTIIO

> The white man says, there is freedom and justice for
> all. We have had "freedom and justice," and that is
> why we have been almost exterminated. We shall
> not forget this.
> —*Grand Council of American Indians, 1927*

*Douglas M. George-Kanentiio, Akwesasne Mohawk author, lecturer,
and former member of the Board of Trustees for the National Museum
of the American Indian, has had a lifelong fascination with the vast
differences in the pursuit of justice between Native peoples and
Westerners. His essay traces the long and venerable history of atonement
among the Mohawk, revealing its connection to the ancient stories,
rituals, and ceremonies that ensured balance and harmony. His distinction
of the Native emphasis on reconciliation and atonement in harsh contrast
with the Western emphasis on retribution and punishment is evidence for
how much indigenous peoples have to teach about truly restorative justice.*

Within the circle of the Haudenosaunee, the Six Nations
Iroquois Confederacy of northeast North America,
atonement, or the making right, the reestablishing of balance,
the restoration of sanity, the alleviation of grief, and the
resumption of life, is of primary concern to our individuals,
families, communities, and nations.

For centuries, those who live with Haudenosaunee culture
have practiced various elaborate rituals to ensure that peace
and harmony are restored with the ebb of conflict. These acts

and ceremonies, songs and customs can be traced to the formation of the confederacy in the twelfth century when a prophet called Skennenrahowi ("He who makes peace," or "the Peacemaker") entered the homeland of the Iroquois to bring an end to war by creating an alliance system of nation-states based on a common set of rules called *Kaïenerekowa*, or "the Great Law of Peace."

Where chaos, violence, and warlords reigned, he established procedures for resolving disputes. Working in concert with his principal disciples Aiionwatha (Hiawatha of the Onondagas) and Jikonsawseh (Seneca), he persuaded the Iroquois to cease fighting among themselves and cede partial authority to a Grand Council of all the Iroquois nations: Mohawk, Oneida, Onondaga, Cayuga, and Seneca, with the Tuscaroras joining after they fled North Carolina in 1715. This "League of the Iroquois" became the most formidable Native organization in North America, its influences being felt far into the continental interior.

The Iroquois Justice System

When offenses occur, the clan leaders—*roïiane*, meaning "nice people" in Mohawk and referred to as "chiefs"—and *kontiianeshon* a "clanmother," serve as arbitrators and judges. Since the Iroquois justice system is based on reconciliation and atonement in contrast to the Western adversarial and punitive system, all efforts are made to have the offending party acknowledge the wrong and make amends to the injured person, to make things whole and complete. Removing the offender from the community is not an option except for serious crimes such as rape and murder, in which instances capital punishment may be imposed. Under traditional law a sentence of death is also considered when children are sexually abused. A person found guilty of a lesser crime must make amends by issuing a formal apology before a public assembly then performing a series of tasks designed to reinforce good behavior while satisfying the person who has been wronged. All victims have a right to determine the degree of punishment, but they must not remove offenders from their normal duties and are required to restore them to good standing. Traditionally, compensation was also ordered by the giving of wampum to the victims, by restoration of stolen goods, or by tendering of physical labor until victims could return to their former condition. Called *anonkoha* in Mohawk, wampum beads were woven into belts and strands, the alignment and patterns having specific meaning. These beads were vital to the culture of the Iroquois and would, in colonial America, be used as currency, a practice quite distinct from the original intent.

In all instances the Iroquois strive to return to a state of mental, emotional, and spiritual clarity called *kanikenriio* ("the good mind"). This can only occur when a person is free from guilt or the compulsions of hatred and revenge. At the time of Skennenrahowi the Iroquois were consumed by wars, which were particularly harsh given their common heritage. After great effort, he convinced many Iroquois that there was an alternative to conflict using the principles of the Great Law of Peace, but he had yet to find a way to alleviate the personal anguish felt by those who had suffered the loss of family and friends. It was Aiionwatha who came up with a solution, in which atonement without revenge, and forgiveness without sacrifice was possible.

Healing Words

Skennenrahowi first spoke the words of healing eight hundred years ago, and the Iroquois have sustained atonement and his chants and procedures, which accompany them, since then. The words were used when the Iroquois as a group approached Atotaho, who used every tactic and power he had to defeat them only to be subdued by the power of Skennenrahowi's songs. He was the last to accept the Great Law of Peace and in recognition of his conversion was given the role of chairperson of the new confederacy. Atotaho had to acknowledge his past before his mind and body were healed. He grasped the string of shells brought by Aiionwatha, then accepted his fate.

Rather than have the sorcerer executed, Skennenrahowi converted his power from evil into a force that propelled the confederacy into being. Skennenrahowi instructed the Iroquois in the rituals they were to preserve if they were to live in a state of peace. He created fifty roiiane with an equal number of kontiianehson (clanmothers). To every one of these he added an assistant called *raterontanonha* ("he takes care of the tree," or subchief), a female faithkeeper called an *iakoterihonton*, and a male faithkeeper *roterihonton*. These two were to advise the roiiane and kontiianehson on spiritual matters while ensuring that the ceremonial activities were conducted in an appropriate time and manner.

The result was that the governing council of the Mohawks, for example, consisted of forty-five individuals (roiiane, kontiianehson, iakoterihonton, and roterihonton) as there were nine roiiane, with each of the three clans having three "titled" male leaders. All roiiane had to have a title name that was decided on at the time of the formation of the confederacy. The names are permanent and clan-specific, and they transferred to a roiiane in a ceremony called a "condolence."

The Condolences

Skennenrahowi created the procedures by which a condolence takes place. On the death of a roiiane the mourning nation will send out strings of wampum to each of the other nations. The person carrying the strings is called a "runner" and will call them to gather in order to replace the deceased roiiane with another. Once the confederate representatives are gathered together, the words of Skennenrahowi are spoken in a long chant, a eulogy of sorts. They begin, symbolically, at "the edge of the woods," just as Skennenrahowi began to emerge from the forest into the clearing before Atotaho. These songs cite the grief felt by all the people at the loss of a clan leader, and then cite the formation of the confederacy. They are called Hai Hai songs and may take hours to complete. They express not only sadness but also joy at the knowledge that the Great Law of Peace endures.

For this event the confederacy divides into two sections: the "younger brothers (or nephews)," meaning the Oneidas, Cayugas, and Tuscaroras, who speak and sing the words of condolence to the "old brothers (or uncles)," the Mohawks, Onondagas, and Senecas. A restoration of the mind is called for along with an alleviation of sorrow. If the older brothers have suffered the death of a roiiane, then the younger ones will conduct the grieving rituals, a situation which is reversed if the younger ones have experienced a death.

The speakers will use symbolic language, such as a fawn skin to wipe the eyes clear of tears, a feather to open the ear channels, and pure spring water to remove the blockage in the throat. They will recite how the confederacy came to be and call off the title names of each of the fifty roiiane. Tobacco is placed into an open fire as part of the ritual; it is an offering meant to carry the words of the people to the universe. Tobacco is used during the condolence ceremony to call all living things to attend to the words of the speaker. But it is smoked in white clay pipes by the roiiane. It is said that the tobacco plant was brought to earth from the skyworld and is the means by which human prayers are most effectively carried, not only to the world but also to the spiritual beings that monitor human activity.

When tobacco is placed into fire and becomes smoke, words become power; thoughts have physical substance. It is considered evil to misuse this power, there being severe repercussions for those who employ it for purposes other than prayer, thanksgiving, or clarity of mind. Tobacco is so closely allied with humans that it is called oionkwa:onwe, has the same root word as "human being." Its Latin name is Nicotiana rustica, and it is very harsh and pungent; hence, those who elect to smoke it may blend the leaf with gentler tobaccos or herbs.

Peace Thinking, Peace Acting

Atonement is at the heart of the Iroquois peacemaking process because it helps in the removal of sorrow and anger, and is a necessary function of all Iroquois social, ceremonial, and political activities. No important session can begin without the recitation of the *ohenten kariwahtekwen*, "the words which come before all else." This is an "address," since it speaks directly to the different elements of the planet, beginning with the earth and proceeding to water, fishes, insects, plants, animals, birds, winds, thunder, moon, stars, spiritual beings, and the creator. Gratitude is expressed to all of these entities and is then carried over to the actual communal function. The address is also meant to remove any feelings of hostility since it places the human experience within a broader natural and spiritual cycle. Once the emotions of the moment are swept away and clarity of mind is restored, the matters at hand may be addressed using thinking that is unencumbered by spite.

The Iroquois have used these methods of peace thinking and peace acting for generations. The historical record lists hundreds of events marked by the "cleansing of the mind" and the "raising of the tree" between the Iroquois and their European neighbors. Beginning with the French explorer Jacques Cartier, in 1534, the Iroquois have used the power of imagery, ritual, and music to effect peace. Wampum diplomacy was initiated with the Dutch in the second decade of the seventeenth century, followed by the use of the "silver covenant chain" between England and the Iroquois Confederacy in 1677. In 1653, a formal treaty of peace and friendship, in which a "maypole tree" was planted in colonial Quebec, and wampum belts were exchanged with the French. Although this compact would not hold, a permanent treaty guaranteeing peace with the French was signed in 1701. That agreement is still held to be in effect by the confederacy.

Atonement in the Confederacy

As part of the formal negotiations with the European nations the confederacy used acts of atonement prior to discussions about the terms of a pending treaty. Speakers would rise, express their sorrow, make an appeal for healing, and then give belts of wampum as compensation for any losses. The rituals and language of formal Indigenous-European treaty making began with the Iroquois. The employment of phrases such as "as long as the grass grows" began in the northeast, as did the smoking of tobacco in "peace pipes." The requirement that no Native lands could be transferred without the consent of national governments stemmed from Iroquois complaints to Britain of avaricious land speculators trespassing on Native territory, entering into fraudulent sales agreements with individuals, and then using force to remove the Natives. This insistence on a formal set of rules led to the enactment of the Royal Proclamation of 1763, which outlawed intrusions onto Indian lands west of the Allegheny Mountains and proved to be a primary cause of the American Revolution.

That war, perceived as a family fight by the confederacy, drove a deep wedge among the Iroquois, as factions within the league elected to fight for or against the rebellious Americans. As brutal as the conflict was on the frontier, it was equally destructive for the Iroquois, who had dozens of their towns destroyed, saw hundreds die from starvation, and were forced to relocate entire populations to Upper Canada (now Ontario). Yet the Haudenosaunee Confederacy endured and summoned sufficient representation to meet with the Americans in western New York State in the fall of 1794. Following the rituals of condolence and atonement, the Iroquois agreed to sign the only valid treaty between the confederacy and the United States. Atonement was essential, as it demonstrated the Iroquois desire to remove retribution as a factor in the relations between the two nations. It acknowledged that violence had taken place but that the Iroquois were grieved and felt great remorse.

In subsequent years, the Iroquois lost most of their lands, the greater part of the population moving north of the Great Lakes or to distant Wisconsin. A group of Senecas and Cayugas settled in northeastern Oklahoma, while a small band of Mohawks secured land in north-central Alberta. Under this stress of displacement and reduced political influence, the Iroquois degenerated into a chaos marked by widespread alcohol abuse. This destructive behavior was brought under control as a result of the religious teachings of Skaniateriio (Handsome Lake), a Seneca prophet. Beginning in 1799, he had a series of visions in which he was shown how the Iroquois might survive in a distinctly different world.

Skaniateriio stressed the need for the public admission of transgressions. He introduced the practice of holding a string of sacred wampum while making a confession during one of the thirteen lunar ceremonies that mark the Iroquois year. He taught that without a purging of guilt there would be severe repercussions in the spirit world. Prior to this, the Iroquois perception of the afterlife was one of release and awareness. The spirit was liberated from the body to return along a star path to a place of living light, an actual planet in the Pleiades cluster. While on this journey the spirit would come to know the mysteries of the universe and would be thereby enlightened. Punishment for acts of evil beyond the clan sanctions occurred at the time of death when the spirit was denied enlighten-ment. Skaniateriio expanded on this, describing in vivid detail a version of Pentecostal hellfire and damnation radical enough to counter the moral anarchy that threatens to overwhelm ancestral customs.

Skaniateriio succeeded in part because he did not try to sup-press Skennenrahowi's principles but rather to strengthen them by emphasizing the need to maintain the traditional rituals. The result was a body of ethics called the "Code of Handsome Lake."

It is recited entirely by memory each year among the Iroquois, and each community sponsors the recital on a rotating basis.

The fundamental elements of Iroquois society have endured into the twenty-first century. Clan affiliation is stable even as the Iroquois language endures great stress. The ceremonial cycle is followed on most territories. The ancient practices of atonement are present, but they are no longer central to resolving disputes. Canadian and American justice methods have supplanted the ancient customs. An Iroquois citizen who breaches the law is more likely to be imprisoned than reconciled. Compensation is difficult to come by as crimes against property have become commonplace. The roiiane and kontiianehson no longer serve as arbitrators, although they carry on with their ceremonial and political functions.

Atonement as witnessed by the community is a whisper of what it once was.

CHAPTER 13

talkin' 'bout my generation

the new face of atonement

STEPHANIE N. VAN HOOK

> Teach this triple truth to all: A generous heart, kind
> speech, and a life of service and compassion are the
> things which renew humanity.
>
> —*The Buddha*

*For two years, Stephanie N. Van Hook served in Bénin, in West
Africa, as a Peace Corps volunteer. She later studied conflict resolution
at Portland State University, in Oregon, graduating in 2009. She is
currently the codirector of the Metta Center for Nonviolence in Berkeley,
California. Her work centers on the need for nonviolent social change
around the globe, and uses the groundwork of atonement, reminding even
those in conflict that they are vitally connected. The stories in this essay
succinctly portray her generation as "concerned world citizens" who are
seeking sustainable development in both the material and spiritual realms,
with atonement at the center of the search for social justice. For her, the
work of Gandhi and Desmond Tutu embodies this ideal, even if theirs are
incomplete visions because "we are still waiting for peace to emerge." If
we embrace the forgiveness of our persecutors and have the courage to go
beyond that to embrace atonement, she says, we may be able to "create a
legacy of atonement for a renewed humanity."*

While serving in the Peace Corps in Bénin from 2005 to
2007, I learned something powerful and life-changing—
how to pray in a mosque. To do so, I learned the Arabic words
to Islamic prayers and I put on a veil. This is the real reason
I decided to join the Peace Corps: to atone for the harmful and
violent foreign policy choices and "war on terror" of the Bush-
Cheney administration by means of a personal commitment
to nonviolence and community-building. I wanted my Islamic

community in particular to know that many concerned citizens of all generations in the United States are genuinely interested in the preservation of other languages, cultures, and religions. I wanted to reinforce to my Catholic family in the United States that change requires action and safety requires harmlessness. These concepts require our very own hands, hearts, and minds. Through my own commitment to atonement, I implicitly gained the commitment and support of others at home and abroad to make the world a safer place. Armed with only love as my weapon, I was very safe, very welcomed, and very loved in return.

This formula of love, I firmly believe, is the necessary condition for atonement.

Through the fruits of my work in Bénin, and in ongoing conversations with my peers, I began to consider examples of the harm that the United States government has inflicted in the world, such as in our relationship with the citizens of Iraq, and to grasp the need of our children and our children's children for a legacy that is better than violence. We need to build a culture of peace—and our part in this greater future is to lay the groundwork for atonement. It is a foundation for establishing our mutual humanity across borders, and it is an idea whose time has come. Through increasing travel and technology, my generation has the sense that we are interconnected with others just like ourselves across the world and that a different country does not imply a difference in human experience.

In essence, the Peace Corps and my peers have taught me that in the twenty-first century our greatest challenge in creating the conditions for peace to emerge is in our enactment of atonement.[1] Just as the Peace Corps promotes sustainable material development, the moral and spiritual development that my generation seeks to promote as concerned world citizens needs to be equally sustainable and long-lasting. A world culture through atonement will lead to peace because its means are nonviolent. We have learned our nonviolence from figures like Gandhi, who have shown us a higher moral process uniting us in heart and mind in the strengths of the human condition. We are learning from Gandhi's legacy that violence is subject to a universal law. When it is used as a means to peace, violence only begets more violence. It remains for us to recognize that this law can help us to understand atonement as well as nonviolence, which both beget peace.

Atonement must be our staff and strength toward a culture of peace. As individuals it makes us stronger in the face of adversity; performed collectively, it embodies our collective integrity to honor humanity the best way we possibly can, namely, by defining cultural strength on its capacity to beget love, not violence. To find an example of this concept in practice, we need look no further than our own lives, to those rare and shining moments when unconditional love triumphs over the harm that we have received or inflicted. This love unifies and redeems us because it raises us above the violence that divides us from one another as friends, coworkers, and neighbors and makes us more human. The potential to enact unconditional love in the face of harm is the force of our soul. This is the truth of atonement. Its secret for a paragon of peace like Gandhi was simple: acts from the soul are never for the weak.

Soul Force

With the gentle leadership of Gandhi, nonviolence defeated the rule of foreign law in India. Desiring a united humanity, he sought to achieve his goal simply through the appeal to the best version of humanity of everyone in India: British and Indian alike. He wanted the citizens of India to find true freedom through action. In doing so, he wanted the British to understand that citizens of India were willing to redefine strength in order to be free. Strength does not come from doing harm; strength comes from the power to honor the unity of life. We cannot truly understand the meaning of this simple truth of Gandhi's without clearly understanding the importance of *ahimsa* and *satyagraha.* These two concepts are at the heart of his life, at the center of his experiments in nonviolence. In essence, ahimsa is a standard for a moral perspective, and satyagraha is a standard for moral action. When used methodologically, ahimsa and satyagraha become tools for freedom, as well as part of my generation's peacemaking toolbox for achieving a legacy of atonement. *Ahimsa* is a Sanskrit word composed of two parts: *a-*, the simple negating prefix, and *himsa,* referring to the desire or intent to harm. Often the word is translated as "nonviolence." In truth, the concept *ahimsa* is much richer and more complex than its translation; it is an active, generative, and positive concept that more closely resembles "unconditional love."

Ahimsa is an ethical standard, a commitment to extinguish our desire and intent to harm, which in turn, is a way of life, a state of being as much as a state of mind. This ethical standard is active; it is a "positive force that holds the solution to most of our major personal, social, and global problems."[2] Violence, on the other hand, is another way of being in the world, which, in contradistinction to ahimsa, is a negative force that creates the dilemmas in most of our major personal, social, and global problems because it is passive. Gandhi's genius was to recognize the formulaic nature of violence as a scientific law for building solutions. He strove to embody ahimsa because he was a pragmatist. He wanted constructive and active, not destructive and passive, solutions. He wanted reason to prevail, but not at the expense of his conscience.

Ahimsa is the secret that helps us to atone because it awakens our hearts. Gandhi's system clearly—and brilliantly—left us this legacy. To harm someone or something is not only doing harm; it means not loving, because violence and harm beget only violence and harm, not love. Together they are a degenerative force that can only be overcome by an active state in the individual and in the culture. Ahimsa is a way of being in the world that goes beyond ending violence to healing it, because it is not only not harming; it is love. Our goal must be to recognize that only love can heal our toughest cultural and individual acts of violence.

By living an attitude of love, or ahimsa, we can obstruct the path of violence through taking the right measures in the present toward a better future, and make peace with our pasts by making right our own violence. This obstructive action, from the individual to the societal scale, is what Gandhi called *satyagraha*. It comes from the words *saty*, or "Truth," and *agraha*, "grasping." Satyagraha is the grasping of Truth. Like ahimsa, it is active. It is not grasping at an illusion, as is violence; it is grasping something deeper and literally felt: Truth. This was no small concept for Gandhi, as he believed that God and Truth are one. To grasp Truth, to engage in satyagraha, is to ignite a powerful force that may change the course of humanity's descent toward a violent future.

Extinguishing harm is easy when we are armed with love and walking with Truth—at least Gandhi made it look that way. Actually, it may be the hardest challenge that any of us can take on, in any generation. Nonviolence is more difficult and requires more emotional and personal strength than violence because we are called to action, not to passivity, using our human energies; and to put our emotions to work for us, not against us. We are called to forgive our enemies; to bless those who curse us; to curb our own desires instead of indulging them; and most important, to go beyond forgiveness and atone for our pasts. Gandhi even expected us to do these things without fear of the consequences. What a great challenge! These simple secrets lead us to create the important conditions for peace. Gandhi reminded us that together, the entire human family will be free when we shake loose the bonds of untruth and violence. He reawakened our sense of our own deeper reserves of love's power, and continues beyond his physical death to plant the seed for a better future.

Finding Unity

After Gandhi, my generation has another example to learn from: Desmond Tutu. In the struggle to come together after apartheid in South Africa, Tutu also sought to lead people toward the nonviolent path. He, like Gandhi, saw that one must hate the sin and not the sinner. If hate we must, we must hate violence—not the person who used violence, for we are all victims of violence. The promise of violence and the intent to harm succeeded in sustaining the divides between black and white South Africans during apartheid. They needed to come together to form a nation; *apartheid*, after all, is Afrikaans for "apartness."

Standing in the wake of structural and direct violence—the consequences of separating some people from other people on the basis of culture and race—the citizens of South Africa knew that there could be no peace, no unified South African identity, without addressing this self-inflicted wound. The conditions were not yet ripe for peace, however. Missing persons haunted the dreams of mothers and fathers; victims of torture and dishonor wanted their stories to be heard. Tutu responded to this collective desire to come together and account for apartheid in order to actively make a future, and he took the opportunity to do something new for all of us. His principle was simple: to be fully free from apartheid and to create a culture of peace, we need the Truth. It was an idea based on the adage, "The truth will set you free." Tutu was an architect of his country's Truth and Reconciliation Commission, and what is now used generally in restorative justice throughout the world But Tutu had more than a philosophical search after truth on his side: he had *ubuntu*.

Ubuntu is a South African legacy. This widely held concept maintains that we are interconnected because we are living human beings. We are interconnected in the same way that pebbles dropped into a pond create outward-reaching waves. It is the recognition that I am human because you make me human, and you are human because I make you human. It is thus a powerful force at the very heart and soul of community.

It is provocative to so many because it honors our ability to think critically about the consequences of our violent and non-violent acts: we can find it quite easy to understand that violent acts separate us and nonviolent acts bring us closer together.

In spite of ubuntu, however, there was a problem. People could not heal from the damage of apartheid without knowing where their missing family members had been buried. Others wanted to show their recognition of having committed violence and become reunited with their communities and themselves. Still others found the entire process inadequate. Finding truth, as Tutu witnessed, was immensely empowering for the South African people in awakening to the greatest horror of apartheid: man's inhumanity to man. They were still left with the seemingly impossible task of reconciliation, and the question remains today as to what could have improved the process altogether.

Tutu's work did not end within the confines of South Africa. He has become one of the world's leading voices for unity through the South African model of the Truth and Reconciliation Commission. In his essay "Without Forgiveness There Is No Future," Tutu declares: "In our African understanding, we set great store by communal peace and harmony. Anything that subverts this harmony is injurious, not just to the community, but to all of us, and therefore forgiveness is an absolute necessity for the continued human existence."[3]

The challenge he leaves us with, however, goes beyond forgiveness. It is atonement. How can we ever "deal adequately with our pasts" without it?

Atonement in the Twenty-First Century

My generation has not lost the ability to grasp the essence of the lawlike nature of violence as Gandhi and Tutu grasped in the twentieth century. We have not lost the spirit of change and the creativity to make it, either. We know that we can become great leaders by using ahimsa, satyagraha, and ubuntu.

These tools inspired social change and helped communities in India and South Africa awaken to the power of the individual to choose nonviolence and see tangible, transformative results from the awareness of that choice. Nevertheless, the results seem incomplete—necessarily so—because we are still waiting for peace to emerge. Gandhi and Tutu gave new faces to old concepts. In the twenty-first century, new leaders must consciously move forward and give a new face to another old concept: atonement. Cultivated mindfully, it will help us create a more excellent story of the human being, and thus a more excellent future for humanity. We are nonetheless confronted with a great challenge on this path of spiritual and ethical excellence: we are required to honor the past as we look ahead.

As the seventeenth-century philosopher and mystic Benedict de Spinoza told us in *The Ethics*, "All things excellent are as difficult as they are rare."[4] If the task of securing our future is to include atonement in our conceptual toolbox, igniting its full force in concert with our work for peace may be the most difficult challenge that any member of my generation will accomplish. But I know it can be done. I have faith that we are well equipped and that we will succeed in creating a legacy of atonement for a renewed humanity.

Notes

1. The Peace Corps was established under the Kennedy administration in 1961 to promote world peace and friendship. For more information on its projects around the world, visit http://www.peacecorps.gov.
2. Michael N. Nagler, *The Search for a Nonviolent Future: A Promise of Peace for Ourselves, Our Families, and Our Worlds* (San Francisco: Inner Ocean, 2004), pp. 44–45.
3. Desmond Tutu, "Without Forgiveness There Is No Future," in Robert D. Enright and Joanna North (eds.), *Exploring Forgiveness* (Madison: University of Wisconsin Press, 1998), p. xiii.
4. Benedict de Spinoza, *The Ethics and Other Works*, ed. and trans. Edwin Curley (Princeton, N.J.: Princeton University Press, 1994), p. 265.

buddhist bowing and atonement

REVEREND HENG SURE

> In the morning, bowing to all;
> In the evening, bowing to all.
> Respecting others is my only duty.
>
> —*Ryokan*

The Reverend Heng Sure, Ph.D., is an American-born Buddhist monk who heads the Berkeley Buddhist monastery, where he carries on the work of Master Hsuan Hua in interfaith harmony. In this probing essay, he provides a unique Buddhist perspective on forgiveness, repentance, and the search for interfaith harmony. His exploration is illuminated by the story of his remarkable eight-hundred-mile "three steps and a bow" pilgrimage, with his companion Heng Chau (Dr. Martin Verhoeven), from South Pasadena to Ukiah, California. Through Buddhist monastic practices, community activism, and musical performances, Heng Sure has created one of the most active spiritual centers on the West Coast.

I'm an American Buddhist monk, ordained in the Chinese Mahayana tradition. In the late 1970s I took a walk, a pilgrimage, for two and a half years up the Pacific Coast Highway in California. The pilgrimage involved making a full prostration to the ground every third step and a prayer of repentance with each bow. I kept a vow of silence for the duration, and focused my thoughts on realizing a more peaceful world through the practice of Buddhist repentance. I maintain that the effort of bowing and humbling the ego, along with the recitation of a repentance verse, is an act of atonement.

Here is the prayer that I repeated—possibly two million times—with each prostration along the eight hundred miles of the journey:

> For all the harmful things I've done, with my body,
> speech and mind, from beginningless greed, anger
> and stupidity, through lifetimes without number, to
> this very day; I now repent and I vow, to change
> entirely.

—*Avatamsaka Sutra*, chapter 40

My wish was to let that verse, originally spoken by Samantabhadra, one of Mahayana Buddhism's most prominent bodhisattvas (awakened beings), filter down to the deep layers of my mind and cleanse away the results of unskillful deeds I had done with words, thoughts, and deeds. The purpose of the silence vow was to give my habitual speech patterns a rest, so that I could get past the words and experience more directly the (often selfish) motives for my talking.

In the Mahayana Buddhist tradition we say that you "bow a repentance." The phrase indicates that the ritual gesture of placing your head, knees, and elbows on the ground is a humbling act in itself and conducive to repentance. Many spiritual classics say that pride is the source of human error, and if that's true, then it's harder to feel proud when your nose is on the ground in a bow.

Bowing is hard work; you have to go low, and the ego suffers a small "death" with each bow. I offer as proof my own experience that the ego resists bowing, especially in public. I didn't like to get down on the ground over and over. It seemed the opposite of getting ahead, of striving to make progress, as my Western cultural values taught me I should do. Bowing down and cleaning out my memory closet seemed to be going backward. Yet after every bowing session I stood a bit taller and felt a bit lighter at heart.

Further, having the head and heart on the same level, close to the vast and tranquil magnet that is the earth, seems to assist in washing up to mind the errors of a lifetime. I can't recall how many times I've bowed to the ground while reciting the repentance verse and, without warning, recalled deeds committed as a self-centered, misguided youth. And the images that arose came with all the senses intact, as if playing in "sense-orama" from some internally stored tape library. It felt as if the repentance verse acted as a mental detergent, flushing up a long-buried misdeed for review in my conscious mind, and scrubbing it clean. The entire experience hinted at the photographic nature of the mind and the senses; it may be that every sense input I've fed to my eyes and ears, wholesome and unwholesome alike, is recorded in my mind with absolute clarity.

I can't say for certain that by repenting and bowing while reciting the verse, I purged my mind of karmic errors, and neutralized the debts I had accrued, but I can say that the experience of bowing Buddhist repentances brought to life the last part of the Avatamsaka Sutra's verse: "I now repent and I vow, to change entirely."

One thing I learned is that four deeds in particular—killing, stealing, lusting, and lying—hurt the doer as much as the receiver. While bowing, I saw, for example, one instance of lying to my mother about smoking cigarettes. I had been smoking in junior high school, in order to be accepted into a group of older tough guys in my neighborhood. I came home with cigarette smoke on my clothes, and my mother smelled it. She asked me if I had been smoking, and fearing a punishment, I said, "Oh, no! Me? Smoking? No way." In fact, I was hiding a pack of Camels in my book bag. That night I tossed and turned in bed, unable to fall asleep. I realized that the deliberate lie to my mother sat on my conscience like a fallen log in a creek, stuck and unable to move along. This episode washed up to consciousness while I was bowing. When I finally confessed to my mother, nearly twenty years after the pilgrimage, she said, "Oh, I knew;

I smelled them on you. Your face was all red. I was sharper than you gave me credit for, you know. I just wanted to see how you handled your fib."

Not very skillfully, until I bowed in repentance and recited the Sutra's verse.

Feeling shame when I make mistakes and then wishing sincerely to change the bad habits that caused them is moving in the right direction. Repentance teaches that the mind is able to reverse itself and spit out negativity; ultimately, one can repent of all past bad karma. This principle gives me hope of genuine atonement for past mistakes. If bowing repentance can heal a mind harmed by thoughtless error, then questions arise: what is the possibility of perfection? How much karma is reversible? How deep does the cleansing of repentance go? Could the teaching on original sin still apply if I can get my mind to regurgitate offenses I've created? The Buddha said that even the heaviest of offenses, of which there are five—the "Cardinal Sins" (patricide, matricide, killing an *Arhat* or Saint, shedding the Buddha's blood, and destroying the harmony of the Buddha's community)—can be atoned for if one can change the wrong view of the existence of the self.

The foundation of Buddhist atonement is the Buddha's insight that the self, the doer of actions, is a fiction. The self doesn't actually exist; it's merely a habitual, pervasive way of viewing the body and mind. The Buddha gave an empirical method for verifying this assertion. He instructed his disciples to look deeply into the existence of *I*, *me*, and *mine*. One finds nothing permanent or substantial. I can't find a "me" in my teeth, my toenails, or my tonsils. No single thought in my mind is mine alone, unique and special to me. When I die, nothing survives but the results of deeds. So questions remain: if the doer of deeds doesn't exist, what about the deeds themselves? Where do they exist? Can they be repented away? What about the individuals I've harmed through my misbehavior?

Cause and effect is always true. It's very fair and never off by the slightest. Further, one is responsible for one's deeds; nobody can transfer mistakes to another, and nobody can escape the results of behavior. There is one exception to this rule. Repentance can erase negative consequences—that is, the ultimate repentance that reveals the true nature of the self.

The Buddha proposed two layers of truth, the provisional and the ultimate. We ordinary people, who have yet to awaken to the ultimate nature of sentient creatures and the ultimate identity of phenomena, still live in the world of duality. In the world of duality, the world of rights and wrongs, of loves and hates, the self is the center of every decision. The self pushes us to strive for petty advantages and to care little about benefiting others.

The Buddha realized, after meditating alone in the forest for six years, that the self is an illusion, merely a faulty perception. When he awoke, he saw through the illusory ego and he was able to let go of its desires, afflictions, and self-important habits. A beautiful verse from the *Dhammapada* sums up his joyful freedom:

> *Craving is the builder of this house (the ego),*
> *Through many a rebirth, in Samsara wandering,*
> *I sought but did not find, the builder of this house;*
> *How painful, how sorrowful to be born again*
> *and again.*
> *Oh! House-builder, I see you at last,*
> *You will build no house any more;*
> *Your ridge pole shatters*
> *Your rafters all fall down;*
> *My mind realizes the unborn,*
> *And craving comes to an end.*

> —*Dhammapada*, section 11,
> verses 153–154

Seeing the ultimate emptiness of the ego that we serve all day long can lead to the second, ultimate, level of truth. The Buddha said that anybody can realize that level of truth, but that it takes hard work. To do this, one must reverse the conditioning that tells us we are unique, special individuals.

Granted, most of us live in the dualistic realm. So if I do an unskillful deed when my mind is firmly in the dualistic realm of "big me in the center of the world," does the deed exist or not? If the Buddha sees through the ego to the non-existence of self and phenomena, does that help me erase my karma when I make big mistakes?

The answer is both yes and no.

The truth of the illusory nature of the ego is set in the context of cause and effect, which is a law of the universe as basic as gravity. The law of cause and effect says that when I kill, I accrue a debt to the person or creature whose life I stole. That debt will follow me until I pay it back.

Deeds done in the world of duality carry a price tag—if I kill and eat the body of a cow, I owe a debt to the animal whose flesh I have consumed. At the same time, there are methods to erase that karma: (1) by meditating until one's wisdom breaks through to the realm of ultimate truth; and (2) by repenting and bowing; by humbling the ego and putting in strenuous work cleansing the mind of selfish desires; by seeing the "builder of this house" of craving that supports the ego and creates wrong views of the ego's central importance. I may have to repay a debt to the cow, but repentance can pull up the seeds of hatred and ignorance that caused me to harm the cow in the first place. Once the debt is repaid, the negative relationship is truly over.

When I finished my pilgrimage, I went to live with two other monks in a tiny cultivation place in Taipei, Taiwan. One person was the monk I did the pilgrimage with, and the other was a new monk, a young man whom I took an instant dislike to—and it was mutual. He wanted to knock me off, and I thought he was a young punk, arrogant and proud. He was a twenty-year-old who had been through high school in a monastery and who knew nothing about the world.

We three were cooped up together in Taiwan, two of us fighting like cats and dogs before the ceremonies, at meals, and after meditation. The third monk kept saying, "What is going on? What are you two doing? How is this in any way Buddhist practice?" It went on like that for three months, including a visit to Hong Kong.

When we came back to the States, Master Hua asked, "How was your trip to Taiwan?" He took one look at the two of us and said, "This is not so simple. You two work it out."

Six months later, with our enmity karma burning hotter than ever, I went to Master Hua and said, "I can't stand it anymore. Why do he and I have this negativity? I don't feel this way about anybody else. Please tell me what to do."

He said, "All right, are you sincere?"

I said, "Yes, I really mean it. Nobody in my life strikes sparks like this guy. I'm so tired of having somebody I can't make peace with. I can't go *on* this way. I'll do anything to atone for whatever I've done to cause this negativity."

He said, "That's what I was waiting to hear. At last you're showing some understanding of principle. A conflict like yours comes from past karma. You and he have been at each other's throats before. It's really mutual. The debts are piled up on both sides. But all it takes to untie it is one person's determination to stop the hatred, or else it will simply roll on forever.

"If you truly want to make a change, here is what you can do. Light a stick of incense and bow in front of the Buddhas at the altar. You know how to bow. Do it with sincerity. With each bow say, 'I want to put an end to all enmity that I have created with this person and with any sentient creature that I may have harmed. May all harm I've done that caused negativity and conflict in the present be neutralized and dispersed. May all wholesome conditions and positive affinities grow and flourish.'"

Master Hua continued, "Bow every day for as long as you can. Do it every day, regularly, and put your heart into it. Really vow to change your thought habits from negative to wholesome. Then every day, when you're done bowing, transfer the merit to all beings, especially those who, like you, have negative affinities. Make the measure of your mind big. Send it beyond you and him. Say, 'May all negative affinities, enmity karma, and hatred that troubles all beings come to an end. And may positive seeds flourish and grow. May all beings live in harmony and in peace.' I want you to transfer the merit like that every day at the end of bowing.

"If you are sincere," he said, "I guarantee you will see a change in the relationship. But you really have to become a different person. Remember the misery of having an endless conflict and stop fighting with yourself. Then transfer the benefits and share the merit with everybody."

My life was miserable, so of course I agreed immediately. I bowed as Master Hua instructed every single day for a month. The young monk was transferred to Seattle, and I was sent to Los Angeles. I saw him six months later when we passed in a corridor, and I didn't even notice him. I looked at him from behind, and then he turned around. When I saw his face, he just looked like a kid. I noticed how young and innocent he looked.

He asked, "How are you doing?" I said, "Fine." He said, "No problem." I said, "No problem." And that was that.

Later he took off his robes and returned to lay life. I saw him years later. We talked and had a great time. He said, "Do you remember when we used to struggle as if our lives depended on it?" I said, "Yes, that was the strangest thing." He said, "Maybe you harmed me in a past life?" I said, "Who knows? I'm sure glad it's over." And that was that.

The Buddhist method begins with the willingness to do something that most people don't think to do, which is to atone for mistakes. That begins with simply taking time to address the relationship, to own my half of the negativity and admit that I am not here on earth to struggle endlessly with this person. I asked that whatever harmful things I had done to him might come up, be cleansed away, and healed. Next, in my heart I wished the young man well; I spoke aloud the wish to do him no further harm; instead, I wished him peace and happiness. Then I transferred the merit of the act of atonement to all beings, especially those having similar situations of interpersonal conflict.

When the seeds of conflict had been made conscious, when I had voiced my wish to bless the person I had been fighting with, he and I became "at one." I was finally able to erase the boundaries between him and me, which yielded *at-one-ment*. But this happened only after I had done the hard work of bowing, reciting the verse, and making conscious the wish to change my attitude. Atonement is more than a wholesome wish; it's hard work.

creative atonement in a time of peril

JAMES O'DEA

> If it is the time of the end, and of great tribulation,
> then it is certainly and above all the time of the
> Great Joy. Eschatology is not finis and punishment,
> the winding up of accounts: it is the final
> beginning, the definitive birth into a new creation.
> —*Thomas Merton*, Raids on the Unspeakable

The former president of the Institute of Noetic Sciences (IONS) and director of the Washington office of Amnesty International, James O'Dea closes this book with a valuable update of the peace and reconciliation projects around the world. O'Dea travels widely to participate in international social healing projects, from the Americas to the Middle East and Africa, which makes him able to trace the resurgence of restorative justice around the world. But he also reports on the influence of the latest research in the evolution of consciousness that suggests cooperation between people is the natural order. His essay elegantly unfolds an advocacy for what he calls "creative atonement," the kind of restitution that reinforces our power to change our destructive behavior toward our fellow human beings and with the planet. Together, his compelling research and vivid stories encourage all of us to creatively engage in the present movements in atonement and reconciliation rather than holding on to the prejudices of the past.

A tonement is a word whose weight and solemnity evoke images of Methodist meetings in Victorian England. It has slate gray tones and ominous undercurrents. It seems to belong to a time when very upright people with moral fortitude atoned for their sins and those who didn't lacked that essential ingredient of *moral fiber*—a spiritual commodity that was held in good supply by "the civilized" and "the saved."

We can go even further back in time into the primary archetypes of Western Judeo-Christian belief where we encounter the call to atonement with all the fulminating gravitas of Old Testament biblical drama. Even those who never attended Sunday school will be vaguely familiar with the idea that plagues were sent as punishment, that clouds opened and people were scorched or turned into pillars of salt for their depravity and refusal to change their ways. Failure to atone implied severe retribution and even today is often accompanied with more than a whiff of brimstone.

The reason the word *atonement* can crash upon the ear with such heavy overtones is due in no small measure to its reverberations with fear, punishment, and damnation. If, however, the sledgehammer of the Almighty is avoided, and sincere repentance is demonstrated through reformed behavior, the path of redemption is one in which the threat of punishment is removed, and replaced by an outpouring of "amazing grace." Embedded in the archetypal templates of the Western psyche there is a line in the sand, on one side of which is *punishment* and, on the other side, *reward*. The punishment is full-blown and sometimes pictured as a psychotic torture chamber of eternal cruelty and suffering, while the reward is, generally speaking, less embellished and couched more vaguely in terms of serenity and bliss.

Despite this freight, atonement is a concept that deserves our attention, not so that it can be forced into a more relevant and contemporary idiom, but because its true potential can be understood and applied creatively in the here-and-now reality of a world facing extreme challenges. In a world of political spin, media cacophony, and seductive advertising, atonement may represent an authentic and reliable indicator of real behavioral change. Let's examine it from a fresh perspective.

Atonement in a New Light

The notion that "as you believe so shall you live" is not new, but maybe we are now more aware how deeply *belief* structures our experience of reality. Belief acts as the primary conditioning lens of our consciousness and influences how we think about ourselves, how we perceive others, and how we organize our families, communities, and nations; and it is at the root of all of our values. As we revise our beliefs, we change our picture of the world around us.

We have all become familiar with the word *paradigm* as coined by Thomas Kuhn: it denotes the model or template we use to integrate our beliefs into a coherent pattern or framework. It comes from the verb *to parse*, which lets us examine the grammar or structure of meaning in ideas. When our paradigms shift, we have occasion to revise our larger worldview. When we talk about exploring atonement in a new light, we are not suggesting a superficial reframing but something that goes deeper into the foundations of our belief system. If we are to examine the concept of atonement from a fresh perspective, we must go to the roots of its connection with the role punishment plays in our worldview.

Let's start with the Western world's relationship to extreme punishment: torture, capital punishment, and corporal punishment. The latter is the easiest. Punishing children by beating them or flogging them is now illegal in the Western world and strongly censured by psychologists. We have come to abhor violent punishment against kids. Equally, the overwhelming majority of people affirms the right of prisoners to humane treatment, and denounces the practice of torture. Looking back over a few millennia of human development, we can affirm significant progress; punishment has been undergoing significant humanization and refinement. But the belief in the efficacy of punishment still runs strong, especially in the United States.

The United States represents less than 5 percent of the world's population, but it houses about 30 percent of the world's prison population; its "three strikes" law is uniquely punitive, and while most of Europe has abolished executions, the United States remains one of the world's leaders in capital punishment. Despite the lack of evidence that executions deter violent crime and despite the clear evidence in recidivism rates that the penal system is failing to rehabilitate or reform a significant percentage of its inmate population, the United States is spending more money building more prisons and expanding the number of prisoners within their walls. Lest you were in doubt, punishment is having a heyday in twenty-first-century America!

How could atonement be seen as a solution to this tragedy? How might we reenvision atonement in relation to this concrete example so that it is not so much coupled with a theology of retribution or perceived as a vindication of vengeance but seen as a modern, enlightened, and efficacious approach to real social problems and challenges? To answer these questions we must be able to see a way out of the false dichotomy represented by the naive polarity between heaven and hell, or the simplistic alternative between damnation and redemption. Such simplification leads to an equally unsophisticated carrot-and-stick psychology with the stick predominating. Let's face it: the threat of punishment is a primitive means of enforcing control.

Atonement prompted by fear of punishment suggests a response that has been induced by coercion or manipulation, not one that has been derived from a genuine appreciation of the nature and consequences of one's actions. Actions that arise out of deep insight and self-reflection, and which are born of new understanding, are more likely to be genuine, spontaneous, and creative. This expression of atonement will arise not out of heavy cultural baggage and conditioning but out of an awareness that more accurately sees the truth of things and from an energy that wishes to honor that truth.

The atonement that arises from fear of the punishment meted out to wrongdoers and sinners is one thing. The atonement that arises out of a realization of ignorance, misdirected will, and wounding, is another. In the latter case, we move away from authoritarian and theological frameworks into educational, therapeutic, and healing approaches. We are invited to experience the full force of truth. But rather than saturating the psyche in fear, guilt, and shame, we can allow truth to revive our conscience and infuse our moral imagination.

Atonement, seen in this light, is something that springs spontaneously from within. It is filled with the energy of *metanoia*—heart opening—and revitalized will. This is atonement ignited in the cauldron of wounding experience, waking up to honestly evaluate the consequences of former beliefs and behaviors, and sparking imaginative engagement in the process of healing whatever has been damaged. Atonement becomes an expression of the creative life force and even a marker of evolutionary change and improvement. While retribution gives back a version of what was received, atonement offers a new path forward. And while a psychologically or theologically coerced atonement may bring some form of relief to the transgressor, creative atonement invites amplified being into unfettered expression. Are we prepared to reenvision atonement so that it is not so much shaped by regret or about attempting to fix the past as it is about demonstrating the kind of resourcefulness and commitment needed to manifest a more enlightened future?

Creative Atonement

Let me share a story of creative atonement. It is about a soldier, a massive, big, burly man, who wakes up in the middle of an operation involving civilians living under military occupation. He was out with his platoon, and they had been fired on but were unable to "take out" or track down their target. Nonetheless, they needed to show the local civilian population that they would be punished for harboring the enemy. Sometimes families would be ordered out of their homes and young men hauled away for interrogation; if the soldiers suspected any member of the family to be involved in resistance to the occupation, they would ransack and even demolish the house. On this day they smashed down several doors, did sweeps, made arrests. During moments like this, soldiers are burning adrenaline; their hearts are pumping fast with a biochemical brew that ignites fear and hostility. Their brain functions are hypervigilant for any signs of aggression or any sudden movements that could endanger their own or a fellow soldier's life.

They had entered by force a house where they found a few older women and three young children. As others searched around, he trained his weapon on the members of the household who were clinging to each other in a corner. The women were screaming, but the children were still, locked in silent defiance, their eyes fixed pools of hatred. Nothing seemed to move inside them; they were statuesque. Each of them was frozen in a deadened representation of enmity. It was an energy that claimed them completely. Neither tears, nor trembling, nor clutching in terror or hiding in their mother's skirts or any of the heart-rending emotion you might expect of children facing the barrel of a machine gun. It was not even personal. They were the antennae of a transpersonal field of hatred that adults on all sides of the conflict had created. He knew he was free to continue to represent the other side of hatred and behave accordingly.

What had appeared to him in the eyes of the children had attempted to lay claim to his soul. It was an invitation to turn their hatred into an even stronger mutual hatred. But he found himself called by his own conscience to wake up and disengage from being the hired gun of an occupying power. The next day he resigned from the military.

As a result of his decision, he was forced to seek work as a laborer at building sites. He had always had a flair for music, and he consoled himself at night by playing the flute and other instruments. It was then that he realized that the best thing he could do with his life would be to offer healing though music rather than carrying a machine gun.

For some months, he found himself working alongside men who had families in many of the places he had patrolled. It was a humbling experience but one which, oddly, was a kind of answer. Working side by side with these men brought him closer to the truth of what he had in common with "the enemy" than he would have thought possible a few months earlier.

Today, his website shows a picture of him as a soldier with his machine gun and another with him carrying his didgeridoo. He works out of a world music store where he offers individual therapeutic healing work that uses Native American flute and didgeridoo. He also puts on plays for schoolchildren.

Maybe this story will seem to some too light on guilt, shame, violation, and transgression, or to be lacking heartfelt apologies, or to indicate a need for more costly or painful repentance. But it short-circuits many of these elements. It does indeed ask us to contemplate the immorality of unjust military occupation, but it also focuses on the light that goes on in the soldier's mind and in the hugely life-affirming choice he makes in response to that awakening.

One might also observe that this man didn't rededicate his life to ending the occupation and its litany of human rights violations. True. But we might contemplate how much would be changed by the soldiers of this world—the ones sent out to enforce wrongful missions—if instead of violating the rights of civilians, they laid down their arms and went to play music for children. Or if instead of enforcing hatred and division, they channeled their creative energy into making world music. After all, if one soldier has the moral imagination to respond in this way, why not more?

Assuming that atonement needs to be part of a very linear and sequential narrative may ultimately confine it to more limited and monotonous responses, and routine apologies. The perspective that invites creative atonement opens itself to the possibility of quantum shifts, deep transformation, and a whole new order of meaning rather than the physics of responses which requires a force equal and opposite to the one that violated and transgressed.

Let us now explore just how a broader creative atonement movement might evolve and how it might even serve to play a role as part of evolutionary change and global transformation.

We Are Accountable for a Planet in Peril

You can call as many character witnesses as you like, but you are in the dock with the rest of us. We drive our cars, fly planes, go to the mall, buy too much stuff, generate lots of trash, take daily showers, consume lots of electricity, and eat a diet that would be totally unsupportable if the whole world attempted to do the same. My apologies to you vegans who live off the grid, who ride your bicycles everywhere, and who would never consider taking a plane anywhere: you are free to go. And you who constitute the majority of the world's citizens who don't drive or fly, who eat simply and live in modest dwellings, you do not belong in the dock. But the rest of us—and we haven't even talked about swimming pools, Hummers, and extravagant lifestyles—we must remain in the dock: Mother Earth cannot support our way of life. Period.

Since the first Earth Day in 1970, human behavior has resulted in wiping out one-third of all species on this planet. It would be something if that were the end of the story and we were collectively waking up with a readiness to atone for our collective unconscious behaviors: tragically, it seems as if many of the economies of the world are just gearing up to accelerate their own versions of rapid unsustainable development with all of its toxic waste and environmental degradation.

A species that destroys its own habitat, abandoning its own long-term survival in favor of temporary excess and at the same time eradicating the majority of other species, is a species that needs more than therapy. It needs deep transformation. At a time of severe global financial collapse, widespread drought, crop failures, destruction of whole communities, frightening indications of serious climate change, and other benchmarks of significant deterioration, some have begun to recognize that we will need interventions that go well beyond systemic adjustments and cosmetic tinkering. The transformation that is now called for must involve a whole system transition from unsustainable development to forms of sustainable development that are eco-friendly, healthy, communally revitalizing, just, far-sighted, and supportive of social and cultural diversity.

To some, global transformation on this scale may seem an impossibility. But the implications of such a view are too bleak to consider. Without such a transformation, we are potentially heading for catastrophic loss of life of a magnitude never witnessed before on Planet Earth. Such a view represents a failure of imagination and a collapse of will. To understand how deeply we can transform present conditions, we must first appreciate the roots of our current crises. Simply put, the seeds of our over-reaching and self-destructive tendencies, as well as our problem-solving abilities and generative creativity, lie within and arise out of the state of our consciousness.

Let's face it: we have simply allowed ourselves to become dazzled and distracted by the seemingly endless possibilities of materialist enjoyment. There is just so much amazing stuff to get, places to go, and things to try on. Every day someone devises new gadgetry to entertain us, and new ways to chat at hyperspeed. Compounding the problem, we have endless media allures and advertising seductions. We are, as the poet T. S. Eliot put it, "distracted from distraction by distraction, filled with fancies and emptied of meaning." And he was referring here to the early part of the twentieth century. Nearly a century later we are hallucinating in a "matrix of distraction." We are in collective attention deficit and seriously adrift from reality. But as the sages of old have ceaselessly reminded us, we should not confuse consciousness with its contents. You are not the experiences you have had in the past or even those you are having right now; you are the one who sees and reflects upon your experiences. Keep tracking your awareness back to its source and you will find in the root of your consciousness a vibrantly alive and awake witness.

As deeply as we may fall into distraction, alienation, and indifference, we can wake up to whatever has been drugging our attention and clouding our perception of reality. Coming to the realization that you have become increasingly numb while the media tries desperately to entertain you with "reality" shows or cajole you with its opinionated pundits is the beginning of waking up. Your sense of nausea may increase as you begin to witness the pervasive nature of our collective social trance. This is the place where you may start to rail against the system and fuel moral outrage at our blindness, insensitivity, and injustice.

But finger-pointing activism cannot be equated with atonement. If you think you are completely outside of the problem, and you ferment an *us* versus *them* mentality, you haven't woken up sufficiently to confess *your* role in the story of modernity.

Once your consciousness shifts from strident accusation to nonjudgmental witnessing, something happens, and you begin to see patterns, not so much of right and wrong, but of wounding and healing. You begin to see more accurately that perpetration often has its roots in cycles of wounding. You begin to see the intergenerational transfer of wounds and deviance, and even begin to appreciate the historical ground in which animosity and hatred are fed and transmitted.

When your capacity to witness becomes skillful and refined, you will see how even subtle ideas take form and manifest as competitive ideology, religious intolerance, cultural supremacy, or spiritual hubris. Now, finally, you will be in a position to see that you might be able to represent a "pattern interrupt," a redesign and change in the flow that offers a departure from the dominant way of doing things. This is a place where your action will flow from compassion for yourself and others because you have come to witness how we are all enmeshed in one another and all connected in the larger story. Once you become fully aware of *the pattern that connects*, you can enter the stream of action as a transformational agent, a paradigm changer, a social healer—a sacred activist—ready to atone creatively in the field of our collective healing and evolutionary advancement. You will be a herald of a movement in consciousness, expressed and manifested as creative atonement, which may change the course of human development on a grand scale.

But before you don the mantle of such a noble purpose, it might be good to refresh your memory about contemporary scientific and spiritual insights into how we catalyze and sustain deep change and even deeper transformation.

We Are Designed for Creative Challenge

There is a reason you can tell me in vivid detail where you were and what you were doing on the morning of 9/11. What happened on that fateful morning triggered for most of us what could be referred to as a "primary amygdala response." Shock and fear sounded the body's alarm system to let you know that the attacks on the Twin Towers represented an unusual level of danger. The amygdala alarm response imprints long-term memory, as if to say, "This event was not routine and you need to keep a separate file on it for quick and easy future reference."

Now the amygdala, like a fire alarm, is designed to ring loud so that its warning is noted, and then to switch off when the danger has passed. It is not supposed to keep ringing. If it does, it is an indicator of a problem such as posttraumatic stress. Our mind-body system is exquisitely designed to be alert and attuned to the present, but because it is so sensitive and subtle it can receive impressions that are difficult to dislodge and which can develop into larger fears, and phobias. The very equipment that can attune to phenomena can also block them and develop blind spots.

Contemporary neuroscience has allowed us to see in brilliant detail how our brains function and how they respond to diverse stimuli. It has produced the simple maxim, "What fires together, wires together." Our brain's neural pathways reflect how we locate and process experience, the way we place our attention, which parts of our brain we use more than others, and where experience and emotional charge configure to etch deeper grooves.

We have all experienced, to some extent, how after some explosive situation or emotionally volatile encounter, our minds go into overdrive and become acutely repetitive. Emotions are ignited in our memory as if they were still happening, words are recalled with echoes reverberating in our head, and our own internal barrister goes to work in our defense, constantly berating those who have long since left the room. It is almost as if the neural firing becomes a hamster wheel that we can't get off.

When this pattern is not overwritten by other more pleasant or peaceful signals, we can find ourselves moving toward recurring negativity and neuroses. We can find ourselves "kindling" a whole neural network of associations and connections until we literally find ourselves in a rut, caught in patterns of thinking and behavior that have been negatively conditioned by our past experiences. These ruts graphically point to where we are stuck. They are places where we spin our wheels, where we are frozen in time, where our attitudes become more fixed and rigid, and where our resistance to change is greatest.

It is generally out of these ruts that our least desirable behaviors emerge, where prejudice ferments and where belief becomes toxically immune to any form of reappraisal or revision. They also mark the places where we refuse to let go of our wounds, where we nurse them in secret caverns of self-pity, and where we formulate those morose convictions about our status as victims.

The rehearsal of atonement out of such places in the psyche reflects little more than a pretense that we are no longer in a rut. It pays homage to the need for change without resurrecting the whole self in the energetic field of new life and expanded being.

And the good news? Well, as it turns out, there is lots of it. Scientific research has been telling us that while we have evolved with "flight or fight" mechanisms solidly ingrained in our emergent design as a species, we are also made for love, deep collaborative play, and social cooperation. In fact, studies reflect that those who are more loving, relationship centered, altruistic, and forgiving live longer and have better quality-of-life indicators. It seems that something in our evolutionary design supports a peaceful mind, a compassionate heart, and service to others. Even comparing the MRI scan of a person meditating to one of someone in a normal state is to witness the difference between coherence and fragmentation.

Slowly, a picture is emerging that affirms that our mind-body system is deeply and positively influenced by what some refer to as higher consciousness and others as spirit.

And it gets even better. Just as we can develop a synchronized field in the brain, the Institute of Heart Math has been showing how to create an equally coherent electromagnetic field in the center of our hearts. Entraining the heart's energy to focus on radiating love not only changes its electromagnetic frequencies; it creates positive shifts in the body's biochemistry. With a peaceful heart and clear mind, we are able to be centered and more capable of responding to challenges with consciousness and compassion.

The world's spiritual traditions have demonstrated numerous approaches to cultivating peace, and increasingly these psychospiritual technologies are readily accessible; they can be practiced without having to pledge allegiance to restrictive religious tenets and dogmas. We can be grateful that the dialogue between science and spirituality provides reassuring evidence that nondogmatic spiritual practice has much to offer. It suggests that atonement may ultimately be best served by ensuring the health and peace of mind needed to rewire our brains away from whatever kindled our more destructive attitudes, beliefs, and behaviors.

But even further evidence suggests that the universe really does want to support our creative engagement in the present rather than maintaining us in the circuitry of the past. Again neuroscientists have observed what has come to be referred to as the "neuroplasticity" of the brain.

In simple terms, this means that our brains will create new circuitry as we rise to meet new challenges and when we give our focused will and attention to exploring new possibilities. Neuroscientist Jerre Levy suggests that perhaps more than anything, we are designed for challenge. Yes, we literally give birth to neurons and new neural pathways when we look at the world with fresh eyes, an open heart, and the will to expand the frontiers of our knowledge and experience.

If you are ready to acknowledge that this planet needs you to wake up and change the way you have been living, if you desire to recreate and redesign the future, there may just be more help than you ever imagined. You are designed for creative engagement in life's possibilities.

A Personal Vision

I remember it well. I was on the metro, and the train was approaching the Pentagon station. I was working for Amnesty International at the time, and heading on this day into its Washington office. I was reading an essay, "Prometheus: A Meditation," in a volume of essays by Thomas Merton titled *Raids on the Unspeakable*. In it Merton pictures Prometheus as an archetype of modern man. He sees Prometheus as one who had to choose an inferior god, a god whom he could steal something from. You may remember that Prometheus stole fire from the gods and his punishment was to be chained to the rocks, where vultures picked out his liver. Merton may be using the myth to hammer home a point: we unconsciously set ourselves up for ruin when we choose something that is less than our highest idealism and imagination; when we make it easy for ourselves by

not creating a direct relationship to our own highest consciousness, and acting from there.

> Not knowing that the fire was his for the asking, a gift of the true
> God, the Living God, not knowing that fire was something God
> did not need for himself, Prometheus felt he was obliged to steal.

And he ends the essay with these words:

> There is nothing we can steal from Him at all, because before we
> can think of stealing it, it has already been given.

As the metro doors opened and people spilled off the train,
and then others filled it up again, tears streamed down my face.
It didn't matter what the commuters thought; these tears could
not be prevented. Everywhere I turned I saw in my mind's eye
people being tortured, murdered, and massacred in the name of
inferior gods: gods of territory, gods of ideology, gods of resources
and material power. The canvas of history was crowded with
suffering. It was as if humanity had put its own limitations on
thrones, high altars, in corporate towers, and that we sent them
around in government limos, armed them with hugely destructive power, and made them superstars. Only so we could tear
them down in the end because we know them to be false idols. I
could see how Merton was trying to pry open the false construct
of civilizations that must fail if they secretly know they have
sidestepped their highest calling.

Rather than recognize that he was created to be *one* with
the Source, Prometheus would claim sacrificial victim status
as the one who gets punished for his heroism. In the twist that
Merton interjects into the myth, Prometheus is actually "guilty,
frustrated, rebellious and fear ridden." Why? Because Merton
is using Prometheus to show us our secret unconscious default
when we refuse to be in the presence of the "Living God" of our
own higher consciousness. "It is our light, not our darkness

that most frightens us," Marianne Williamson reminds us. "We ask ourselves: Who am I to be brilliant, gorgeous, talented, fabulous?"

So here we are on the edge of a precipice, witnessing severe climate disruption, and systemic crises affecting food, sustainable economies, and peaceful coexistence. We must ask ourselves, "Are there not human ideals that can 'template' planetary civilization and reach beyond the waste and ruin we see around us? Within the spacious possibilities of our own consciousness can we not envision something greater, more perfect, and truly worthy of the beings we are?"

The answer is assuredly, "Yes!"

For in reality the birth of the subtler, wiser, more tolerant, and forgiving human race is already under way. We cannot see it so clearly because we collectively fixate on the bad news. But it is there, reaching toward the next spiral movement of evolution itself, and it invites you to shed all the things you know in your heart need to go, all the false gods and the neuroses that hold you in the prison of the victim. You are invited to be the exquisitely subtle, ingenious, and loving eyes and ears, hands and feet of universal consciousness creating through you. Whenever you feel like retreating into the narrower, pettier, and smaller version of yourself, with all of its cozy materialist idolatry, let your atonement be some act of creativity that affirms who it is you really are. I dare you to stand in the fire of your own greatness. And believe me, that will be all the atonement you need or that anyone needs from you.

However you do it, standing fearlessly in your own light is the essence of creative atonement. Indeed, to do so requires us to overcome fear, conditioned responses, and perhaps shame. These elements can sucker us into surrendering our power to the status quo. Creative atonement overturns the status quo; it steps into a power that was held back and an affirmation of worthiness that may have hidden itself from its fullest and most beautiful expression. Remember, we are designed for growth and for the steep climb that is necessary if we are to realize our full potential. And when we get to the highest place we can go, there is always a higher place. That is when we discover that there are many ahead of us on the path who have lived their highest ideals.

When the view for a sufficient number of humanity is truly breathtaking, and we can see that there really is higher ground we all can share, we will no longer be in peril.

Michael Bernard Beckwith is a world leader and teacher in the New Thought–Ancient Wisdom tradition of spirituality, the founder of the Agape International Spiritual Center in Los Angeles, and cofounder of the Season for Nonviolence. He is also the author of several books, including *A Manifesto of Peace* and *Spiritual Liberation: Fulfilling Your Soul's Potential*.

Kate Dahlstedt is codirector of Soldier's Heart, a veterans healing program, centered in Troy, New York. She is a psychotherapist, group facilitator, and journey guide as well as a writer. She can be contacted at kate@soldiersheart.net.

Katharine Dever is a London-based speaker, workshop leader, and CEO of Bonny Doon Ltd., an organization dedicated to helping individuals find their vocation. She is the author of *Bettermorphosis: A Transformation Handbook for Awakening Women* and a featured contributor in *The Indigo Children Ten Years Later* by Lee Carroll and Jan Tober.

Arun Gandhi is one of nine surviving grandchildren of Mohandas and Kastur Gandhi. For almost twenty years he has traveled around the world speaking at universities and colleges and sharing with youth the lessons he learned from his parents and grandparents. President of the board of the Gandhi Worldwide Education Institute (http://www.gandhiforchildren.org), he currently resides in Rochester, New York.

Douglas M. George-Kanentiio was born and raised on the Mohawk territory of Akwesasne. He is the former editor of the journal *Akwesasne Notes* and a cofounder of the Native American Journalists Association, which presented him with the Wassaja Award for journalism excellence. He is a former member of the board of trustees for the National Museum of the American Indian and is the author of *Iroquois on Fire: A Voice from the Mohawk Nation*, a narrative on contemporary Iroquois issues. He is currently a columnist with *News from Indian Country* (http://www.IndianCountryNews.com). He resides on Iroquois territory with his wife, musician Joanne Shenandoah.

Azim Noordin Khamisa is an author, activist, international speaker, and president of the Tariq Khamisa Foundation in Southern California (http://www.tkf.org). He has delivered more than four hundred keynote address speeches around the world on the topic of halting the tragic cycle of youth violence. His books include *Azim's Bardo: A Father's Journey from Murder to Forgiveness*, *From Forgiveness to Fulfillment*, and *The Secrets of the Bulletproof Spirit: How to Bounce Back from Life's Hardest Hits* (with Jillian Quinn). His tireless advocacy for peace and reconciliation has been recognized by the National Crime Victims Special Community Service Award, the Search for Common Ground Award, the international award for Building Peaceful Communities, the Crazy Horse Award, and the Freedom Heroes Award.

Michael Lerner is an American rabbi and political activist. The editor of *Tikkun* magazine (http://www.tikkun.org), a progressive Jewish and interfaith magazine, he is the rabbi of Beyt Tikkun Synagogue in Berkeley and the author of the 2006 *New York Times* best seller *The Left Hand of God: Taking Back Our Country from the Religious Right*.

Michael N. Nagler has devoted his life to exploring nonviolence as an alternative to war. Professor emeritus of languages at the University of California, Berkeley, and founder and former chair of the university's Peace and Conflict Studies Program, Nagler has become one of the world's most widely respected peace scholars and activists. He is the author of several books, including *America Without Violence* and *The Upanishads*. His book *Is There No Other Way? The Search for a Nonviolent Future* received an American Book Award. Nagler is on the editorial board of *The Acorn: Journal of the Gandhi-King Society* and also serves on the advisory board of *Tikkun* magazine.

Jacob Needleman is professor of philosophy at San Francisco State University, former director of the Center for the Study of Religions at the Graduate Theological Union in Berkeley, and guest professor of religious studies at the Sorbonne in Paris. He is the author of many books, including *The New Religions*, *The Wisdom of Love*, *Money and the Meaning of Life*, *Time and the Soul*, *The Essential Marcus Aurelius*, *The American Soul*, *Why Can't We Be Good?* and *What Is God?* He has been featured on Bill Moyers's acclaimed PBS series *A World of Ideas*. His website is http://www.jacobneedleman.com.

James O'Dea is currently involved in international social healing work, building on several years of dialogues funded by the Fetzer Institute. He is on the extended faculty of the Institute of Noetic Sciences, which he served as president. He is the former Washington office director of Amnesty International and CEO of the Seva Foundation. He is a member of the Evolutionary Leaders Group, founded by Deepak Chopra, and author of numerous published essays. His most recent book is *Creative Stress: A Path for Evolving Souls Living Through Personal and Planetary Upheaval*.

Diane Hennacy Powell, M.D., is a strong advocate for human rights. As founder of the psychiatric program at Survivors of Torture, International, in San Diego, she has worked with victims of genocide, torture, sexual abuse, and postpartum depression, as well as refugees and asylum seekers. Her clinical practice is in Medford, Oregon.

Huston Smith is the Thomas J. Watson Professor of Religion and Distinguished Adjunct Professor of Philosophy, Emeritus, at Syracuse University. His many books include *Forgotten Truth: The Common Vision of the World's Religions*, *Beyond the Post-Modern Mind*, and *Why Religion Matters: The Fate of the Human Spirit in an Age of Disbelief*, as well as the classic *The World's Religions*. His discovery of Tibetan multiphonic chanting was lauded as "an important landmark in the study of music," and his film documentaries of Hinduism, Tibetan Buddhism, and Sufism have all won international awards. His latest book is *Tales of Wonder, Tales of Delight: Adventures Chasing the Divine*.

Heng Sure is an American Buddhist monk from Ohio. He ordained with the late Chan Master Hsuan Hua in 1976. Currently, Dharma Master Heng Sure is the director of the Berkeley Buddhist Monastery, in Berkeley, California, where he lives and teaches on the staff at the Institute for World Religions.

Edward Tick is a mythologist, poet, writer, educator, and psychotherapist who applies his innovative model of posttraumatic stress syndrome treatment among war veterans. Tick is the founder and director of Soldier's Heart and the author of the award-winning study *War and the Soul*, as well as *The Practice of Dream Healing: Bringing Ancient Greek Mysteries into Modern Medicine* and *The Golden Tortoise: Journeys in Vietnam*. He can be reached at info@soldiersheart.net.

Stephanie N. Van Hook is a returned Peace Corps volunteer who served in Bénin. She studied conflict resolution at Portland State University in Oregon, graduating in 2009, and is currently the codirector of the Metta Center for Nonviolence in Berkeley, California. Her interests in nonviolence and forgiveness have intersected with activists and academics working for nonviolent social change in the global peace and justice community.

Phil Cousineau is a freelance writer, independent filmmaker, photographer, travel leader, and worldwide lecturer. Over the past twenty years he has published more than twenty-five books, including *The Art of Pilgrimage*, *Stoking the Creative Fires*, *Once and Future Myths*, and *Wordcatcher: An Odyssey into the World of Weird and Wonderful Words*. His book *The Olympic Odyssey: Rekindling the True Spirit of the Great Games* was selected by the United States Olympic Committee as a gift for American athletes at the 2004 Summer Games in Athens. His other books include *Deadlines: A Rhapsody on a Theme of Famous Last Words* (winner of the Fallot Literary Award), *The Blue Museum*, *Night Train*, and *The Way Things Are: Conversations with Huston Smith on the Spiritual Life*.

Cousineau has also earned more than twenty documentary film credits, including *The Hero's Journey: The World of Joseph Campbell*; *Ecological Design: Inventing the Future*; *Forever Activists: Stories from the Abraham Lincoln Brigade* (1991 Academy Award nominee); and a collaboration with Huston Smith and Gary Rhine, *A Seat at the Table: The Struggle for American Indian Religious Freedom*. Currently, Cousineau is host of the national television series *Global Spirit* on Link TV. He lives with his family on Telegraph Hill in San Francisco, where he coaches youth baseball. For more information about his books, films, television work, lectures, and literary tours, visit his website, http://www.philcousineau.net.

And if he comes to me with sins equivalent to the
whole world, I will greet him with forgiveness equal
to it.

—*Mishkat Al-Masabi*

The Beyond Forgiveness project was inspired by Richard Meyer, a businessman from Southern California, who after a chance meeting with Azim Noordin Khamisa, was compelled to support a book on the subject of atonement. Rich was so moved by Azim's stance that "peace can be restored no matter what has gone on before" that he approached author and editor Phil Cousineau to create a collection of essays and interviews on atonement, "the next step in reconciliation." In Azim's tradition, Sufism, atonement is deeply important; seen from Rich's broad spiritual background and intensive studies, atonement is a connecting thread. For many contemporary people, however, atonement is a remote theological idea, and it is for them that this project has been created.

The mission of the Beyond Forgiveness project is to explore and create inspiring dialogue around the practice of atonement as an integral step in the process of reconciliation and healing. The project promotes building community, sharing stories, and offering resources for personal action and transformation—including this book, *Beyond Forgiveness*, and its companion website at http://www.BeyondForgiveness.org. The site has been designed to provide an interactive community place for those who would like to share their experiences surrounding forgiveness and atonement. As part of the project we provide a compelling range of insights into the various ways that creative and compassionate acts of atonement can help individuals, families, groups, and nations break tragic cycles of violence and vengeance. By offering an alternative to the traditional fallback positions of retribution and punishment, and a complement to the burgeoning forgiveness movement, we hope to inspire participants to share their own stories and take action in their own lives and communities to move beyond forgiveness, towards atonement.

Healing Through Storytelling

To contribute your personal story to the Beyond Forgiveness project, visit our website. Explore this site to learn more about how others have healed the past and restored balance in their lives, and the world, through the practices of compassion, forgiveness, and atonement. Share your story and discover the stories of others—in books, songs, movies, recent news reports, and accounts of people's lives around the world. Come along with us on a healing journey that will educate and inspire one another through sharing our stories. It is a journey that will foster sustainable change because, as the great American proverb reminds us, "People don't change when they see the light; they change when they feel the heat." In our case, the fire of our collective passion for fusing forgiveness and atonement.

Please log on at http://www.BeyondForgiveness.org and join the growing movement of peaceful and long-lasting reconciliation.

First and foremost, I would like to acknowledge Richard J. Meyer, the inspired and inspiring heart and soul of this atonement project. His devotion to the cause of peaceful reconciliation is unbounded, and my admiration for his selfless dedication to this cause knows no limits. I would also like to thank the contributors to this volume, who have kindly given of their time in creating these essays and interviews; they are Michael Bernard Beckwith, Kate Dahlstedt, Katharine Dever, Arun Gandhi, Douglas M. George-Kanentiio, Azim Noordin Khamisa, Michael Lerner, Michael Nagler, Jacob Needleman, James O'Dea, Diane Hennacy Powell, Heng Sure, Ed Tick, and Stephanie N. Van Hook. Profuse thanks also to my friend, spiritual mentor, and my son's honorary godfather Huston Smith, who not only graced this volume with a wonderful Foreword, but has encouraged me to plumb the depths of what he believes is a "profoundly important subject."

To all those at Jossey-Bass I wish to express my gratitude and admiration for so enthusiastically taking on this project, especially my all-forgiving editor, Sheryl Fullerton, who immediately recognized the numinous niche that our book might fill. My thanks, too, to my punctilious copyeditor, Jeffrey Wyneken; to Jeff Puda, for his glorious cover art; to Paula Goldstein, for her elegant interior design; to Joanne Clapp Fullagar, for her fabulous management of the book's production; to Sandy Siegle, for her marketing expertise; and to Alison Knowles, for her graceful assistance in all matters regarding this book.

Many thanks as well to everyone on the BeyondForgiveness .org website team, including Jo Beaton and Shannon Wills, for coproducing the powerful site, which serves to highlight reflections and stories from around the world; Michael Yap for his beautiful design; and Ann Oyama for her expert programming skills.

I would also like to express my gratitude to my agile agent, Amy Rennert, who recognized the potential of this project from the beginning, and found the best possible home for this book. And deepest thanks to Jo Beaton and Jack Cousineau, my family, who gracefully dealt with my attempts at atoning for my long absences and struggles as I wove the threads of this tapestry of reflections into a book that I hope will make a vital contribution to the peace and reconciliation projects that are teeming around the world.

Other Books of Interest

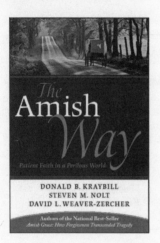

The Amish Way

Patient Faith in a Perilous World

Donald B. Kraybill, Steven M. Nolt, &
David L. Weaver-Zercher

Hardcover
ISBN: 978-0-470-52069-7

"*The Amish Way* is enlightening, practical, and well-researched. A wonderful read!"
—**Beverly Lewis**, *New York Times* bestselling author of Amish fiction

"With detailed personal anecdotes and explanations straight from the Amish themselves, *The Amish Way* illustrates the simplicity and grace with which the Amish live their lives, and proves that those of us who have our own questions with faith might well learn from their example."
—**Jodi Picoult**, author, *Plain Truth* and *House Rules*

In this follow-up to the bestselling *Amish Grace: How Forgiveness Transcended Tragedy*, the authors explain how Amish faith is intertwined with community and commitment, child rearing, home life, material possessions, the natural world, evil, and sorrow. The authors explore the complicated question, "Is there anything the Amish can teach the rest of us about living meaningfully in the modern world?"

Written in a lively and engaging style, *The Amish Way* holds appeal for anyone who wants to learn more about the spiritual and religious impulse that energizes the Amish way of life.

DONALD B. KRAYBILL, Ph.D., is senior fellow at the Young Center of Elizabethtown College in Elizabethtown, Pennsylvania.

STEVEN M. NOLT, Ph.D., is professor of history at Goshen College in Goshen, Indiana.

DAVID L. WEAVER-ZERCHER, Ph.D., is professor of American religious history at Messiah College in Grantham, Pennsylvania.

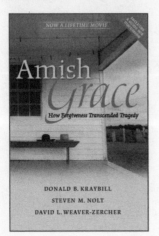

Amish Grace

How Forgiveness Transcended Tragedy

Donald B. Kraybill, Steven M. Nolt, &
David L. Weaver-Zercher

Paperback
ISBN: 978-0-470-34404-0

"A story our polarized country needs to hear: It is still grace that saves."
—**Bill Moyers**, Public Affairs Television

"In a world where repaying evil with evil is almost second nature, the Amish remind us there's a better way. In plain and beautiful prose, *Amish Grace* recounts the Amish witness and connects it to the heart of their spirituality."
—**Sister Helen Prejean**, author, *Dead Man Walking*

"Professors Kraybill, Nolt, and Weaver-Zercher have written a superb book—a model of clear, forceful writing about a tragedy and its aftermath. They have an obvious affection for the Amish yet ask tough questions, weigh contradictions, and explore conundrums such as how a loving God could permit schoolgirls to be massacred."
—**National Catholic Reporter**

The remarkable response of the Amish community to the horrific shooting of ten schoolgirls at Nickel Mines, Pennsylvania, in October 2006 stunned the larger world. *Amish Grace* tells the incredible story of this community's reaction to this senseless shooting and explores its profoundly countercultural practice of forgiveness.

Now in paperback, this extraordinary, award-winning account of Amish forgiveness includes an afterword by the authors along with an interview with the mother of the man responsible for the shootings, and a guide for discussion.

Other Books of Interest

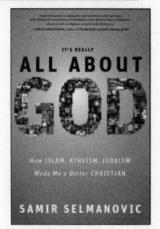

It's Really All About God

How Islam, Atheism, Judaism Made Me a Better Christian

Samir Selmanovic

Paper
ISBN: 978-0-470-92341-2

"Samir Selmanovic is asking the right questions at the right time, and refusing the consolations of certainty at a time when strident orthodoxies—atheists as well as religious—are perilously dividing us."

—**Karen Armstrong**, author, *The Case for God*, *A History of God*, and *The Great Transformation*

"Why are thousands not saying what this man is saying? Such obvious truth must be made even more obvious, and this is exactly what Samir Selmanovic is doing for all of us and for the future of humanity. After you read this wise book, you will say, 'Of course!' and 'Thank God!'"

—**Fr. Richard Rohr**, O.F.M., Center for Action and Contemplation, Albuquerque, New Mexico

"We need a million more Samirs on the planet—people of conviction and humility who know that the vast mystery called God calls us not to the arrogance of 'ownership' but to the beloved community."

—**Parker J. Palmer**, author, *A Hidden Wholeness*, *Let Your Life Speak*, and *The Courage to Teach*

It's Really All About God is a very personal story and a thrilling exploration of a redeeming, dynamic, and radically different way of treasuring one's own religion while discovering God, goodness, and grace in others and in their traditions.

SAMIR SELMANOVIC (Ph.D) is a founder of Faith House Manhattan, an interfaith "community of communities" that brings together forward-looking Christians, Muslims, Jews, atheists and others who seek to thrive interdependently. Samir is also the director of a Christian community called Citylights and serves on the Interfaith Relations Commission of the National Council of Churches and speaks nationally and internationally. He has been profiled in a number of local and national media, including the *New York Times*. Learn more about him at www.samirselmanovic.com.